THE TRAGEDY OF
HAMLET,
PRINCE OF
DENMARK

BROADVIEW / INTERNET SHAKESPEARE EDITIONS

Broadview Editions Series Editor
Martin R. Boyne
Internet Shakespeare Editions Coordinating Editors
Michael Best and Janelle Jenstad
Internet Shakespeare Editions General Textual Editors
Eric Rasmussen and James Mardock

THE TRAGEDY OF
HAMLET,
PRINCE OF
DENMARK

William Shakespeare

EDITED BY

David Bevington

BROADVIEW / INTERNET SHAKESPEARE EDITIONS

BROADVIEW PRESS – www.broadviewpress.com
Peterborough, Ontario, Canada

Founded in 1985, Broadview Press remains a wholly independent publishing house. Broadview's focus is on academic publishing; our titles are accessible to university and college students as well as scholars and general readers. With over 600 titles in print, Broadview has become a leading international publisher in the humanities, with world-wide distribution. Broadview is committed to environmentally responsible publishing and fair business practices.

The interior of this book is printed on 100% recycled paper.

PERMANENT   100%   **BIO GAS**   Ancient Forest Friendly™
                           E N E R G Y

Library and Archives Canada Cataloguing in Publication

Shakespeare, William, 1564–1616
[Hamlet]
    The tragedy of Hamlet, Prince of Denmark / William Shakespeare ; edited by David Bevington.

(Broadview / Internet Shakespeare Editions)
Includes bibliographical references.
ISBN 978-1-55481-378-0 (softcover)

    I. Bevington, David M., editor II. Title. III. Title: Hamlet
V. Series: Broadview / Internet Shakespeare Editions

PR2807.A2B48 2018   822.3'3   C2018-903068-2

Broadview Press handles its own distribution in North America:
PO Box 1243, Peterborough, Ontario K9J 7H5, Canada
555 Riverwalk Parkway, Tonawanda, NY 14150, USA
Tel: (705) 743-8990; Fax: (705) 743-8353
email: customerservice@broadviewpress.com

Distribution is handled by Eurospan Group in the UK, Europe, Central Asia, Middle East, Africa, India, Southeast Asia, Central America, South America, and the Caribbean. Distribution is handled by Footprint Books in Australia and New Zealand.

Canadä

Broadview Press acknowledges the financial support of the Government of Canada for our publishing activities.

Copy-edited by Denis Johnston
Book design by Michel Vrana
Typeset in MVB Verdigris Pro

PRINTED IN CANADA

CONTENTS

FOREWORD

The Internet Shakespeare Editions (http://internetshakespeare.uvic. ca) and Broadview Press are pleased to collaborate on a series of Shakespeare editions in book form, creating for each volume an "integrated text" designed to meet the needs of today's students.

The texts, introductions, and other materials for these editions are drawn from those prepared by leading scholars for the Internet Shakespeare Editions, modified to suit the demands of publication in book form. The print editions are integrated with the fuller resources and research materials that are available electronically on the site of the Internet Shakespeare Editions. Consistent with other volumes in the Broadview Editions series, each of these Shakespeare editions includes a wide range of background materials, providing information on the play's historical and intellectual context, in addition to the text itself, introduction, chronology, essays on Shakespeare's life and theater, and bibliography; all these will be found in more extensive form on the website.

The Internet Shakespeare Editions, a non-profit organization founded in 1996, creates and publishes works for the student, scholar, actor, and general reader in a form native to the medium of the Internet: scholarly, fully annotated texts of Shakespeare's plays, multimedia explorations of the context of Shakespeare's life and works, and records of his plays in performance. The Internet Shakespeare Editions is affiliated with the University of Victoria.

The Broadview Editions series was founded in 1992 under the title "Broadview Literary Texts." Under the guidance of executive editors Julia Gaunce and Marjorie Mather, of series editors Eugene Benson, Leonard Conolly, and Martin Boyne, and of managing editors Barbara Conolly and Tara Lowes, it has grown to include several hundred volumes—lesser-known works of cultural significance as well as canonical texts. Designed with the needs of undergraduate students in mind, the series has also appealed widely to scholars—and to readers in general.

Janelle Jenstad and Michael Best, Coordinating Editors, University of Victoria
Eric Rasmussen, General Textual Editor, University of Nevada, Reno
James Mardock, General Textual Editor, University of Nevada, Reno
Don LePan, Company Founder and CEO, Broadview Press

ACKNOWLEDGEMENTS

I am more indebted than I can easily say to Michael Best as the now-retired Coordinating Editor of Internet Shakespeare Editions, and to Denis Johnston as tireless and wonderfully careful copy editor for Broadview Press, for their exact and patient help with this edition of *Hamlet*. Both Michael and Denis also helped me immensely with my earlier edition of *As You Like It*. I am both grateful and impressed that they have been willing to continue their labors as they have done. In the final stages of this editing project, I have had splendid assistance from Janelle Jenstad, Coordinating Editor of Internet Shakespeare Editions, and Tara Trueman, Production Editor, Broadview Press.

Hamlet may well be Shakespeare's best-known play. It is also crucial to our understanding of his development as a playwright. He evidently wrote it in 1599–1601, after he had devoted himself primarily to romantic comedies in the 1590s, including *The Comedy of Errors*, *The Taming of the Shrew*, *A Midsummer Night's Dream*, *Much Ado About Nothing*, and *As You Like It*, culminating in *Twelfth Night*, written at about the same time as *Hamlet*. Throughout the 1590s Shakespeare also excelled in writing English history plays, a genre he helped to create: *Henry VI* in three parts, *Richard III*, *King John*, *Richard II*, *Henry IV* in two parts, and *Henry V* in 1599, more or less at the rate of one a year. Again, the last play of this series provides in distilled form the definition and culmination of the genre; and again it is nearly the last of its kind for the remainder of Shakespeare's career.

With the beginning of the seventeenth century, Shakespeare turned to problem plays—including *Troilus and Cressida*, *All's Well That Ends Well*, and *Measure for Measure* in 1601–04—and especially to tragedy. He had collaborated in writing the early *Titus Andronicus* and achieved a stunning success in 1594–96 with *Romeo and Juliet*, but the latter is almost as much a love comedy as a tragedy. With *Julius Caesar* in 1599, followed by *Hamlet*, Shakespeare became the great tragedian of the English stage. *Hamlet* is followed in breathtaking succession by *Othello*, *King Lear*, *Macbeth*, and *Antony and Cleopatra*, until in his late years of 1608–11 he revisited comedy in the genre of what is often called romance or sometimes tragicomedy: *Pericles*, *Cymbeline*, *The Winter's Tale*, and *The Tempest*. *King Henry VIII* followed in 1613.

Hamlet is thus pivotal in Shakespeare's career as a playwright. Its story was well known and retold by 1600, beginning with a Scandinavian epic of the late twelfth century by Saxo Grammaticus entitled *Historia Danica*, and thereafter reformulated by François de Belleforest in 1576, and by others (see Appendix C). A stage version appears to have been performed in the late 1580s. A comparison of Shakespeare's play with his possible sources helps reveal some of his intent in turning to this ancient pagan account. Saxo gives us the plot line of a hero named Amleth whose wicked uncle murders his own brother, Amleth's father, in order to seize the Danish throne and marry his sister-in-law, Amleth's mother. The moral perspective of the story is, however, transformed.

Saxo's hero is bloody, resolute, and crafty. He adopts a guise of madness as a way of outmaneuvering his baleful enemy. He acts in accord with an ancient code of revenge demanding that fratricide and adultery be punished by cold-blooded murder. No moral constraints hinder Amleth: on his return from England, where he has been sent to be executed, he conspires with his penitent mother to throw an ingenious net over the uncle's royal banqueting hall. A fire consumes the drunken inhabitants; Amleth finishes off his uncle, Feng, with that hated uncle's own sword. "By this skillful defense of himself, and strenuous revenge for his parent," writes Saxo, "he has left it doubtful whether we are to think more of his wit or his bravery." Amleth is unambiguously a hero of pagan revenge.

In Shakespeare's play, Hamlet's uncle Claudius is an adulterer and slayer of his brother, like his ancestor in Saxo, but he is vastly more complex and interesting. We quickly perceive that he is an adroit politician. He evidently planned the murder of his royal brother carefully, at a time when young Hamlet was far away from Denmark studying at Wittenberg with his friend Horatio. In his first appearance in the play, in 1.2, Claudius demonstrates his rhetorical skill in seeking endorsement of his unexpected ascent to the throne. Denmark finds itself suddenly threatened by an invasion led by young Fortinbras, nephew to the Norwegian king. In what is apparently his first public appearance at court in the wake of his brother's sudden death, Claudius handles this emergency with aplomb. The occasion calls forth both tears for the deceased monarch and a resolute call to action: Denmark must not appear weak and unprepared. Under Claudius's firm direction, Denmark is busily defending itself. The new king justifies his sudden marriage to his sister-in-law as part of his plan for arming against the Norwegians: the marriage will provide stability and continuity, allowing Gertrude to continue as consort of the ruling monarch. Privately, Hamlet and his ghostly father regard the marriage as incestuous; to them, Claudius is "that incestuous, that adulterate beast" (1.5.43, TLN 729). In public, to the contrary, the marriage is a political stroke of genius. Claudius knows how to win his people and courtiers over to his side.

We can infer how Claudius has solidified his position as new monarch. He is superb at flattering men like Polonius. We quickly sense in this play that Polonius is much happier with Claudius as king than he would be with Hamlet, who does not suffer fools gladly—and to him Polonius is one of "these tedious old fools" (2.2.216, TLN 1262).

Claudius is expert at deals. He lives by the creed of promising to scratch someone's back if that person will scratch his. He makes a great point of allowing Polonius's son Laertes an exit visa to go to Paris. "What wouldst thou beg, Laertes," he says to the young man, "That shall not be my offer, not thy asking?" (1.2.45–46, TLN 225–26). No courtier, says the King, has been more "instrumental" to "the throne of Denmark" than Polonius (1.2.47–48, TLN 228–29); such a man can hope to be paid for his loyalty by royal favors. The King mentions the name "Laertes" no fewer than four times in this brief conversation: a good politician knows the power that is to be found in such intimacies of address.

Denmark, we learn, is an elective monarchy; that is, the choice of monarch is determined by a select and highly patrician oligarchical group of "electors." The emperor of the Holy Roman Empire was chosen thus in the sixteenth century, much as today a Roman Catholic pope is elected by the College of Cardinals. Perhaps Polonius is such an elector in Denmark. A candidate for the office of king would do well to curry favor with those who will do the electing. We can see that Claudius has done just that. Hamlet is outraged by the deal that has been engineered so quickly while he was abroad, in Wittenberg. He complains later to Horatio that Claudius "hath killed my King and whored my mother, / Popped in between th'election and my hopes" (5.2.64–65, TLN 3568–69). Claudius has apparently managed to rig the "election" in his favor by his offers of deals and promises. Hamlet here indicates that he does indeed regard the throne of Denmark as his proper due. He was, after all, the only son and heir of the now-dead monarch; even in an elective monarchy his candidacy would have seemed formidable.

Whether Hamlet really would have wished to be king is a complex matter. He roundly despises so much of what goes with high office: "Th'oppressor's wrong, the proud man's contumely, / ... the law's delay, / The insolence of office" (3.1.72–74, TLN 1725–27), and still more. Hamlet seems at times better suited to the intellectual's study than to the throne. Shakespeare seems to be puzzling out the paradox that has worried humanity since the time of Plato: whether any person can be both king and philosopher at the same time. The Emperor Alexander is said to have raised the question with Diogenes, the crabbed philosopher who scorned pomp and circumstance in favor of honest poverty and intellectual independence. Hamlet seems more a critic of power than a candidate for office.

Hamlet idealizes his dead father as a great king, the kind of ruler Hamlet would have wished to be. A son in such circumstances can be forgiven if his hero-worship goes so far as to deny any failings: to Hamlet, his father was, among his other admirable traits, "so loving to my mother / That he might not beteem the winds of heaven / Visit her face too roughly" (1.2.140–42, TLN 324–26). In any case, the play as a whole tends to confirm Hamlet's estimate of his father as a mighty and chivalrous monarch. From Horatio we learn how Hamlet Senior accepted a challenge by the King of Norway to personal combat, man to man, with each of their kingdoms pledged to the outcome of the duel (1.1.84–99, TLN 97–112). Hamlet Senior won, with the result that Norway has been a client state to Denmark ever since. The dare might seem to us hardy to the point of recklessness, but it certainly casts Hamlet Senior in the role of dauntless Saxon warlord. Claudius is, in contrast, shrewd and calculating as a royal administrator. He handles the threat of Norwegian invasion by sending a delegation to the King of Norway, offering that king's young nephew Fortinbras free passage through Denmark to Poland in return for a promise not to invade Denmark itself. This is brilliant diplomacy, and it succeeds. We might today tend to prefer diplomatic negotiation to heroic chivalry with a naked sword, and many of Claudius's subjects appear grateful for his skill at the bargaining table. Can any one person hope to be both wise and dauntless, diplomatic and fiercely warlike?

The play of *Hamlet* thus offers us radically contrastive models of kingship. In Hamlet's view, to speak of Hamlet Senior and Claudius in the same breath is to compare "Hyperion to a satyr" (1.2.140, TLN 324). Claudius, Hamlet says, is "no more like my father / Than I to Hercules" (152–53, TLN 336–37). Hamlet urges his mother to compare likenesses of the two, one featuring "Hyperion's curls, the front of Jove himself, / An eye like Mars to threaten and command," while Claudius is "like a mildewed ear, / Blasting his wholesome brother" (3.4.57–66, TLN 2440–49).

How is one to act in such a world as Hamlet sees all around him, a world that is an "unweeded garden / That grows to seed," so depraved indeed that "things rank and gross in nature / Possess it merely" (1.2.135–37, TLN 319–21)? Critics often view Hamlet as paralyzed into inaction by a morbid sensitivity, better at expressing himself in marvelous poetic language than in getting on with the business at hand.

And indeed Hamlet is unsparingly critical of his own failure to act. When he learns from his dead father's ghost what Claudius has done in murdering his brother and whoring that brother's wife, Hamlet's response is unflinching: "Haste me to know 't, that I with wings as swift / As meditation or the thoughts of love / May sweep to my revenge" (1.5.30–32, TLN 714–17). But later, when a touring actor recites the sad tale of Queen Hecuba's passionate lament for the slaughter of her husband, King Priam of Troy, Hamlet cries out in utter dismay at his own passivity. "Oh, what a rogue and peasant slave am I! ,... This is most brave, / That I, the son of a dear father murdered, / Prompted to my revenge by heaven and hell, / Must like a whore unpack my heart with words, / And fall a-cursing like a very drab, / A scullion. Fie upon 't, foh!" (2.2.518–56, TLN 1588–1628). In another soliloquy he ponders how "the native hue of resolution / Is sicklied o'er with the pale cast of thought" (3.1.85–86, TLN 1738–39). In still another, Hamlet reflects on Fortinbras's readiness for direct military action against Poland as a model that should teach him, Hamlet, how to "spur my dull revenge" (4.4.34, TLN 2743.27).

Yet Hamlet is often capable of speedy and even violent action. He is directly responsible for the deaths of others, much more so than any other major figure in the play. He stabs Polonius through a curtain in his mother's private chambers, thinking him to be Claudius; Polonius is not the victim Hamlet intended to slay, but the intent and the act itself are bloody. Moments earlier, when he comes upon the guilty Claudius in prayer, he perceives what appears to be a golden opportunity for bloody revenge, but desists solely because he fears that if he kills the man at prayer he might send him to heaven. "Why, this is hire and salary, not revenge," he reflects. He will postpone the vengeful act until his uncle is "drunk asleep, or in his rage, / Or in th'incestuous pleasure of his bed" (3.3.79–90, TLN 2355–65), so that his soul will surely go to hell. Nineteenth-century productions of *Hamlet* tended to omit this passage because it made Hamlet seem so remorselessly bloody. When Hamlet boasts to Horatio of his cleverly having arranged the execution of his escorts to England, Rosencrantz and Guildenstern, by exchanging their names for his in the document ordering sudden death, he does so without scruple: "Why, man," he says to Horatio, "they did make love to this employment. / They are not near my conscience" (5.2.57–58, TLN 3560–61). When, in his final duel with Laertes, Hamlet discovers that his opponent has wounded him with an unbated sword (that is, one without a button on the point), he wrests the weapon from Laertes and delivers a death blow. Laertes acknowledges at last that he is "justly killed with mine own treachery" (5.2.293, TLN 3785). No gentleman should do such a secret and skulking thing as to use a lethal weapon in a fencing match. "The point envenomed too?" (line 307) cries Hamlet, whereupon he uses the sword to stab the King fatally and then forces the dying man to drink from the poisoned cup intended for Hamlet's own demise. The Queen is already dead from this poison, as an unintended consequence of the plotting against Hamlet. Earlier, Ophelia has lost her sanity and has drowned, again as a direct if unintended consequence of Hamlet's fatal struggle with his uncle. Hamlet is certainly capable of swift action. But when is the right time to act?

Hamlet fully grasps the nature of this dilemma. "Rightly to be great / Is not to stir without great argument, / But greatly to find quarrel in a straw / When honor's at the stake," he observes as he ponders the career of Fortinbras (4.4.18–67, TLN 2743.18–60). Here is a young prince, Hamlet's equivalent in the Norwegian hierarchy, whose very name, "strong in arms," embodies the idea of resolute action. But does Fortinbras's bold career inspire unambiguous admiration? Hamlet plainly sees that Fortinbras, on his way to Poland to fight for "a little patch of ground / That hath in it no profit but the name," is ready to risk "Two thousand souls and twenty thousand ducats" to "debate the question of this straw." His soldiers will fight for a plot of land "Which is not tomb enough and continent / To hide the slain." This is brave, all right, but is it sane? Does it provide a cogent model to Hamlet as to when he should act against Claudius?

The play approaches this weighty problem in a number of ways, often by inviting us to reflect on contrasting pairs of characters. Hamlet Senior and Claudius serve this purpose, the first a "Hyperion" or a "Mars" in Hamlet's view, the other a "mildewed ear," a "murderer and a villain." This contrast embodies features of the Calvinist theology that was so prevalent in Shakespeare's day. Hamlet is intensely aware of the fallen moral state of most humans. "We are arrant knaves, all; believe none of us," he tells Ophelia (3.1.126–27, TLN 1784). He regards himself as "indifferent honest" (that is, reasonably virtuous) and yet, he says, "I could accuse me of such things that it were better my mother had not borne me" (3.1.121–23, TLN 1777–79). Claudius, in these terms, comes across as a reprobate—a Calvinist term for a man wholly incapable of salvation. When he attempts in fervent prayer to seek the forgiveness that Christianity offers to anyone who is truly penitent, we realize that Claudius is a Christian in the sense of having been born into a Christian world; he knows what God demands of one who seeks forgiveness. "But, oh," he ponders, "what form of prayer / Can serve my turn? 'Forgive me my foul murder'? / That cannot be, since I am still possessed / Of those effects for which I did the murder: / My crown, mine own ambition, and my queen" (3.3.51–55, TLN 2327–31). Claudius understands perfectly what he would have to do to be saved. He understands the fierce penalty he faces if he cannot do this: eternal damnation. Why, possessing such knowledge, is Claudius unable to pray? Calvinism provides an answer: Claudius is not one of the elect. He is a reprobate. He cannot will himself to give up the crown and his new wife, despite his realization that the penalty for failure will be unutterably terrible. He is a worldling.

To Hamlet, this polarity of opposites, of the reprobate and the virtuous in human nature, defines the fallen world in which Hamlet finds himself. He is keenly aware that the devil exists, capable of tempting him to undo his own eternal destiny by behaving foully. Perhaps, Hamlet ponders, the spirit he has encountered of his father's ghost was a demon. Hamlet is not being fanciful to suppose the devil capable of such deception: this was standard lore in the work of learned clerics. "The spirit that I have seen / May be the devil," he reasons, "and the devil hath power / T'assume a pleasing shape; yea, and perhaps, / Out of my weakness and my melancholy, ... Abuses me to damn me" (2.2.567–72, TLN 1638–43). That is why Hamlet must devise a test that will unambiguously reveal whether Claudius is guilty or not. Hamlet's test is the play-within-the-play. It works precisely as Hamlet predicts. The play-within-the-play's representation of a man murdering his own brother to win that brother's wife and throne is too vivid for Claudius not to give away his dark secret by his guilty response. "I'll take the Ghost's word for a thousand pound" (3.2.268–69, TLN 2158–59), crows Hamlet to Horatio, who is no less convinced.

Once the truth is proven beyond doubt, Hamlet acts swiftly. Having been sent to England in the custody of Rosencrantz and Guildenstern, he evades their practices, returns to Denmark by boarding a pirate ship in the course of a sea battle and then enlisting the pirates to help him regain his native country—all of this sounding rather like a Hollywood action film. When he accepts the challenge to a fencing match with Laertes, the play comes to a thunderous conclusion, with corpses bestrewing the stage. To see Hamlet as incapable of action flies in the face of the plot.

The women in *Hamlet* offer contrasting models in the puzzle of action and inaction. Ophelia is an obedient daughter of her father, Polonius. Young women are supposed to be obedient. She turns over to her father Hamlet's love letters, whereupon Polonius triumphantly takes them to the King as evidence that Hamlet suffers from love madness. Polonius fatuously insists that he recognizes the symptoms and the disease; he suffered himself, he says, from love melancholy in his youth (2.2.189–90, TLN 1227–28). This comic misdiagnosis points up for us the huge difficulty that attends any attempt to analyze human behavior. Hamlet scoffs at Polonius's simple-mindedness, just as he also jeers at Rosencrantz and Guildenstern for their innocent supposition that Hamlet's erratic behavior is a consequence of frustrated political ambition. "Why, look you now, how unworthy a thing you make of me!" he exults. "You would play upon me, you would seem to know my stops, you would pluck out the heart of my mystery" (3.2.337–39, TLN 2234–37). Human beings are more complex than that, and Hamlet sees himself as especially so. Part of his appeal as a character is his awareness of how infinitely difficult it is to know oneself and to know when it is time to act.

Ophelia is a pitiable victim in these terms: obedience to her father yields her nothing but Hamlet's rejection of her. Her father's death is so unbearably hard on her that she loses her mind and perhaps takes her own life. The play is ambiguous about this, and yet suicide remains throughout the play as a plausible if finally unacceptable alternative to action when the right action seems unattainable. Hamlet contemplates suicide even as he rejects it on religious grounds: "Oh, that this too too solid flesh would melt, / Thaw, and resolve itself into a dew! / Or that the Everlasting had not fixed / His canon 'gainst self-slaughter!" (1.2.129–32, TLN 313–16). To die, to sleep, is "a consummation / Devoutly to be wished." Why would anyone bear the "whips and scorns of time" and so much else, "When he himself might his quietus make / With a bare bodkin?" (3.1.64–77, TLN 1717–30). Suicide is the extreme form of passivity. Hamlet resists it, but the option is always there for him.

Queen Gertrude, Ophelia's counterpart, is another woman whose passivity and obedience to men are seen by Hamlet, and arguably by us as audience, as deeply problematic. "Frailty, thy name is woman!" exclaims Hamlet, as he reflects morbidly on the "wicked speed" with which his mother has posted "With such dexterity to incestuous sheets," "or ere those shoes were old / With which she followed my poor father's body" (1.2.146–57, TLN 330–41). Hamlet's ghostly father is no less blunt in condemning the way in which Claudius has "won to his shameful lust / The will of my most seeming virtuous queen" (1.5.46–47, TLN 732–33). Was she complicit in the crime of murder? This seems unlikely, perhaps, but scarcely less blameworthy in the eyes of Hamlet and his father is her having consented to a marriage that was distressingly sudden. In medieval and Elizabethan times, mourning duties would normally have called on her to refrain from remarrying for at least two years. Was it an incestuous union? Clerical strictures on that troublesome subject have varied from time to time (see Appendix D1), but at the very least the close relationship of brother- and sister-in-law has made for an awkward and unseemly proposition. Claudius must have known that he could prevail on Gertrude to marry him once he had killed her husband, much as he doubtless also knew that he could talk his courtiers and citizens into welcoming him as their new king. Claudius has prepared his way on both fronts. We can perhaps surmise, then, why the weeping and distraught queen, wilting under the barrage of her son's accusations, cries out in heartfelt confession: "Thou turn'st mine eyes into my very soul, / And there I see such black and grainèd spots / As will not leave their tinct" (3.4.91–93, TLN 2465–67).

What is she confessing? Perhaps nothing more than she did agree to the marriage with unseemly and deplorable haste, and in such a way as to appear guilty of illicit sexual desire. Sometimes in production, as when Glenn Close shows passionate feelings for Alan Bates as Claudius in Franco Zeffirelli's film of *Hamlet* (1990), the motivation is overtly sexual, but Gertrude can also be played as a woman like Queen Jocasta in Sophocles' *Oedipus Rex*, who may see her marriage as a means of holding onto her high status as the king's royal consort in a perilous time of regime change. Gertrude feels guiltily anxious about her son, defensive about his criticisms of her, and then truly penitent to the best of her ability. Her dead husband's ghost, though deeply disappointed in her and revulsed by her disloyalty to him, is ready to forgive her if she can beg forgiveness of him and of heaven. Though Hamlet Senior yearns to have his murderous brother executed and sent to hell for what he has done, the Ghost begs his son to be more tender with Gertrude. "Taint not thy mind, nor let thy soul contrive / Against thy mother aught," he instructs Hamlet; "leave her to heaven / And to those thorns that in her bosom lodge / To prick and sting her" (1.5.85–88. TLN 770–73). Penitence is necessarily and healthily sharp and painful, but it can work its cure. If Claudius is a reprobate in Calvinist terms, Gertrude is not. The Ghost returns later to chide his son for being too brusque with Gertrude in his forcing her to confront her own guilt, but arguably Hamlet knows just what he is doing. "Confess yourself to heaven," he urges his mother. "Repent what's past, avoid what is to come" (3.4.156–57, TLN 2532–33). This is the timeless counsel of penitence that Christianity offers to anyone who is troubled with guilt but finally willing to be spiritually reborn.

Evidently, Gertrude now does what Hamlet bids her do for her soul's safety. She not only repents; she heeds Hamlet's stern injunction not to tell her husband Hamlet's great secret, that his madness is a stratagem and a cover.[1] She understands that she must not reveal to Claudius that Hamlet "essentially" is not mad, but "mad in craft" (3.4.194–95, TLN 2563–64). When in the following scene Claudius enters to ask of Gertrude, "How does Hamlet?" her answer is a deliberate prevarication: "Mad as the sea and wind when both contend / Which is the mightier" (4.1.6–8, TLN 2592–94). What is more, in the play's final scene she publicly disobeys her husband. "Gertrude, do not drink" (5.2.276, TLN 3760), Claudius bids her, knowing the wine she holds in her hand to be the poisoned wine that he has prepared for Hamlet to drink during the duel with Laertes. Claudius sees that he is doomed to become the agent of his own undoing, but he can say nothing to stop her. Does she, having witnessed her husband's reaction to the play-within-the-play, come finally to a realization that the man she married is a villain, and that he may have poisoned her dead husband? Does she consume the wine now to spare the life of her son, by drinking what was intended for him? Or is her drinking of the wine one last penitent act, a suicide in fact, and thus a way of ending a life she now wishes to leave? Just as plausibly, or perhaps even more plausibly, does she die

---

1   See Appendix E3, p. 299, for Q1's support for this interpretation.

as a kind of innocent victim of a murderous plot that her husband did not intend for her? In any case, Gertrude has lied to her husband and has disobeyed him as a way of asserting her loyalty to her dear son. We can hope that mother and son are reconciled in death.

The play of *Hamlet* is thus filled with theatrically edifying instances of paired characters. More such comparisons can be adduced. Rosencrantz and Guildenstern are untrustworthy friends of Hamlet as compared with Horatio, the one person to whom Hamlet can willingly trust all his secrets and his life itself. Rosencrantz and Guildenstern act according to their own principles as loyal and ambitious young courtiers glad to serve a king whose life appears to be imperiled by his wild-mannered nephew, but to Hamlet they are time-servers and yes-men. Polonius is another courtier whom Hamlet mistrusts and despises, given as he is to windy and complacent advice. Polonius fancies himself as a master spy and analyst of the human condition. "If circumstances lead me, I will find / Where truth is hid, though it were hid indeed / Within the center," he fatuously boasts to the King (2.2.158–60, TLN 1188–90). The implicit contrast between this foolish self-assurance and the honest counsel of a person like Horatio has much to suggest about the nature of true friendship and loyalty. True friendship in Horatio is also an implicit rebuke of most romantic attachment and sexual love, which Hamlet finds inadequate at every turn.

No set of comparisons and contrasts is more vital to *Hamlet* than the paired fortunes of three young men who find themselves obligated to revenge the death of a revered father: Hamlet himself, Laertes, and Fortinbras. The comparison is profoundly instructive about family ties and about the demands that are laid upon a son whose father has been murdered. The story that Shakespeare inherited from Saxo Gammaticus is one of the duty of revenge and of dire demands placed upon the revenger. To Saxo, Hamlet's duty is morally clear and unambiguous: the ancient code of vengeance is a sacred obligation that must override all feelings of compunction.

The story in *Hamlet* that most nearly resembles this standard model of revenge is the story of Laertes. He knows that his father has been slain by Hamlet. Whether extenuating circumstances might pertain is of no concern to Laertes. Especially when he beholds how terribly his sister has suffered from the death of their father, Laertes renounces all mercy. "To hell, allegiance!" he shouts. "Vows, to the blackest devil!

/ Conscience and grace, to the profoundest pit! / I dare damnation" (4.5.131–33, TLN 2878–80). Is not Laertes justified in this? Hamlet did kill Polonius. The revenge code demands an eye for an eye. What this seemingly plain interpretation of the event leaves out, however, is the crux of the matter: the trouble all began with Claudius's murder of his brother. Laertes makes the fatal mistake of trusting the King's plausible insinuations. Laertes is so driven by the revenge code that he agrees to duel with Hamlet with an unbated sword and ups the ante by offering to anoint its lethal point with a deadly poison. Such secret behavior is both criminal and offensive to the code of honor that Laertes also cherishes: "'tis almost 'gainst my conscience" (5.2.282, TLN 3769), he ponders to himself, as the duel with Hamlet begins to turn against him. He sees too late that he has fallen into a trap of his own devising: he is "a woodcock to mine own springe" (292, TLN 3783–84). His atonement is to accept the blame he deserves, while also revealing to Hamlet and the Danish court where the evil truly lies: "The King, the King's to blame" (307, TLN 3801). He exchanges forgiveness with Hamlet, and dies. Laertes's story is thus an exemplary warning in terms of trying to figure when to act decisively and when to learn more about the true nature of things. Laertes acts rashly and must pay the penalty.

Hamlet faces this dilemma of action with similar puzzles and consequences. He kills the man whose voice he hears behind a curtain in his mother's chambers. Who could this possibly be but the King? Hamlet seizes this moment as ideally attuned to his bloody determination to kill Claudius, but his victim turns out to be Polonius instead. Rash action, as in Laertes's case, turns to catastrophe. Hamlet's response is to recognize that he will have to pay for his killing of Polonius. "I do repent," he tells his mother; "but heaven hath pleased it so / To punish me with this, and this with me, / That I must be their scourge and minister" (3.4.180–82, TLN 2549–51). He perceives that heaven is at work: although what he did was not what he intended, the deed must have some ultimate purpose in providence's great scheme of things. And indeed Hamlet follows this idea to the end of his story. In response to the obligation thrust upon him to slay Claudius, Hamlet has acted swiftly. He sees at once that his willful act was wrong in its premise. Yet, he reasons, providence must have intended that his misdirected action will mysteriously turn out to be a part of heaven's plan. Hamlet comes to believe that "There's a special providence in the fall of a sparrow. If it be now, 'tis not to come; if it be not to come, it will be now; if it be not now, yet it will come" (5.2.200–02, TLN 3668–70). Hamlet has learned from his own failures and aborted planning that "Our indiscretion sometime serves us well / When our deep plots do pall." That should prove to us, he insists to Horatio, that "There's a divinity that shapes our ends, / Rough-hew them how we will" (5.2.8–11, TLN 3507–10).

Instead of pursuing the active role of the avenger, sword in hand, Hamlet now submits himself to the promptings of providence. Some heavenly plan, he trusts, will accomplish its purpose in ways that Hamlet could not have contrived. At least this is how he figures out what it all means. Having been sent to England, then managing to get back to Denmark and reveal himself to the King and to Laertes, Hamlet accepts a challenge to fence with Laertes. He enters into this contest with innocent intent. Why should he now wish to harm or kill Laertes, whom he has already grievously wronged? In a way that he could not have foreseen, the duel and its sudden exchanging of weapons delivers into his hand the chance to defend himself against Laertes and then, most importantly of all, to slay the King. Providence has shown a way. Hamlet has avenged his father's death without premeditation. He has slain his and his father's great enemy, not through cunning and calculation but virtually as an act of self-defense. And he finds the death he longs for not through a willful act of suicide, which he would consider deeply and even damnably sinful, but through trusting to providence. The story is of course profoundly tragic, but it is not a story of murderous intent guiltily fulfilled.

Fortinbras, the third son charged with avenging the death of a father, presents to us a strikingly different resolution of the problem of when to act and when not to act. He acts decisively throughout, and without scruple. His military career against Poland strikes Hamlet as bizarre and even absurd, but it is the consistent career of a military figure who does not waste time with some "craven scruple" of "thinking too precisely on th'event" (4.4.41–42, TLN 2743.34–35). His is a story of pure action, uncomplicated by the kinds of meditation that Hamlet broods over. And, in this case, Fortinbras's forthrightness turns out to be right on target, according to his own appraisal of what he wants. He does indeed succeed in avenging his father's loss to Hamlet Senior through which Norway became a feudal client state of Denmark. Now the Norwegian king will be king of Denmark as well. Hamlet's last utterance is to "prophesy th'election lights / On Fortinbras. He has my dying voice" (5.2.340–41, TLN 3844–45). What an absurd ending, it might seem, for the victory to go to the one who is simply ruthless! Why would Hamlet endorse this resolution of turning Denmark over to the son of the very enemy whom Hamlet's father had defeated in winner-take-all combat?

But what this remarkable conclusion can do for *Hamlet* is perhaps as wonderful and right-minded as it is unexpected: it offers a reading of history that is radically counter to Hamlet's own interpretation of what has happened to him, so much so that we are left with huge questions of how we are to understand Hamlet's tragedy. At certain times, it appears, forthright ruthless action may be the necessary and appropriate choice. Horatio, too, in the final scene, offers a reading of history wholly at variance with that of his dear now-dead friend. To Horatio, the story that has unfolded is one "Of carnal, bloody, and unnatural acts, / Of accidental judgments, casual slaughters, / Of deaths put on by cunning and forced cause, / And, in this upshot, purposes mistook / Fall'n on th'inventors' heads" (5.2.367–71, TLN 3876–80). This is the view of the skeptical humanist, the friend to whom Hamlet has insisted that "There are more things in heaven and earth ... Than are dreamt of in your philosophy" (1.5.174–75, TLN 863–64). Hamlet's own serenely providential reading of his own story is all the more memorable and challenging for being only one perspective on human destiny. *Hamlet* is beautiful for the questions it refuses to address with unequivocal answers.

CRITICAL APPROACHES TO *HAMLET*

Hamlet was a very real success in its own day. An unauthorized quarto, Q1, was published in 1603, so corrupt and abbreviated that it prompted the publication in 1604 of a quarto (Q2) that was, according to its title page, "Newly imprinted and enlarged to almost as much again as it was, according to the true and perfect copy." Other quartos followed in 1611 and some time before 1623, suggesting a strong demand by the reading public. In 1598–1601 the classical scholar Gabriel Harvey lauded the play as having the capacity "to please the wisest sort." Anthony Scoloker, in 1604, described true literary excellence as something that "should please all, like Prince Hamlet." Ben Jonson, though he faulted Shakespeare for having "small Latin, and less Greek," and for too often ignoring the classical unities, generously allowed, in his commendatory tribute in the First Folio collection of 1623, that Shakespeare was worthy of comparison as a tragic writer with ancient Greek dramatists Aeschylus, Sophocles, and Euripides, and without a rival as a comic dramatist even in "insolent Greece or haughty Rome." During the Restoration in 1660 and afterwards, *Hamlet* was accorded the unusual respect of being performed without extensive adaptation, though it was substantially shortened. Samuel Pepys, in his famous Diary, greatly admired the play, as performed repeatedly by Thomas Betterton from 1661 until 1709; in 1688 he praised the role of Hamlet as "the best part, I believe, that ever man acted."

The Earl of Shaftesbury appears to have spoken on behalf of other eighteenth-century observers when, in his *Characteristic Advice to an Author* (1710), he praised *Hamlet* as "almost one continued moral, a series of deep reflections, drawn from the mouth upon the subject of one single accident and calamity, naturally fitted to move horror and compassion." *Hamlet* "appears to have most affected English hearts, and has perhaps been oftenest acted of any which have come upon the stage." Thomas Hanmer, in *Some Remarks on the Tragedy of Hamlet, Prince of Denmark* (1736), similarly found an instructive universality in the play that demonstrated brilliantly how it conforms with the demands of poetic justice. Samuel Johnson, in his preface to the plays (1765), commended Shakespeare's "just representation of general nature." These comments are notably consistent in their view of the play as morally instructive and universal.

Romantic criticism of the late eighteenth and early nineteenth centuries turned in quite a new direction, toward a study of character and emotion. Goethe was perhaps the first to focus on Hamlet's hesitation to act. "Amazement and sorrow overwhelm the solitary young man," wrote Goethe in his *Wilhelm Meister's Apprenticeship* (1795). Many critics have wondered if Goethe was not talking at least partly about the brooding melancholic protagonist of his own autobiographical meditation, *The Sorrows of Young Werther* (1774). The same suspicion lingers in an appraisal of Samuel Taylor Coleridge's *Notes and Lectures upon Shakespeare* (1808), in which the author frankly admits that to understand Hamlet fully "it is essential that we should reflect on the constitution of our own minds." "I have a smack of Hamlet in myself," Coleridge wrote. The writer who was addicted to laudanum and who, according to legend at least, composed his poem "Kubla Khan" following an opium-induced dream and then left it unfinished, might be expected to see Hamlet as one who "vacillates from sensibility, and procrastinates from thought, and loses the power of action in the energy of resolve." The critical sentiment is all the more powerful in that it reflects Romantic sensibility in many other writers. Charles Lamb, in his *On the Tragedies of Shakespeare* (1811) reflected on his desire "to know the internal workings and movements of a great mind, of an Othello or a Hamlet for instance, the *when* and the *why* and the *how far* they should be moved." William Hazlitt declared, in *Characters of Shakespeare's Plays* (1817), that "It is we who are Hamlet," most of all in the way in which his "powers have been eaten up by thought." For August W. von Schlegel, in *Lectures on Dramatic Art and Literature* (1809), the burden that Hamlet faces "cripples the power of thought."

This fascination with character as the central concern of drama spilled over onto other characters in *Hamlet* too, particularly Ophelia. "Poor Ophelia!" wrote Anna Jameson in *Characteristics of Women* (1832). "Oh, far too soft, too good, too fair to be cast among the briers of this working-day world, and fall and bleed upon the thorns of life!" Critics such as Thomas Campbell lambasted Hamlet for his insensitivity in his dealings with Ophelia. A new interest in women was to be seen everywhere. Her drowning, as described by Gertrude, became the subject for many paintings by eighteenth- and nineteenth-century artists such as Henry Tresham, Richard Westall, and John Everett Millais. Mary Cowden Clarke imagined what the girlhood of Ophelia might have been like in her *Girlhood of Shakespeare's Heroines* (1851–52). The Victorian actor and writer Helena Faucit similarly wondered about the afterlife of Ophelia in *On Some of Shakespeare's Female Characters* (1885). George Eliot (pen name of the novelist Mary Anne Evans) proposed in *The Mill on the Floss* (1860) that "we can conceive of Hamlet's having married Ophelia" and then managing to get through life "with a reputation for sanity." In such writings, and with many readers and audience members, the characters of *Hamlet*, along with other vivid creations such as Falstaff and Cleopatra, took on lives of their own. Critics delighted in wondering what it would have been like to know these characters and to pursue their destinies outside the bounds of

Ophelia, John Everett Millais, 1851–52.

the plays as Shakespeare had written them. The interweaving of author, character, reader, and viewer was seen as a fundamental quality of dramatic creation through which Shakespeare became intensely personal. By the nineteenth century, Shakespeare had grown into England's great national poet through whom the nation could celebrate its cultural and political greatness. *Hamlet* stood as his quintessential play at the center of this cultural triumph.

A landmark of literary criticism of *Hamlet* arrived early in the twentieth century: A.C. Bradley's *Shakespearean Tragedy* (1904). For Bradley, *Hamlet* is one of the four "great" Shakespearean tragedies, along with *Othello*, *King Lear*, and *Macbeth*, in their embrace of universal issues: good and evil, temptation and sin, self-knowledge and betrayal. Hamlet stands revealed in this broad moral context as an idealist, deeply sensitive, vulnerable to the shocks of a father's murder and a mother's hasty remarriage. He generalizes philosophically in ways that resonate with our longing to understand ourselves and the universe we inhabit. Bradley deftly incorporates the resources of "character" criticism that the nineteenth century had found so compatible and enlightening. Character criticism continued to be a major focus of critics, especially in Ernest Jones's *Hamlet and Oedipus* (1910), in which this disciple of Sigmund Freud enlarged upon the psychoanalytical thesis that Freud had himself propounded in *The Interpretation of Dreams* (1899)—namely, that Hamlet is driven subconsciously by an incestuous desire for his mother which complicates his task of avenging the murder of his father: how can he kill the hated uncle for having taken sexual possession of the mother whom Hamlet himself yearns for? The classical scholar Gilbert Murray, in *Hamlet and Orestes* (1914), pursued a parallel method of psychological and anthropological analysis by studying *Hamlet* as a kind of ritual drama that is profoundly related to ancient tribal customs and ceremonies. (This approach owed much to the work of Freud's fellow psychologist Carl Jung.) Such ideas also informed Northrop Frye's *Anatomy of Criticism* (1957), which proposed that drama can be seen as a response to mythic patterns that include the seasonal changes of the year: *Hamlet*, in these terms, is autumnal, wintry, and melancholic. Similarly, Maynard Mack's "The World of *Hamlet*" (1952) sees the play as dominated by the interrogative mood, by questions, riddles, enigmas, and mysteries.

At the same time, critical responses to "character" criticism were emerging. One of the most insistent was that of historical criticism. Practiced in good part by academic scholars motivated by a new professionalism in their ranks, the method insisted, as did Sir Walter Raleigh (a professor of English Literature at Oxford, not related to the courtier who served Queen Elizabeth and James I), that "[a] play is not a collection of the biographies of those who appear in it," nor is it a moral play (*Shakespeare*, 1907). Instead, a play is a kind of artifice arising out of a particular historical milieu. E.E. Stoll's *Art and Artifice in Shakespeare* (1933) adroitly captures this critical point of view. *Hamlet*, for Stoll, is not a study of psychological types: it is a revenge play, the resources for which are provided by dramatic conventions. Hamlet's delay is, in these terms, necessary in order that Hamlet may test whether Claudius is indeed the murderer that the Ghost has declared him to be. Lily Bess Campbell's *Shakespeare's Tragic Heroes: Slaves of Passion* (1952) declares in its title a commitment to historical circumstances, and especially to Elizabethan "understandings" of melancholy. John Dover Wilson, in *What Happens in "Hamlet"* (1935), locates the play in the Elizabethan playhouse as a way of asking, among other matters, whether Hamlet perceives that he is being overheard by the King and Polonius during his painful interview with Ophelia. In *Shakespeare and the Nature of Man* (1942), Theodore Spencer, a professor at Harvard, looks closely at Shakespeare's indebtedness to innovative and heterodox thinkers in the Renaissance such as Copernicus, Montaigne, Mirandola, and Machiavelli. Historical criticism continues to this day.

The 1930s saw another critical revolution, this time expressing itself as a critique of historical criticism. The so-called "New" critics, such as G. Wilson Knight (*The Wheel of Fire*, 1930; *The Shakespearian Tempest*, 1953), Derek Traversi (*An Approach to Shakespeare*, 1938), and L.C. Knights (*Explorations*, 1946; *An Approach to Hamlet*, 1960), insisted that historical criticism was too often dry and philological in its quest for factual information about writers' biographies and other historical concerns. Surely criticism should turn its attention instead to close reading of texts, to image patterns, to the sounds of poetry. Caroline Spurgeon's *Shakespeare's Imagery and What It Tells Us* (1935) catalogued Shakespeare's images in related clusters: diseases, poison, ulcers, blisters, and the like. Maurice Charney's *Style in "Hamlet"* (1969) turned the new interest in imagery to the theater, where stage picture, gesture, props, and all that is scenic could be seen as creating a language of theatrical gesture. Historical critics quickly realized that they could contribute to such theatrical insights rather than simply allowing themselves to be pilloried as academic pedants. Andrew Gurr (*Playgoing in Shakespeare's London*, 1987) and Ann Jennalie Cook (*The Privileged Playgoers of Shakespeare's London, 1576–1642*, 1981) provided a wealth of new information and insight about those who came to see the plays of Shakespeare and his contemporaries.

In the 1960s and afterwards, with cultural upheaval brought about by protests against the Vietnam War, racial conflict, social unrest, the assassinations of John and Bobby Kennedy and Martin Luther King Jr., and so much more, literary criticism of *Hamlet* found several new forms of expression. One was the so-called "New Historicism," championed by Stephen Greenblatt, Louis Montrose, Jonathan Goldberg, and others such as Stephen Orgel and Richard Helgerson who were more or less loosely allied to the movement. The New Historicists owed much in theoretical terms to Clifford Geertz's *Negara* (1980), and to Lawrence Stone's *The Crisis of the Aristocracy, 1558–1641* (1965), in which critics could find eloquent models of how public ceremonials of statecraft offered themselves as myths about the creation and manipulation of political power. Prompted by their resistance to the governorship of California and then the US presidency of Ronald Reagan in the 1980s, the New Historicists formed a close relationship with the Cultural Materialism of continental and British critics that included Raymond Williams, Jonathan Dollimore, Alan Sinfield, Terry Eagleton, and others. These critics devoted their energies to politically radical interpretations of texts as expressive of rapid political and social change. They took sustenance from the galvanizing new insights offered by Jan Kott, a Polish political activist who viewed *Hamlet* and other Shakespearean plays against the apocalyptic background of a Europe divided by the Iron Curtain after World War II. In *Shakespeare Our Contemporary* (1964), Kott describes *Hamlet* as "a drama of political crime." Its protagonist was one who was "deeply involved in politics, sarcastic, passionate and brutal"; like the persona of movie star James Dean, he was a young rebel intent on "action, not reflection." Kott was clearly indebted to the absurdist drama and existential philosophy of such twentieth-century playwrights and dramatic theorists as Antonin Artaud, Jean-Paul Sartre, Eugène Ionesco, Albert Camus, and Jerzy Grotowski. *Hamlet*, according to Kott, was a bleak comedy of the absurd through which "we ought to get at our modern experience, anxiety and sensibility."

Feminist criticism took on new energy in these late-twentieth-century years of experiment and rebellion. Juliet Dusinberre's *Shakespeare and the Nature of Women* (1975) was an inspirational study that brought the feminist concerns of the nineteenth century into a new political context. Lisa Jardine's *Still Harping on Daughters* (1983), with its title derived from Polonius's response to Hamlet's "mad" discourse, turned the focus of feminist criticism in *Hamlet* to fulminations against patriarchal interference in the lives of young women. Claude Lévi-Strauss, in his *The Elementary Structures of Kinship* (1969), offered a bracing model of new ways of thinking about family relationships, in which men are so often the controlling force, making use of daughters as resources to be pawned and traded in commercial and political negotiations among men. Arnold Van Gennep (*The Rites of Passage*, 1960) and Victor Turner (*The Ritual Process*, 1969) offered further anthropological models for exploring the transitional moments in human life—birth, puberty, marriage, death—that made for such compelling and threatening conflicts in the lives especially of women. Both Ophelia and Gertrude provided splendid materials for analyses by Coppélia Kahn, Lynda Boose, Marjorie Garber, Madelon Sprengnether, Jean Howard, Gail Paster, Phyllis Rackin, Dympna Callaghan, Jyotsna Singh, Marianne

Novy, Carol Neely, Valerie Traub, and many others. Some feminist critics such as Ania Loomba brought to this lively discourse the perspective of third world experience. Still others, such as Kim Hall and Margo Hendricks, looked at gender in terms of race relations. Same-sex relationships became the concern of Bruce Smith, Laurie Shannon, Jonathan Goldberg, Mario DiGangi, and still others. *Hamlet* has been a central text in all these explorations.

Post-structural criticism, or deconstruction, arrived on the scene at more or less the same time in the late twentieth century. It owed its philosophical and critical origins especially to the linguistic and semiotic work on the Continent, notably in France, of Ferdinand de Saussure, Michel Foucault, and Jacques Derrida. For such thinkers, "meaning" and "authorial intent" were protean and indeterminate concepts, best understood as arbitrary signifiers in a complex system of difference. Patricia Parker and Geoffrey Hartman, in *Shakespeare and the Question of Theory* (1985), showed how infinitely supple Shakespeare's poetic language could be, with its incessant play of words and its delight in punning. Hamlet, viewed in this light, could be seen as a superb practitioner in the art of verbal play. Deconstruction has led to new and challenging insights in editing, as well; by insisting, in Foucaultian fashion, that texts are multiple and evolving, especially in the theater. *Hamlet*, with its extensive differences between the authorized versions of Q2 and F1 (see A Note on the Text, pp. 57–59), and then even more remarkably by the variations embodied in the unauthorized Q1, continues to be a battleground for rival textual theories as to how this great work came into being and then evolved.

In the late twentieth and early twenty-first centuries, literary appraisals of *Hamlet* have had the advantage of being able to make use of New Historicist, feminist, and deconstructive methodologies, along with theatrical analysis and still other perspectives, often in combination. Examples include Leah Marcus's *Puzzling Shakespeare* (1988), Annabel Patterson's *Shakespeare and the Popular Voice* (1989), Janet Adelman's "Man and Wife Is One Flesh: *Hamlet* and the Confrontation with the Maternal Body" (*Suffocating Mothers*, 1992), Stephen Greenblatt's *Hamlet in Purgatory* (2001), William Hamlin's *Tragedy and Scepticism in Shakespeare's England* (2005), Linda Charnes's *Hamlet's Heirs: Shakespeare and the Politics of a New Millennium* (2006), Lars Engle's "Moral Agency in *Hamlet*" (*Shakespeare Studies*, 2012), Richard McCoy's *Faith in*

Shakespeare (2013), and Andrew Cutrofello's *All for Nothing: Hamlet's Negativity* (2014).

Hamlet was first performed, probably in 1599–1601, by the Lord Chamberlain's Men, who were to become the King's Men in 1603 when James VI of Scotland came to the throne as James I of England. Richard Burbage, the company's leading actor, took the role of Hamlet. Tradition proposes, with uncertain authority, that Shakespeare may have played the Ghost of Hamlet's father. Other actor sharers included John Heminges, Henry Condell, Thomas Pope, Augustine Phillips, and Will Sly. Robert Armin, who had joined the company in 1598, seems to have specialized in comic roles, including probably the Gravedigger in this play. *Hamlet* may have been one of the plays used in 1599 to open the company's new theater, the Globe, on the south bank of the River Thames. The company regulars took the important speaking roles, while hired extras were retained to play the soldiers on watch, ambassadors, attendants, and the like. Boy actors portrayed Gertrude, Ophelia, and the Player Queen.

The famous 1596 illustration of the Swan Theatre (see p. 49) gives us the best evidence we have as to the theatrical space available for the first performances of *Hamlet*, even though we cannot assume that the Globe Theatre resembled the Swan in every detail. (See Shakespeare's Theater, pp. 47–51.) A trap door in the main stage must have provided a space for Ophelia's grave in Act 5: a tribute to Richard Burbage in 1619 observed, "Oft have I seen him jump into the grave." The unauthorized 1603 quarto (Q1) supports this evidence with its stage directions, "*Laertes leaps into the grave*," followed then by "*Hamlet leaps in after Laertes*." Earlier, as we learn from Q2, the Ghost's voice could be heard "*under the stage*" (1.5.156, TLN 845) as he moved from place to place. The appearances of the Ghost in Act 1 were probably located on the main stage, as the gallery was too small for such complex action.

Large props probably included thrones for the King and Queen. Hand-held props were plentiful: spades, swords, tables, cushions, bouquets of flowers, skulls, recorders, and still more. Musical effects included Ophelia's singing, and numerous fanfares of trumpet and drum celebrating royal entrances and toasts of wine. Since lighting effects were essentially unknown, and since the stage action was open to the heavens, the suggestion of nighttime and ghostly visitations must have been achieved by gesture and terse conversation. Hamlet's remarks to the players on how to practice their art (3.2.1–37, TLN 1848–93) tell us much about the company's acting ability and its fervent intent to improve on the practices of previous generations of actors.

Hamlet was performed often in its early years, including a performance at court in 1619. When the theaters reopened in London, after being closed from 1642 to 1660 during the Puritan Commonwealth, Hamlet was among the first plays to be shown in revival. It had become the property of William Davenant, impresario of the Duke of York's Company. This Hamlet, though it was less altered than some other Shakespeare plays, was shortened from the original by some 841 lines. Gone was most of the action involving Fortinbras, Rosencrantz, and Guildenstern, along with Hamlet's advice to the players and his encounter with the Captain of Fortinbras's army, and a good deal else. Performances were now indoors, at the Lincoln's Inn Fields theater, with a proscenium arch, artificial lighting, and scenic effects showing views in perspective by means of movable painted flats. Thomas Betterton was the reigning actor-manager of the Restoration period, meaning that he starred in the play's title role while also managing the company in which he owned a major share. Betterton was greatly admired, by the diarist Samuel Pepys and others, for his ability to convey "an almost breathless astonishment, or an impatience, limited by filial obedience," in his encounters with his father's Ghost. Gertrude was played by Elizabeth Barry, one of the famous actresses who had by now replaced the boy actors of Shakespeare's era. Elegance and refinement were the order of the day, in accord with manners that had been largely imported from France with the Restoration of England's monarchy in 1660. Betterton was the Hamlet of the London stage from 1661 until 1709, when he was 74. He was succeeded by Robert Wilks, who played Hamlet until 1732.

David Garrick, the pre-eminent actor-manager of his time, excelled in the role of Hamlet from the 1740s until his retirement in 1776. Garrick aided materially in raising Shakespeare to the iconic status of being England's greatest writer; Stratford-upon-Avon became a place of pilgrimage in 1769, when Garrick staged a three-day Shakespeare Jubilee centered mainly on Garrick's stirring recital of his own "Ode upon Dedicating the Town Hall, and Erecting a Statue to Shakespeare." (No plays were performed on this occasion.) His Hamlet thrilled audiences to the core, most of all when a specially made wig caused his hair to stand on end (see extended note, p. 182). A trick chair fell over, in a piece of stage business inherited from Betterton. Garrick trembled so at the appearance of the Ghost that his knees knocked together, his hat fell off, his mouth stood open, and he looked so petrified with terror that his friends feared he would fall to the ground. Despite this great success, Garrick undertook in 1772 to revise the text of *Hamlet* in a way not previously attempted. In this version, Hamlet never embarks for England at all, and Laertes does not conspire with Claudius to kill Hamlet. When the King attempts to intervene in the duel between Laertes and Hamlet, he is fatally stabbed by Hamlet. Hamlet is slain by Laertes but forgives him, whereupon Laertes agrees to rule jointly in Denmark with Horatio. Fortinbras, Rosencrantz, and Guildenstern are omitted from this ending. Gertrude lives on, though in a remorseful trance of near madness. Garrick soon regretted having undertaken this revision, and it quickly disappeared from stage history.

Romantic authors such as William Hazlitt, intent upon portraying Hamlet as a melancholy and sensitive poet incapable of forthright action, considered *Hamlet* a play ill suited for performance. Though Hazlitt admired John Philip Kemble and Edmund Kean as the great Shakespearean actors of the day, he considered them largely incapable of portraying Hamlet as a man "wrapped up in his own reflections" who only "*thinks aloud.*" He should be acted with "a pensive air of sadness," in Hazlitt's view, "full of weakness and melancholy," "the most amiable of misanthropes" (*Characters of Shakespeare's Plays*, 1817). Kemble's sister, Sarah Siddons, played Gertrude in 1796 and even undertook Hamlet in a "breeches" (i.e., cross-dressed) performance. Middle-class audiences were increasingly large in these early years of the industrial revolution. These audiences, demanding more elaborate and expensive scenery, were gratified by new scenic effects, especially those introduced by Edmund Kean at Drury Lane. William Charles Macready expanded this new opulent style of presentation, first at Covent Garden and then at Drury Lane. His *Hamlet* in 1837 was lauded by one reviewer as "a series of glorious pictures." The background for the scene at Ophelia's grave featured a Gothic-windowed building and masonry archway flanked by trees. Macready located the play-within-the-play in an elaborate theatrical structure ornamented with drapes, curtains, statuary, and carved paneling, surrounded by an onstage audience that included the King and Queen, Hamlet, Horatio, Ophelia, numerous courtiers, and spear-carrying guards. Macready's other great contribution to theater history was to restore the text to something more approaching its original features than had been the revisionary custom for nearly two centuries. (He also abandoned the happy ending of *King Lear* that had held the stage since Nahum Tate's production of 1681.)

Later Victorian productions were the work of actor-managers such as Samuel Phelps, Charles Kean, and Henry Irving, whose reign as Hamlet at the Lyceum from 1871 to 1902 achieved new heights of opulent and expensive set-building. The battlements of Elsinore Castle and surrounding massive rocks were bathed in the soft light of the moon, shimmering over an expanse of water as dawn approached. Ellen Terry, touchingly triumphant in her mad scenes, played Ophelia for Irving in a production that ran for 108 performances in 1878–79. Like other actor-managers before him, Irving ended the play with Hamlet's "the rest is silence," thereby giving him, rather than Fortinbras, the last word.

The early twentieth century saw a marked departure from this opulent and expensive staging, even if that tradition still persisted in the lavish productions of Herbert Beerbohm Tree in 1909 and 1910. William Poel introduced a revolutionary return to something like Renaissance staging when he directed a reading of *Hamlet* at St. George's Hall on Regent Street, London, in 1881 and again in 1914, based on the unauthorized Q1. Poel employed an unadorned stage framed on four sides by red curtains. George Bernard Shaw enthusiastically endorsed the restoration of Shakespearean staging to something like its original mode of production. Inspired by these new promptings, Harley Granville-Barker championed the cause of a bare-stage production unencumbered by the neoclassical preconceptions that had made for long delays at the presumed scene divisions of nineteenth-century Shakespearean productions. The first known modern-dress *Hamlet* took place at the Birmingham Repertory Theatre in 1925, under the direction of Barry Jackson and H.K. Ayliff. Muriel Hewitt, dressed in the style of the flapper generation of the 1920s, interpreted Ophelia as both fascinated by and anxious about the prospect of an enlarged sexual freedom.

Sigmund Freud's psychoanalytic interpretation of Hamlet (see above, pp. 27–28) was adopted by some directors, notably by Tyrone Guthrie in his 1937–38 production that featured Laurence Olivier in the title role. Because of weather, a VIP performance intended for an outdoor courtyard at Kronborg Castle (i.e., Elsinore) in Denmark had to be moved into the ballroom of the hotel where the company was staying and was therefore improvised in the round, with such startlingly revolutionary effects that a new mode of staging came into being. Olivier's famous film version of 1948 was inevitably influenced by the Guthrie production (see below, "*Hamlet* on Film and Television"). Michael Benthall set the play in Victorian England in his 1948 production at Stratford-upon-Avon, with two actors, Paul Scofield and Robert Helpmann, in the role of Hamlet on alternate nights. Once the precedent had been established of transferring the mise en scène from Renaissance Denmark to more modern locations, other experiments followed. Richard Burton's Electronovision enactment of the title role in 1964 rejected the melancholy and pensive interpretation insisted upon by Goethe, Coleridge, and Ernest Jones in favor of a virile and rough-edged Hamlet dressed informally as if at a rehearsal. Burton was, after all, the son of a Welsh coal-miner who had found his theatrical calling in the Oxford University Dramatic Society.

Disaffection with social and political life in the 1960s and 1970s prompted a number of productions of *Hamlet* caught up in a mood of disillusionment and cynicism. Peter Hall's *Hamlet* at Stratford-upon-Avon in 1965 dwelt, in Hall's words, on "an apathy of the will so deep that commitment to politics, to religion or to life is impossible." Glenda Jackson as Ophelia was a neurotic shrew, and the observation of Hamlet (played by David Warner) that "Denmark's a prison" (2.2.240, TLN 1289) seemed painfully appropriate to a Europe divided by an Iron Curtain. Jan Kott's *Shakespeare Our Contemporary* (see above, p. 30) inspired a number of directors to speak through *Hamlet* about a nightmare world of existential impasse. Nicol Williamson, in Tony Richardson's 1969 production at London's Roundhouse Theatre, was a snarling, ill-tempered working-class rebel against the British Establishment, speaking in the guttural rhythms of his social class. Buzz Goodbody, the first female director to work for the Royal Shakespeare Company, in 1975 converted The Other Place at Stratford-upon-Avon into a prison by shutting the theater doors and not allowing the audience to exit for any reason until the show was over. In the United States, Joseph Papp opened his 1968 production at the Public Theater with Hamlet (Martin Sheen) in a coffin-like cradle at the foot of Claudius's and Gertrude's bed, thereby invoking a nightmare atmosphere of Oedipal and incestuous conflict. Heiner Müller's *Die Hamletmaschine*, first produced in Paris in 1979, took the point of view of artists and intellectuals alienated from the police state of Soviet-dominated eastern Europe. An expanded version of over seven hours at Berlin in 1989–90 turned the play into an avant-garde disquisition between a schizophrenically impotent Hamlet and a revolutionary Ophelia.

The rise to prominence in 1980 and afterwards of New Historicism, feminism, and deconstruction, among other new schools of criticism (see above, pp. 29–32), was sure to find theatrical expression. Jonathan Miller's 1982 production at London's Warehouse Theatre presented Hamlet (Anton Lesser) as a tiresome and unattractive character, clever enough but immature and dirty-minded. Adrian Noble's production in 1992–93 with Kenneth Branagh in the title role was highly self-referential in a way that suggested that everything in life is staged and hollow. Alexandru Tocilescu, at Bucharest's Bulandra Theatre in 1985, saw the world of Denmark as a theatrical version of Nicolae Ceauşescu's Stalinist regime in Rumania; the part of Hamlet was taken by Ion Caramitru, who was soon to become the leader of the revolution overthrowing Ceauşescu in 1989. In John Caird's Royal National Theatre production of 2001–02, the set was simultaneously a prison and a cathedral. For Steven Pimlott, directing the play at Stratford-upon-Avon in 2001, Hamlet was a killer, the embodiment of a youth culture rebelling against an unfeeling world. Surveillance cameras and search-lights looked down upon the drab, gray world of Denmark. Larry Lamb as Claudius was a master of "spin-doctoring" in a way that invoked the political world of George W. Bush and Tony Blair. Rosencrantz and Guildenstern shared a marijuana joint with Hamlet. Hamlet dispatched Claudius with a revolver, whereupon those who survived the catastrophe at the end of the play fawningly greeted Fortinbras as the new strongman of the hour. *Hamlet* has proved to be a powerful weapon for devastating productions in Egypt criticizing President Gamal Abdel Nasser in the 1950s and 1960s until his overthrow in 1970.

Jude Law, as Hamlet in Michael Grandage's production at the Donmar Warehouse in 2009, was a media sensation, Law himself having been identified as one of the ten most handsome males in show business. David Tennant's interpretation of Hamlet, under the direction of

Gregory Doran in 2008–09, was intense and intelligent. A filmed version was set in a nineteenth-century missionary school chapel. Another insightful production, starring Benedict Cumberbatch at the Barbican Theatre in London under the direction of Lyndsey Turner, was made available on live television in 2015, enabling large audiences to see a show that was quickly sold out in London. War in this production was imminent in the many bomb blasts and battlefield carnage brought about by Fortinbras's huge army.

HAMLET ON FILM AND TELEVISION

Hamlet has been filmed more often than any other Shakespeare play, and justly so. The early Danish movie star Asta Nielsen played Hamlet in a 78-minute silent version filmed in 1920. Laurence Olivier directed and starred in a celebrated film version of 1948, which imagined *Hamlet* (in Olivier's own voice-over comment) as "the tragedy of a man who could not make up his mind." It was nominated for seven Academy Awards and won four, including Best Picture and Best Actor. In 1954 a powerful film version in Russian directed by Grigori Kozintsev, with a translation by Boris Pasternak and a musical score by Dmitri Shostakovich, looked at the play in the light of Stalin's prison camps: the Hamlet of this film was heroic in his resistance to oppression.

Other notable film adaptations include a 1980 BBC version, with Derek Jacobi as Hamlet, and Franco Zeffirelli's film of 1990, with Mel Gibson as an action hero, along with Alan Bates as Claudius, Glenn Close as a Gertrude who is deeply attracted to her new husband, Helena Bonham Carter as a jittery and unhappy Ophelia, Ian Holm as Polonius, and Paul Scofield as the Ghost. Such star power and the film's pictorial handsomeness ensured a commercial success. Kenneth Branagh's four-hour uncut *Hamlet* (1996–97) featured Derek Jacobi, who had played Hamlet in 1980, as Claudius, along with Julie Christie as Gertrude and Kate Winslet as a distraught Ophelia. It also included celebrity star turns for Robin Williams as Osric, Charlton Heston as the Player King, Jack Lemmon as Marcellus, Gérard Depardieu as Reynaldo, and Billy Crystal as the Gravedigger, which again contributed to financial success, even if some of the individual performances were disappointing. Michael Almereyda set *Hamlet* (2000) in a New York skyscraper housing the Denmark Corporation, of which Claudius (Kyle MacLachlan) was chief executive officer, with Gertrude (Diane Venora), his wife, a svelte suburbanite well placed in a world of luxurious comforts such as private swimming pools and stretch limousines. Hamlet was played by Ethan Hawke as a film geek deeply alienated from the materialistic world of his mother and stepfather. The playwright Sam Shepard took the role of the Ghost, appearing eerily on the building's closed-circuit security system. Nicholas Hytner's 2010–11 production of the play at London's National Theatre was shown on film to good effect. Kevin Kline and Kirk Browning filmed a *Hamlet* in 1989, with Kline himself in the title role, that was low-budget and has accordingly been generally forgotten today, but managed to be wonderfully intelligent. The role of Hamlet continues to serve as a supreme theatrical challenge and achievement for so many great actors, including Maurice Evans, John Gielgud, John Neville, Christopher Plummer, and Rory Kinnear, along with those already named here.

The website of the Internet Shakespeare Editions (http://internetshakespeare. uvic.ca), in the section "Life & Times," has further information on many topics mentioned here: Shakespeare's education, his religion, the lives and work of his contemporaries, and the rival acting companies in London.

William Shakespeare was baptized on 26 April 1564, in Holy Trinity Church, Stratford-upon-Avon. He is traditionally assumed to have been born three days earlier, on 23 April, the feast day of St. George, England's patron saint. His father, John Shakespeare, prospering for years as a tanner, glover, and dealer in commodities such as wool and grain, rose to become city chamberlain or treasurer, alderman, and high bailiff, the town's highest municipal position. Beginning in 1577, John Shakespeare encountered financial difficulties, with the result that he was obliged to mortgage his wife's property and miss council meetings. Although some scholars argue that he was secretly a Catholic, absenting himself also from Anglican church services for that reason, the greater likelihood is that he stayed at home for fear of being prosecuted for debt. His wife, Mary, did come from a family with ongoing Catholic connections, but most of the evidence suggests that Shakespeare's parents were respected members of the Established Church. John's civic duties involved him in carrying out practices of the Protestant Reformation. John and Mary baptized all their children at the Anglican Holy Trinity Church and were buried there.

As a civic official, John must have sent his son William to the King Edward VI grammar school close to their house on Henley Street. Student records from the period have perished, but information about the program of education is plentifully available. William would have studied Latin grammar and authors, including Ovid, Virgil, Plautus, Seneca, and others that left an indelible mark on the plays he wrote in his early years.

Shakespeare did not, however, go to university. The reasons are presumably two: his father's financial difficulties, and, perhaps even more crucially, Shakespeare's own marriage at the age of eighteen to Anne Hathaway, since neither Oxford nor Cambridge would ordinarily admit married students. Anne was eight years older than William. She was also three months pregnant when they were married in November 1582. A special license had to be obtained from the Bishop of Worcester to allow them to marry quickly, without the customary readings on three successive Sundays in church of the banns, or announcements of intent to marry. The couple's first child, Susanna, was born in late May 1583. Twins, named Hamnet and Judith, the last of their children, followed in February 1585. Thereafter, evidence is scarce as to Shakespeare's whereabouts or occupation for about seven years. Perhaps he taught school, or was apprenticed to his father, or joined some company of traveling actors. At any event, he turns up in London in 1592. In that year, he was subjected to a vitriolic printed attack by a fellow drama- tist, Robert Greene (1558–92), who seems to have been driven by pro- fessional envy to accuse Shakespeare of being an "upstart crow" who had beautified himself with the feathers of other writers for the stage, including Christopher Marlowe (1564–93), George Peele (1556–96), Thomas Nashe (1567–1601), and Greene himself.

Shakespeare was indeed well established as a playwright in London by the time of this incident in 1592. In the same year, Nashe paid trib- ute to the huge success of the tragic death of Lord Talbot in a play, and the only play we know that includes Talbot is Shakespeare's *1 Henry VI*. We do not know for what acting company or companies Shakespeare wrote in the years before 1594, or just how he got started, but he seems to have been an actor as well as a dramatist. Two other plays about the reign of Henry VI also belong to those early years, along with his triumphantly successful *Richard III*. These four plays, forming his first historical tetralogy, were instrumental in defining the genre of the English history play. Following shortly after the great defeat of the Spanish Armada in 1588, they celebrated England's ascent from a century of devastating civil wars to the accession in 1485 of the Tudor Henry VII, grandfather of Queen Elizabeth I. Shakespeare's early work also includes some fine ventures into comedy, including *The Comedy of Errors*, *The Two Gentlemen of Verona*, *Love's Labor's Lost*, and *The Taming of the Shrew*. He wrote only one tragedy at this time, *Titus Andronicus*, a revenge tragedy based on fictional early Roman history. Shakespeare also turned his hand to narrative poetry in these early years. *Venus and Adonis* in 1593 and *The Rape of Lucrece* in 1594, both dedicated to the Earl of Southampton, seem to show Shakespeare's interest in becoming a published poet, though ultimately he chose drama as more fulfilling and lucrative. He probably wrote some of his sonnets in these years, perhaps to the Earl of Southampton, though they were not published until 1609 and then without Shakespeare's authorization.

Shakespeare joined the newly formed Lord Chamberlain's Men, as an actor-sharer and playwright, in 1594, along with Richard Burbage (c. 1567–1619), his leading man. This group quickly became the premier acting company in London, in stiff competition with Edward Alleyn and the Lord Admiral's Men. For the Lord Chamberlain's group, Shakespeare wrote his second and more artistically mature tetralogy of English histories, including *Richard II* and the two *Henry IV* plays, centered on the Prince who then becomes the monarch and victor at Agincourt in *Henry V* (1599). He also wrote another history play, *King John*, in these years. Concurrently, Shakespeare achieved great success in romantic comedy, with *A Midsummer Night's Dream*, *The Merchant of Venice*, and *The Merry Wives of Windsor*. He hit the top of his form in romantic comedy in three plays of 1598–1600 with similar throw-away titles: *Much Ado About Nothing*, *As You Like It*, and *Twelfth Night, or What You Will*. Having fulfilled that amazing task, he set romantic comedy aside until some years later.

During this time Shakespeare lived in London, apart from his family in Stratford. He saw to it that they were handsomely housed and provided for; he bought New Place, one of the two finest houses in town. Presumably he went home to Stratford when he could. He was comfortably well off, owning one share among ten in an acting company that enjoyed remarkable artistic and financial success. He suffered a terrible tragedy in 1596 when his only son and heir, Hamnet, died at the age of eleven. In that year, Shakespeare applied successfully for a coat of arms for his father, so that John, and William too, could each style himself as a gentleman. John died in 1601, Shakespeare's mother in 1608.

Having set aside romantic comedy and patriotic English history at the end of the 1590s, Shakespeare turned instead to problematic plays such as *All's Well That Ends Well*, *Measure for Measure*, and *Troilus and Cressida*, the last of which is ambivalently a tragedy (with the death of Hector), a history play about the Trojan War, and a bleak existential drama about a failed love relationship. He also took up writing tragedies in earnest. *Romeo and Juliet*, in 1594–96, is a justly famous play, but in its early acts it is more a comedy than a tragedy, and its central figures are not tragic protagonists of the stature of those he created in plays from 1599 onward: *Julius Caesar, Hamlet, Othello, King Lear, Macbeth, Timon of Athens, Antony and Cleopatra*, and *Coriolanus*, this last play written in about 1608. Whether Shakespeare was moved to write these great tragedies by sad personal experiences, or by a shifting of the national mood in 1603 with the death of Queen Elizabeth and the accession to the throne of James VI of Scotland to become James I of England (when the Lord Chamberlain's Men became the King's Men), or by a growing skepticism and philosophical pessimism on his part, is impossible to say; perhaps he felt invigorated artistically by the challenge of excelling in the relatively new (for him) genre of tragedy.

Equally hard to answer with any certainty is the question of why he then turned, in his late years as a dramatist, to a form of comedy usually called romance, or tragicomedy. The genre was made popular by his contemporaries Francis Beaumont (1584–1616) and John Fletcher (1579–1625), and it is worth noting that the long indigenous tradition of English drama, comprising the cycles of mystery plays and the morality plays, was essentially tragicomic in form. The plays of this phase, from *Pericles* (c. 1606–08) to *Cymbeline, The Winter's Tale*, and *The Tempest* (c. 1608–11), would seem to overlap somewhat the late tragedies in dates of composition. These romances are like the early romantic comedies in many ways: young heroines in disguise, plots of adventure and separation leading to tearfully joyful reunions, comic highjinks, and so on. Yet these late romances are also tinged with the tragic vision that the dramatist had portrayed so vividly: death threatens or actually occurs in these plays, the emotional struggles of the male protagonists are nearly tragic in their psychic dimensions, and the restored happiness of the endings is apt to seem miraculous.

Shakespeare seems to have retired from London to Stratford-upon-Avon some time around 1611; *The Tempest* may have been designed as his farewell to the theater and his career as dramatist, after which he appears to have collaborated with Fletcher, his successor at the King's Men, in *Henry VIII* and *The Two Noble Kinsmen* (1613–14). His elder daughter, Susanna, had married the successful physician John Hall in 1607. In his last will and testament Shakespeare left various bequests to friends and colleagues, but to Anne, his wife, nothing other than his "second-best bed." Whether this betokens any estrangement between him and Anne, whom he had married under the necessity of her pregnancy and from whom he then lived apart during the two decades or so when he resided and worked in London, is a matter of hot debate. Divorce was impossible, whether contemplated or not. He did take good care of her and his family, and he did retire to Stratford. Anne lived on with Susanna and John until she died in 1623. Shakespeare was buried on 25 April 1616. Tradition assumes that he died on 23 April, since he would have left the world on the very feast day (of St. George, England's patron saint) that had probably witnessed his birth some 52 years earlier. He lies buried under the altar of Holy Trinity, next to his wife and other family members. A memorial bust, erected some time before 1623, is mounted on the chancel wall.

The website of the Internet Shakespeare Editions (http://internetshakespeare. uvic.ca) includes an extensive discussion of the theaters of Shakespeare's time, and of the audiences that attended them: click on "Life & Times" and choose the menu item "Stage."

Where Shakespeare's plays of the early 1590s were performed we do not know. When he joined the newly formed Lord Chamberlain's Men in 1594, with Richard Burbage as his leading man, most public performances of Shakespeare's plays would have been put on in a building called The Theatre, since, when it was erected in 1576 by Richard Burbage's father James Burbage (c. 1530–97), it was the only structure in London designed specifically for the performance of plays, and indeed the first such building in the history of English theater. Earlier, plays were staged by itinerant companies in inns and innyards, great houses, churchyards, public squares, and any other place that could be commandeered for dramatic presentation. In Shakespeare's time the professional companies still toured, but to a lesser extent, and several of them also derived part of their income from private performances at court.

The Theatre had been erected in Shoreditch (also called Moorfields), a short walking distance north of London's walls, in order to evade the too often censorious regulations of the city's governing council. There, spectators might have chosen to see *Romeo and Juliet*, *A Midsummer Night's Dream*, *The Merchant of Venice*, *King John*, or *Richard II*. They would also have seen some earlier Shakespeare plays that he had brought with him (perhaps as the price needed to pay for a share in the company) when he joined the Lord Chamberlain's Men: plays such as *Richard III* and *The Taming of the Shrew*. When in the late 1590s the Puritan-leaning owner of the land on which the building stood, Giles Allen, refused to renew their lease because he wished "to pull down the same, and to convert the wood and timber thereof to some better use," the Lord Chamberlain's Men performed for a while in the nearby Curtain Theatre. Eventually, in 1599, they solved their problem with the landlord by dismantling The Theatre and moving it across the River Thames to the shore opposite from London, just to the west of London Bridge, where audiences could reach the new theater—the Globe—by bridge or by water taxi, and where the players were still outside the authority of the city of London. At the time of this move, the River Thames was frozen over in an especially harsh winter, so possibly they slid the timbers of their theater across on the ice.

At any event, the Globe Theatre that they erected in Southwark, not far from the location of today's reconstructed Globe, was in the main the same building they had acted in before. Because timbers were all hand-hewn and fitted, the best plan was to reassemble them as much as was feasible. No doubt the company decided on some modifications, especially in the acting area, based on their theatrical experience, but the house remained essentially as before.

No pictures exist today of the interiors of the Theatre, the Curtain, or the Globe. We do have Visscher's View of London (1616) and other representations showing the exteriors of some theatrical buildings, but for the important matter of the interior design we have only a drawing of the Swan Theatre, copied by a Dutchman, Arend van Buchel (1565–1641), from a lost original by another Dutchman, Johannes de Witt, who visited London in about 1596–98. In many respects, the Swan seems to have been typical of such buildings. As seen in the accompanying illustration, the building appears to be circular or polygonal, with a thatched roof (called *tectum* in the illustration's labels) over the galleries containing seats and another roof over the stage, but leaving the space for standing spectators open to the heavens. (In the modern Globe, similarly constructed, spectators intending to stand in the yard for a performance can purchase a plastic rain poncho to ward off London's frequent rain showers.) From other kinds of information about Elizabethan playhouses, we can estimate a diameter of about 70 feet for the interior space. A large rectangular stage labeled the *proscaenium* (literally, "that which stands before the scene"), approximately 43 feet wide and 27 feet deep, juts out from one portion of the wall into the yard, or *planities siue arena* ("the plain place or arena"). The stage stands about 5 ½ feet above the surface of the yard. Two pillars support the roof over the stage, which in turn is surmounted by a hut. A flag is flying at the top, while a trumpeter at a door in the hut is presumably announcing the performance of a play. The spectators' seats are arrayed in three tiers of galleries. Stairway entrances (*ingressus*) are provided for spectators to gain access from the yard to the seats, labeled *orchestra* on the first level and nearest the stage, and *porticus* above.

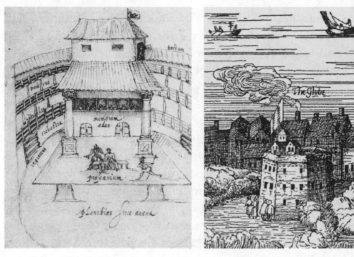

ABOVE, LEFT: This sketch of the Swan is the most complete we have of any theater of
the time. The Swan was built in 1596; Shakespeare's company, The Chamberlain's Men,
played there in the same year. RIGHT: This view of the first Globe by the Dutch engraver
J.C. Visscher (1586–1652) was printed in 1625, but must be taken from an earlier
drawing, since the first Globe burned to the ground in 1613 at the first performance
of Shakespeare's *Henry VIII*. There is substantial evidence that Visscher simplified the
appearance of the theater by portraying it as octagonal: most scholars now believe that
it had twenty sides, thus making it seem more circular than in this engraving.

The stage area is of greatest concern, and here the Swan drawing evidently does not show everything needed for performance in a theater
such as the Globe. No trapdoor is visible, though one is needed in a
number of Renaissance plays for appearances by ghostly or diabolical visitations from the infernal regions imagined to lie beneath the
earth. The underside of the stage roof is not visible in this drawing, but
from the plays themselves and other sources of information we gather
that this underside above the actors' heads, known as the "heavens,"
displayed representations of the sun, moon, planets, and stars (as in
today's Globe in London). The back wall of the stage in the drawing,
labeled *mimorum ades* or "housing for the actors," provides a visual
barrier between the stage itself and what was commonly known as the
"tiring house" or place where the actors could attire themselves and be
ready for their entrances. The two doors shown in this wall confirm
an arrangement evidently found in other theaters like the Globe, but
the absence of any other means of access to the tiring house raises

important questions. Many plays, by Shakespeare and others, seem to require some kind of "discovery space," located perhaps between the two doors, to accommodate a London shop, or a place where in *The Tempest* Prospero can pull back a curtain to "discover" Miranda and Ferdinand playing chess, or a place to which Falstaff, in the great tavern scene of *1 Henry IV,* can retire to avoid the Sheriff's visit and then be heard snoring offstage before he exits at scene's end into the tiring house. The modern Globe has such a discovery space.

Above the stage in the Swan drawing is what appears to be a gallery of six bays in which we can see seated figures watching the actors on the main stage, thereby surrounding those actors with spectators on all sides. But did theaters such as the Swan or the Globe regularly seat spectators above the stage like this? Were such seats reserved for dignitaries and persons of wealth? Other documents refer to a "lords' room" in such theaters. The problem is complicated by the fact that many Elizabethan plays require some upper acting area for the play itself, as when Juliet, in Act II of *Romeo and Juliet,* appears "above" at her "window" to be heard by Romeo and then converses with him, or later, when Romeo and Juliet are seen together "aloft" at her "window" before Romeo descends, presumably by means of a rope ladder in full view of the audience, to go to banishment (3.5). Richard II appears *"on the walls"* of Flint Castle when he is surrounded by his enemies and is obliged to descend (behind the scenes) and then enter on the main stage to Bolingbroke (*Richard II,* 3.3). Instances are numerous. The gallery above the stage, shown in the Swan drawing, must have provided the necessary acting area "above." On those many occasions when the space was needed for action of this sort, seemingly the acting company would not seat spectators there. It is unclear how spectators sitting above would have seen action in the "discovery space," since it may have been beneath them.

On stage, in the drawing, a well-dressed lady, seated on a bench and accompanied perhaps by her lady-in-waiting, receives the addresses of a courtier or soldier with a long-handled weapon or staff of office. Even though the sketch is rough and imperfect, it does suggest the extent to which the plays of Shakespeare and his contemporaries were acted on this broad, open stage with a minimum of scenic effects. The actors would identify their fictional roles and their location by their dialogue, their costumes, and their gestures. On other occasions, when, for example, a throne was needed for a throne scene, extras could bring on such large objects and then remove them when they were no longer needed. Beds, as in the final scene of *Othello*, were apparently thrust on stage from the tiring house. The building itself was handsomely decorated and picturesque, such that the stage picture was by no means unimpressive, yet the visual effects were not designed to inform the audience about setting or time of the action. The play texts and the actors took care of that.

We have a verbal description of the Globe Theatre by Thomas Platter, a visitor to London in 1599, on the occasion of a performance of *Julius Caesar*. The description unfortunately says little about the stage, but it is otherwise very informative about the London playhouses:

> The playhouses are so constructed that they play on a raised platform, so that everyone has a good view. There are different galleries and places, however, where the seating is better and more comfortable and therefore more expensive. For whoever cares to stand below pays only one English penny, but if he wishes to sit, he enters by another door and pays another penny, while if he desires to sit in the most comfortable seats, which are cushioned, where he not only sees everything well but can also be seen, then he pays yet another English penny at another door. And during the performance food and drink are carried around the audience, so that for what one cares to pay one may also have refreshment.

Shakespeare's company may have included ten or so actor-sharers, who owned the company jointly and distributed important roles among themselves. Richard Burbage was Shakespeare's leading man from 1594 until Shakespeare's retirement from the theater. Other actor-sharers, such as John Heminges (1566–1630) and Henry Condell (d. 1627), who would edit the First Folio collection of Shakespeare's plays in 1623, were his longtime professional associates. The quality of performance appears to have been high. Hired men generally took minor roles of messengers, soldiers, and servants. The women's parts were played by boys, who were trained by the major actors in a kind of apprenticeship and remained as actors of women's parts until their voices changed. Many went on in later years to be adult actors.

WILLIAM SHAKESPEARE AND *HAMLET*:
A BRIEF CHRONOLOGY

(Some dates are approximate, notably those of the plays)

c. 1200　　*Hamlet*'s earliest source written by Saxo Grammaticus in his *Historia Danica* (*History of the Danes*), first printed in Paris in 1514.

1509–47　　Reign of Henry VIII.

1534　　Act of Supremacy declares Henry VIII head of the Church of England.

1547–53　　Reign of Edward VI.

1553–58　　Reign of Mary I; England returns to Catholicism.

1558–1603　Reign of Elizabeth I; England returns to Protestantism.

1563　　Adoption of the Thirty-Nine Articles, establishing Anglicanism as a middle path between Roman Catholicism and more fundamentalist Protestantism.

1564　　William Shakespeare born, c. 23 April, christened 26 April.

1569　　Suppression of Northern Rebellion of Catholic earls.

1576　　James Burbage builds The Theatre.
　　　　François de Belleforest, in his *Histoires Tragiques*, translates Saxo Grammaticus's story of Hamlet into French.

1582　　Shakespeare marries Anne Hathaway, late November.

1583　　Birth of Susanna, Shakespeare's first child, c. 26 May.

1583–84　　Plots against Elizabeth on behalf of Mary Queen of Scots.

1585　　Birth of Shakespeare's twins, Hamnet and Judith, early February.
　　　　Earl of Leicester sent to aid the Dutch against the Spanish.

1587　　Execution of Mary Queen of Scots, 8 February.

1588　　At some point, Shakespeare moves to London; family remains in Stratford.
　　　　War with Spain; the Spanish Armada fleet destroyed in July.

1588–94　　*The Two Gentlemen of Verona, 1 Henry VI, 2 Henry VI, 3 Henry VI, The Taming of the Shrew, Titus Andronicus,*

	Richard III, Venus and Adonis (poem), *The Rape of Lucrece* (poem), *The Comedy of Errors, Love's Labor's Lost.*
1589	Thomas Nashe, in his *Menaphon*, refers to "whole Hamlets, I should say handfuls, of tragical speeches."
1592	Shakespeare attacked in print by Robert Greene.
1593–1603	*The Sonnets.*
1594	Shakespeare joins the Lord Chamberlain's Men. Reference to a play called *Hamlet* being performed at Newington Butts.
1594–95	*A Midsummer Night's Dream, Richard II, Romeo and Juliet.*
1596–98	*The Merchant of Venice, 1 Henry IV, 2 Henry IV.*
1597	Earl of Essex sent to Ireland to put down a rebellion led by the Earl of Tyrone. George Chapman, *An Humorous Day's Mirth.*
1598	Ben Jonson, *Every Man in His Humor.*
1598–99	*Much Ado About Nothing, The Merry Wives of Windsor.*
1599	Shakespeare's company moves to the Globe; *As You Like It, Henry V, Julius Caesar.* Prohibition and public burning of satires.
1599–1602	*Twelfth Night, Troilus and Cressida, Hamlet, All's Well That Ends Well.*
1601	Shakespeare's father dies. Essex's abortive rebellion and subsequent execution.
1603	Death of Elizabeth I; coronation of James I, 24 March. Shakespeare's company, the Lord Chamberlain's Men, is renamed the King's Men. Publication of the unauthorized first quarto (Q1) of *Hamlet* under the title *The Tragicall Historie of Hamlet Prince of Denmarke.*
1603–04	*Measure for Measure, Othello.*
1604	James's confrontation of the Puritans at the Hampton Court Conference. Peace with Spain. Publication of the second quarto (Q2) of *Hamlet.*
1605	The Gunpowder Plot foiled, 5 November.
1605–06	*King Lear.*
1606–07	*Macbeth, Timon of Athens, Antony and Cleopatra, Pericles.*

1607	A performance of *Hamlet*, which may have differed materially from any surviving texts we have, evidently occurred on board a ship anchored off the coast of Africa.
1608	*Coriolanus.*
1609–11	*Cymbeline, The Winter's Tale, The Tempest.*
1613–14	*Henry VIII, The Two Noble Kinsmen.*
	Globe burns down, soon rebuilt.
	Shakespeare in retirement, living in Stratford.
1616	Shakespeare dies c. 23 April, buried on 25 April.
1623	Publication of the First Folio (F1), a collection of 36 plays by Shakespeare, of which 18 had not been published before and probably would have been lost.

A NOTE ON THE TEXT

On 26 July 1602, the printer James Roberts entered into the official record book of the London Company of Stationers (known as the Stationers' Register) "A Booke called the Revenge of Hamlett Prince Denmarke as yt was latelie Acted by the Lord Chamberlayne his seruants." These "seruants" were the acting company to which Shakespeare belonged as actor and as its chief playwright. *Hamlet*, only recently performed, was so successful that it soon appeared in an unauthorized edition in 1603, published not by Roberts but by Nicholas Ling and John Trundell. Its title page described the play as follows:

> THE Tragicall Historie of HAMLET *Prince of Denmarke* By William Shake-speare. As it hath beene diuerse times acted by his Highnesse seruants in the Cittie of London: as also in the two Vniversities of Cambridge and Oxford, and else-where.

By this time, Shakespeare's company had become "his Highnesse seruants," i.e., the King's Men, following the accession to the throne of James I of England in 1603. This quarto volume of 1603 (Q1) shows many signs of being unauthorized. Portions appear to be corrupt, and the text substantially abbreviated and rearranged. One theory is that it was assembled surreptitiously with the help of minor actors in the company. Another theory is that Q1 is related to an earlier text, one that may have contained passages based on an older play of *Hamlet* by Thomas Kyd, and perhaps close to what was presented on stage in 1603. Whatever the case, Q1 offers occasional insights that are textually valuable, especially with stage directions that seem to come from witnesses who were present at public performances.

A new and corrected edition was plainly called for. It appeared in 1604 (and in some copies dated 1605) with the following title:

> *THE* Tragicall Historie of HAMLET, *Prince of Denmarke.* By William Shakespeare. Newly imprinted and enlarged to almost as much again as it was, according to the true and perfect Coppie. AT LONDON, Printed by I. R. [James Roberts] for N. L. [Nicholas Ling] and are to be sold at his shoppe vnder Saint Dunstons Church in Fleetstreet. 1604.

This text (Q2) appears to have been based on Shakespeare's own papers, with annotations by the "bookkeeper" in charge of stage management. This second quarto served as copy for a third quarto (Q3) in 1611, published by John Smethwick, to whom Ling had transferred his rights to the play. A fourth undated quarto (Q4), based on the third, was published some time before 1623. These last two quartos do not bear signs of authorial intervention.

The text printed in the First Folio of 1623 (F1) omits more than two hundred lines of Q2, while at the same time adding substantial new materials, especially in a passage in 2.2 in which Hamlet interrogates his companions, Rosencrantz and Guildenstern, about a theatrical rivalry between the adult acting companies of "the city" (plainly with relevance to London) and juvenile actors whose satirical plays had proven to be immensely popular (see extended note, pp. 124–25). Whether the cuts were designed to reduce the playing time of an unusually long play is a matter of debate among textual scholars. The lines in question are undoubtedly Shakespearean, in any case, and are kept in the present edition. At the same time, many shorter alterations from Q2 to F1 appear to be authorial; when they are not likely to have been the work of a copyist or compositor, they are retained here as plausibly Shakespearean. Anyone wishing to compare the three early editions of Hamlet—Q1, Q2, and F1—in all their rich and complex diversity, may do so by consulting them online in the Internet Shakespeare Editions (ISE).

The 1623 Folio text contains some obvious flaws. It appears to have been set from a scribal copy of a text containing the cuts, additions, and alterations described in the previous paragraph. The scribe responsible for this text appears to have taken liberties, and introduced some new errors. The Folio compositors evidently consulted Q4 occasionally but not often. These circumstances lend the weight of authority to Q2 when Folio readings appear to be erroneous.

The text of Hamlet in this present edition is undoubtedly longer than any version ever acted by Shakespeare's company, and cannot claim to represent the play as it was seen by London audiences at any particular moment in the play's stage history. At the same time, the materials included in this text are all genuinely Shakespearean, and are parts of the play as Shakespeare worked on it at various stages. The cuts in F1 could represent authorial choices in revision, but they could also be choices dictated by the need to keep playing time within practical limits.

About line numbering in the text of this present edition: "TLN" means "through line numbering." This is the numbering system created by Charlton Hinman in *The Norton Facsimile: The First Folio of Shakespeare* (New York: Norton, 1968), in which each play is numbered from start to finish; for example, *Hamlet* runs from line number 1 to 3906. Every printed line in this fine facsimile edition is numbered: the spoken text, all stage directions, and all indications of act and scene. This TLN system has the advantage of being universal: it can be applied to any modern edition, where the line numbering varies because prose is set in columns of varying width and thus occupies varying amounts of space. In addition, this system has to provide for numbering lines that do not appear in F1. For example, most editions of *Hamlet* include passages from Q2 that do not appear in F1. Here the TLN system provides added numbers as a decimal suffix. For example, when in 1.4.18, Hamlet, conversing with Marcellus and Horatio, ends his speech in the F1 version by saying, about the Danes' reputation for heavy drinking, "it is a custom / More honored in the breach than the observance," Q2 has a version of this speech that is 22 lines longer, clearly by Shakespeare. (Why it is left out of the Folio text is unclear.) In the present edition, as in the online ISE edition, this extended speech is included and is numbered TLN 621.1–22.

The line numbers in this edition begin again at 1 in each new scene. Each line of verse or prose receives a line number; stage directions or scene headings do not. Ranges of both TLNs and traditional act-scene-line numbers appear in running heads for each page.

THE TRAGEDY OF HAMLET,
PRINCE OF DENMARK

[CHARACTERS IN THE PLAY

THE GHOST *of Hamlet, the former King of Denmark*
CLAUDIUS, *King of Denmark*
GERTRUDE, *Queen of Denmark, his wife, widow of the former King*
HAMLET, *Prince of Denmark, son of the late King and of Gertrude*

POLONIUS, *counselor to King Claudius*
LAERTES, *his son*
OPHELIA, *his daughter*
REYNALDO, *his servant*

HORATIO, *Hamlet's friend*

VOLTEMAND
CORNELIUS } *courtiers and ambassadors*

ROSENCRANTZ
GUILDENSTERN } *courtiers, once boyhood friends of Hamlet*

OSRIC, *an obsequious courtier*
A GENTLEMAN
A LORD

BARNARDO
FRANCESCO } *officers and sentinels on watch*
MARCELLUS

FORTINBRAS, *Prince of Norway*
CAPTAIN *in his army*

FIRST PLAYER *and three or four others, taking the roles of* PROLOGUE, PLAYER KING, PLAYER QUEEN, *and* LUCIANUS *in the play put on before the King and Queen*
Two MESSENGERS
FIRST SAILOR
Two CLOWNS, *a gravedigger and his companion*
PRIEST
AMBASSADOR *from England*

Lords, Soldiers, Attendants, Guards, other Players, Followers of Laertes, other Sailors, another Ambassador or Ambassadors from England

SCENE: *Denmark*]

[1.1 ELSINORE CASTLE, DENMARK.
A GUARD PLATFORM]

Enter Barnardo and Francisco, two sentinels.

BARNARDO. Who's there?

FRANCISCO. Nay, answer me. Stand and unfold yourself.[1]

BARNARDO. Long live the King!

FRANCISCO. Barnardo?

BARNARDO. He.   5

FRANCISCO. You come most carefully upon your hour.

BARNARDO. 'Tis now struck twelve. Get thee to bed, Francisco.

FRANCISCO. For this relief much thanks. 'Tis bitter cold,
  And I am sick at heart.

BARNARDO. Have you had quiet guard?   10

FRANCISCO. Not a mouse stirring.

BARNARDO. Well, good night.
  If you do meet Horatio and Marcellus,
  The rivals° of my watch, bid them make haste.   *partners*

Enter Horatio and Marcellus.

FRANCISCO. I think I hear them.—Stand, ho! Who is there?   15

HORATIO. Friends to this ground.°   *country, land*

MARCELLUS. And liegemen to the Dane.°   *subjects of the Danish king*

FRANCISCO. Give° you good night.   *may God give*

MARCELLUS. Oh, farewell, honest soldier. Who hath relieved you?

FRANCISCO. Barnardo hath my place. Give you good night.   20

                                         Exit Francisco.

MARCELLUS. Holla, Barnardo!

BARNARDO. Say, what, is Horatio there?

HORATIO. A piece of him.

BARNARDO. Welcome, Horatio. Welcome, good Marcellus.

HORATIO. What, has this thing appeared again tonight?   25

BARNARDO. I have seen nothing.

MARCELLUS. Horatio says 'tis but our fantasy,°   *fantastic imaginings*
  And will not let belief take hold of him,
  Touching° this dreaded sight twice seen of us.   *regarding, concerning*

---

1 Identify who you are.

30 Therefore I have entreated him along
   With us to watch the minutes of this night[1]
   That if again this apparition come
   He may approve° our eyes and speak to it.   *confirm, corroborate*
   HORATIO. Tush, tush, 'twill not appear.
   BARNARDO.   Sit down awhile,
35 And let us once again assail your ears,
   That are so fortified against our story,
   What we two nights have seen.
   HORATIO.   Well, sit we down,
   And let us hear Barnardo speak of this.
   BARNARDO. Last night of all,[2]
40 When yond same star that's westward from the pole[3]
   Had made his° course t'illume[4] that part of heaven   *its*
   Where now it burns, Marcellus and myself,
   The bell then beating one—

Enter the Ghost.

   MARCELLUS. Peace, break thee off! Look where it comes again!
45 BARNARDO. In the same figure like the King that's dead.
   MARCELLUS. Thou art a scholar.[5] Speak to it, Horatio.
   BARNARDO. Looks it not like the King? Mark it, Horatio.
   HORATIO. Most like. It harrows me with fear and wonder.
   BARNARDO. It would be spoke to.
   MARCELLUS.   Question it, Horatio.
50 HORATIO. What art thou that usurp'st[6] this time of night,
   Together with that fair and warlike form
   In which the majesty of buried Denmark[7]
   Did sometimes[8] march? By heaven, I charge thee speak!
   MARCELLUS. It is offended.

---

1 To come along and stand watch with us this evening.
2 In the night just before the present one.
3 Probably Arcturus, a bright star just to the west of the Big Dipper.
4 To illuminate.
5 One trained in the Latin of the Church and thus qualified to interrogate a
ghost.
6 Who are you that thus wrongfully assert your authority over.
7 I.e., in which the buried former King of Denmark, Hamlet's dead father.
8 Formerly.

BARNARDO.   See, it stalks away.

HORATIO. Stay, speak, speak, I charge thee speak!   55

Exit the Ghost.

MARCELLUS. 'Tis gone, and will not answer.

BARNARDO. How now, Horatio, you tremble and look pale.
  Is not this something more than fantasy?
  What think you on't?°   *of it*

HORATIO. Before my God, I might not this believe   60
  Without the sensible[1] and true avouch°   *authority, confirmation*
  Of mine own eyes.

MARCELLUS.   Is it not like the King?

HORATIO. As thou art to thyself.
  Such was the very armor he had on
  When he the ambitious Norway° combated.   *King of Norway*   65
  So frowned he once, when in an angry parle[2]
  He smote the sledded Polacks[3] on the ice.
  'Tis strange.

MARCELLUS. Thus twice before, and jump[4] at this dead hour,
  With martial stalk° hath he gone by our watch.   *stride*   70

HORATIO. In what particular thought to work[5] I know not,
  But in the gross and scope of mine opinion[6]
  This bodes° some strange eruption to our state.   *foretells*

MARCELLUS. Good now,[7] sit down, and tell me, he that knows,
  Why this same strict and most observant watch   75
  So nightly toils the subject[8] of the land,
  And why such daily cast° of brazen° cannon   *casting / brass*
  And foreign mart[9] for implements of war,
  Why such impress[10] of shipwrights, whose sore task

---

1 Evident to the senses (especially sight).
2 Parley, conference with the enemy.
3 Polish soldiers traveling on sleds.
4 Precisely.
5 To organize my thoughts.
6 In my opinion, as I consider the whole topic.
7 I.e., I implore you all.
8 Imposes toil on the subjects, the citizens.
9 Shopping abroad.
10 Impressment, conscription.

80   Does not divide the Sunday from the week:[1]
       What might be toward,° that this sweaty haste   *about to happen*
       Doth make the night joint-laborer with the day?[2]
       Who is't that can inform me?
HORATIO.   That can I.
       At least the whisper goes so: our last King,

---

1   I.e., requires them to work on Sunday just like every other day of the week.
2   I.e., demands that work continue all 24 hours.

1.1.44:   "ENTER THE GHOST" (TLN 51)

Ghost lore is especially vivid in *Hamlet*. When the Ghost of Hamlet's father appears to the soldiers on watch and then to Horatio and Hamlet in Act 1, scenes 1 and 4–5, he wears the armor and headgear of the dead king, complete with a "beaver" or visor that is up so that his face is visible (1.2.231–32, TLN 425–26). He makes his visitations at night and must return to his ghostly dwelling place before daybreak; the scent of "the morning's air" (1.5.58, TLN 743) and the "glow-worm" showing "the matin to be near" (1.5.89, TLN 774) are signals that his time is up.

The Ghost refuses to speak to anyone until Hamlet joins the watch in order to talk with him. In this matter the scene appears to reflect a commonly held belief that ghosts could not speak until spoken to (see 1.4.65, TLN 651). The Ghost cannot be struck or harmed by the soldiers with their weapons; he is "as the air, invulnerable" (1.1.151, TLN 144). The Ghost is able to move quickly from place to place, or indeed to seem to be everywhere at once: as Hamlet says, in Latin, "Hic et ubique?" (Here and everywhere), at 1.5.163 (TLN 853). Often in production, Horatio and then Hamlet hold up a sword, with its hilt in the form of a cross, to ward off evil.

The effect of the Ghost's appearance is so intense and graphic that it convinces the skeptical Horatio that this ghost is real. Whether ghosts were real was a much-debated topic at the time the play was written; King James VI of Scotland, soon to become King James I of England as well, argued for the existence of demons and witches in his *Demonology* (1597) in reply to the skeptical arguments of Reginald Scot in *The Discovery of Witchcraft* (1584). The earlier *Malleus Maleficarum* or *Hammer of the*

Whose image even but now appeared to us, 85
Was as you know by Fortinbras of Norway,[1]
Thereto pricked on° by a most emulate[2] pride,   *egged on, incited*
Dared to the combat;[3] in which our valiant Hamlet—

---

1 Old Fortinbras, King of Norway (with whom old Hamlet fought, as described
in lines 64–65 (TLN 76–77); not young Fortinbras, nephew of this present king.
2 Competitive, rivalrous.
3 Challenged to fight, one on one.

Hamlet, Prince of Denmark, Act I, Scene IV, Henry Fuseli, c. 1780.

Witches (1486) offered instruction on how to identify witches and other
evil spirits. In *Hamlet*, the Ghost is certainly real in dramatic terms: he
appears before the audience, he converses with his son, and he tells a
powerful story of how he was murdered. But real or not, is this an evil
or a beneficent spirit? Hamlet himself voices his concern that this spirit
"May be the devil, and the devil hath power / T'assume a pleasing shape,"
especially in the overwrought and melancholic state of Hamlet's mind
(2.2.567–72, TLN 1638–43). Hamlet is ultimately convinced, like his friend
Horatio, that the Ghost is real.

For so this side of our known world[1] esteemed him—
90   Did slay this Fortinbras, who by a sealed[2] compact
Well ratified by law and heraldry[3]
Did forfeit, with his life, all those his lands
Which he stood seized of,° to the conqueror;   *possessed of*
Against the which a moiety competent
95   Was gagèd by our King,[4] which had returned[5]
To the inheritance of Fortinbras
Had he been vanquisher, as, by the same cov'nant[6]
And carriage of the article design[ed][7]
His fell to Hamlet.[8] Now, sir, young Fortinbras,
100   Of unimprovèd mettle hot and full,°   *full of untested fiery spirits*
Hath in the skirts° of Norway here and there   *outskirts*
Sharked up a list of landless resolutes[9]
For food and diet to some enterprise
That hath a stomach in't,[10] which is no other,
105   As it doth well appear unto our state,
But to recover of us° by strong hand   *from us*
And terms compulsative those foresaid lands
So by his father[11] lost. And this, I take it,
Is the main motive of our preparations,
110   The source° of this our watch, and the chief head   *motivation*
Of this post-haste and rummage[12] in the land.
BARNARDO. I think it be no other but e'en so.

---

1   I.e., all of Western Europe.
2   Confirmed by an official seal.
3   The laws and pageant customs of chivalry.
4   In return for which a comparable portion of land was pledged by our King of Denmark.
5   Which was to have been assigned.
6   Contractual agreement.
7   And intent of the contact in question.
8   Old Fortinbras's lands would have been transferred to old Hamlet.
9   Rounded up a troop of restlessly ambitious younger sons and other gentry without landed title.
10 To feed and supply a bold enterprise demanding appetite and raw courage for such a venture.
11 The old Fortinbras, late King of Norway, brother of the present King of Norway.
12 Frenetic activity and bustle.

Well may it sort that[1] this portentous figure
Comes armèd through our watch so like the King
That was and is the question° of these wars.   *focus of contention*   115
HORATIO. A mote° it is to trouble the mind's eye.   *speck of dust*
   In the most high and palmy[2] state of Rome,
   A little ere° the mightiest Julius[3] fell,   *before*
   The graves stood tenantless,° and the sheeted[4] dead   *unoccupied*
   Did squeak and gibber in the Roman streets,   120
   As stars with trains of fire and dews of blood,[5]
   Disasters[6] in the sun; and the moist star,[7]
   Upon whose influence Neptune's empire stands,[8]
   Was sick almost to doomsday with eclipse.[9]
   And even the like precurse of feared events,   125
   As harbingers preceding still the fates
   And prologue to the omen coming on,
   Have heaven and earth together demonstrated
   Unto our climatures and countrymen.[10]

Enter Ghost again.

   But soft,° behold, lo, where it comes again!   *i.e., gently, wait, hold on*   130
   I'll cross it[11] though it blast me.[12]—Stay, illusion!
It spreads his° arms.   *its*
   If thou hast any sound or use of voice,

---

1 That could well explain why.
2 Flourishing, prosperous, worthy to "bear the palm" in a conventional symbol
of victory.
3 Julius Caesar. See Appendix A, p. 249.
4 Shrouded in grave-clothes.
5 Just like comets with their trails drizzling blood.
6 Unfavorable astrological signs or aspects.
7 I.e., the Moon, governess of tides.
8 Upon the influence of which the sea depends. On Neptune, see Appendix A, p. 257.
9 The moon in eclipse was a foreboding sign of the day of Judgment and second coming of Christ predicted in Matthew 24:29 and Revelation 6:12. See Appendix B, p. 269.
10 And no less fearful predictions of frightening happenings, serving as prognos-
ticators and prologues incessantly preceding the calamitous events that are fated
to come, are the means by which heaven and earth together make manifest to our
regions and peoples what they can expect.
11 I.e., stand in its way, confront it; also, hold up a Christian cross in front of it
(as Horatio may do here).
12 Strike or wither me with a curse.

Speak to me!
If there be any good thing to be done
135 That may to thee do ease and grace to me,
Speak to me!
If thou art privy to¹ thy country's fate,
Which happily foreknowing may avoid,
Oh, speak!
140 Or if thou hast uphoarded in thy life
Extorted treasure in the womb of earth,
For which, they say, you spirits oft walk in death,
Speak of it. Stay and speak!
The cock crows.
                                    Stop it, Marcellus!
MARCELLUS. Shall I strike at it with my partisan?²
145 HORATIO. Do, if it will not stand.
BARNARDO. 'Tis here.
HORATIO. 'Tis here.

                                                    Exit Ghost.

MARCELLUS. 'Tis gone.
We do it wrong, being so majestical,
150 To offer it the show of violence,
For it is as the air, invulnerable,
And our vain blows malicious mockery.
BARNARDO. It was about to speak when the cock crew.
HORATIO. And then it started³ like a guilty thing
155 Upon a fearful summons. I have heard
The cock, that is the trumpet° to the morn,   *trumpeter, herald*
Doth with his lofty and shrill-sounding throat
Awake the god of day,⁴ and, at his warning,
Whether in sea or fire, in earth or air,
160 Th'extravagant and erring° spirit hies°   *wandering, unrestrained / hastens*
To his confine; and of the truth herein
This present object made probation.°   *proof*

---

1 Are possessed with secret knowledge of.
2 Long-handled, broad-bladed spear.
3 Moved suddenly and violently.
4 The sun god, Phoebus Apollo (see Appendix A, p. 248); or possibly Eos or
Aurora, goddess of the dawn.

MARCELLUS. It faded on the crowing of the cock.
    Some say that ever 'gainst° that season comes   *just before*
    Wherein our Savior's birth is celebrated,   165
    The bird of dawning° singeth all night long,   *the cock or rooster*
    And then they say no spirit can walk abroad;
    The nights are wholesome, then no planets strike,[1]
    No fairy takes,° nor witch hath power to charm,[2]   *bewitches*
    So hallowed and so gracious° is that time.   *suffused with divine grace* 170
HORATIO. So have I heard and do in part believe it.
    But look, the morn in russet° mantle clad   *reddish-brown*
    Walks o'er the dew of yon high eastward hill.
    Break we our watch up, and by my advice
    Let us impart what we have seen tonight   175
    Unto young Hamlet, for, upon my life,
    This spirit, dumb to us, will speak to him.
    Do you consent we shall acquaint him with it
    As needful in our loves, fitting our duty?
MARCELLUS. Let's do't, I pray, and I this morning know   180
    Where we shall find him most conveniently.

                                          Exeunt.

[1.2 A ROOM OF STATE IN THE CASTLE]

*Flourish.[3] Enter Claudius, King of Denmark, Gertrude the Queen,
Hamlet, Polonius, Laertes, and his sister Ophelia, Lords attendant
[including Voltemand and Cornelius].*
KING. Though yet of Hamlet our° dear brother's death   *my*
    The memory be green, and that it us befitted
    To bear our hearts in grief, and our whole kingdom
    To be contracted in one brow of woe,
    Yet so far hath discretion fought with nature   5
    That we with wisest sorrow think on him
    Together with remembrance of ourselves.

---

1   No planets exert their baleful influence.
2   Cast a spell, enchant.
3   A trumpet fanfare announcing the arrival of royalty or other important
persons.

Therefore our sometime sister,[1] now our queen,
Th'imperial jointress[2] of this warlike state,
10   Have we as 'twere with a defeated joy,
With one auspicious and one dropping eye,[3]
With mirth in funeral and with dirge in marriage,
In equal scale weighing delight and dole,°   sorrow
Taken to wife. Nor have we herein barred
15   Your better wisdoms,[4] which have freely gone
With this affair along.[5] For all, our thanks.
Now follows that you know:[6] young Fortinbras,
Holding a weak supposal of our worth,[7]
Or thinking by our late° dear brother's death   recent
20   Our state to be disjoint and out of frame,°   totally disordered
Co-leaguèd with this dream of his advantage,[8]
He hath not failed to pester us with message
Importing° the surrender of those lands   concerning, signifying
Lost by his father, with all bonds of law,[9]
25   To our most valiant brother. So much for him.
Now for ourself, and for this time of meeting,
Thus much the business is: we have here writ
To Norway, uncle of young Fortinbras,
Who, impotent and bed-rid,[10] scarcely hears
30   Of this his nephew's purpose, to suppress
His further gait herein, in that the levies,
The lists, and full proportions are all made
Out of his subject;[11] and we here dispatch
You, good Cornelius, and you, Voltemand,

---

1 My former sister-in-law.
2 Joint possessor of the throne.
3 With one eye smiling and the other tear-stained and lowered in grief.
4 The sage advice of you elders and statesmen (such as Polonius).
5 Who have freely given consent to this marriage.
6 You need to be aware of the following circumstances.
7 Having a low estimate of our power and authority.
8 Combined with this illusory dream of his having us at a disadvantage.
9 "Well ratified by law and heraldry," as Horatio put it at 1.1.91 (TLN 104).
10 Wasted by disease and confined to bed.
11 I.e., insisting that the Norwegian king put an end to Fortinbras's proceeding
any further in this business, since the raising of troops and supplies is all made up
out of the King of Norway's subjects (who are therefore at his disposal for military
purposes, not young Fortinbras's). ("The lists" means "The roster of the troops
levied.")

For bearers° of this greeting to old Norway,   *to serve as bearers* 35
Giving to you no further personal power
To business with the King more than the scope
Of these dilated[1] articles allow.
Farewell, and let your haste commend your duty.[2]

CORNELIUS AND VOLTEMAND.
    In that and all things will we show our duty.   40
KING. We doubt it nothing.[3] Heartily farewell.

                  Exeunt Voltemand and Cornelius.

And now, Laertes, what's the news with you?
You told us of some suit. What is't, Laertes?
You cannot speak of reason to the Dane°   *the Danish king*
And lose your voice.[4] What wouldst thou beg, Laertes, 45
That shall not be my offer, not thy asking?[5]
The head is not more native° to the heart,   *closely related*
The hand more instrumental to the mouth,[6]
Than is the throne of Denmark to thy father.
What wouldst thou have, Laertes?

LAERTES.   Dread my lord,[7]   50
Your leave and favor[8] to return to France,
From whence though willingly I came to Denmark
To show my duty in your coronation,
Yet now I must confess, that duty done,
My thoughts and wishes bend again toward France   55
And bow them to your gracious leave and pardon.[9]
KING. Have you your father's leave? What says Polonius?
POLONIUS. H'ath,° my lord, wrung from me my slow leave   *he has*
    By laborsome petition, and at last

---

1   Expanded, set out at length; but if the word is meant to be "delated" (Q2's spelling), it would mean "offered for your acceptance, presented to you as herein limited and defined."
2   Let your swift carrying out of my command give testimony of your dutiful obedience.
3   Not in the slightest.
4   Waste your speech.
5   I.e., that I will offer almost before you ask.
6   Useful in carrying out what is verbally commanded.
7   My awe-inspiring lord and master.
8   Your gracious permission.
9   And submissively ask your gracious permission and forgiveness for my having asked such a favor.

60   Upon his will I sealed my hard consent.[1]
     I do beseech you, give him leave to go.
     KING. Take thy fair hour,[2] Laertes. Time be thine,
     And thy best graces spend it at thy will.[3]
     But now, my cousin[4] Hamlet, and my son—
65   HAMLET. A little more than kin, and less than kind.[5]
     KING. How is it that the clouds still hang on you?
     HAMLET. Not so, my lord, I am too much i'th' sun.[6]
     QUEEN. Good Hamlet, cast thy nighted color[7] off
     And let thine eye look like a friend on Denmark.[8]
70   Do not forever with thy vailèd lids°   *lowered eyelids*
     Seek for thy noble father in the dust.[9]
     Thou know'st 'tis common:[10] all that lives must die,
     Passing through nature to eternity.
     HAMLET. Ay, madam, it is common.
     QUEEN.   If it be,
75   Why seems it so particular° with thee?   *personal*
     HAMLET. "Seems," madam? Nay, it is, I know not "seems."
     'Tis not alone my inky cloak, good mother,
     Nor customary[11] suits of solemn black,
     Nor windy suspiration° of forced breath,   *sighing*
80   No, nor the fruitful river° in the eye,   *abundance of tears*
     Nor the dejected havior° of the visage,   *expression*
     Together with all forms, moods, shapes of grief
     That can denote me truly. These indeed seem,
     For they are actions that a man might play.

---

1 I gave my reluctant consent, as though affixing a seal to a document of approval.
2 Seize your opportunity while there is still time, while you are young.
3 And may you spend your time guided by your best qualities and inclinations.
4 Anyone related by blood or kinship but not of the immediate family.
5 I.e., involved in a family relationship that is at once too close and yet lacking in loving affection.
6 I.e., (1) I am too closely related as step-son to Claudius; (2) I am too much in the sunshine of royal favor.
7 (1) Dark mourning garments; (2) melancholy.
8 The King of Denmark.
9 See Appendix B, pp. 269–70.
10 (1) A common occurrence; (2) as Hamlet uses the term, "vulgar, disgusting."
11 Traditional on a mourning occasion.

But I have that within which passeth show;   85
These but the trappings[1] and the suits of woe.
KING. 'Tis sweet and commendable in your nature, Hamlet,
    To give these mourning duties to your father.
    But you must know your father lost a father;
    That father lost,[2] lost his, and the survivor bound   90
    In filial obligation for some term
    To do obsequious[3] sorrow; but to persever
    In obstinate condolement° is a course   *grieving, lamentation*
    Of impious stubbornness. 'Tis unmanly grief.
    It shows a will most incorrect to heaven,   95
    A heart unfortified,[4] a mind impatient,
    An understanding simple° and unschooled;   *ignorant*
    For what we know must be and is as common
    As any the most vulgar thing to sense,[5]
    Why should we in our peevish opposition   100
    Take it to heart? Fie, 'tis a fault to heaven,
    A fault against the dead, a fault to nature,
    To reason most absurd, whose common theme
    Is death of fathers, and who still[6] hath cried
    From the first corpse[7] till he that died today   105
    "This must be so." We pray you throw to earth
    This unprevailing° woe, and think of us   *profitless*
    As of a father; for let the world take note
    You are the most immediate° to our throne,   *next in succession*
    And with no less nobility of love   110
    Than that which dearest father bears his son
    Do I impart toward you. For° your intent   *as for*
    In going back to school in Wittenberg,
    It is most retrograde° to our desire,   *contrary*
    And we beseech you bend you° to remain   *yield to our wishes*   115

---

1 Outward decorative signs.
2 That father who is now dead.
3 Appropriate to obsequies or funerals.
4 Insufficiently armed against adversity.
5 For since everything that happens to us must be as common as the most ordinary experiences as we perceive them.
6 Continually, always.
7 From the body of the first human ever to have died. See Appendix B, p. 270.

In 1517 in this German city on the River Elbe, also home to a famous university, Martin Luther (1483–1546) is supposed to have posted his 95 theses on the door of the Schlosskirke in what is conventionally regarded as the opening salvo of the Protestant Reformation. In these theses, Luther excoriated corrupt practices of the Roman Catholic Church, including nepotism, simony (the making of profit out of sacred offices), usury, pluralism (the simultaneous holding of multiple ecclesiastical offices), and most of all the practice of demanding payment in return for the granting of "indulgences" for the forgiveness of sins. The Papacy was currently granting these "indulgences" on a large scale as a means of raising funds for renovation of St. Peter's Basilica in Rome. Luther was excommunicated by Pope Leo X in 1521. As the play begins, Hamlet has returned from Wittenberg for his father's funeral and mother's marriage; he longs to go "back to school" there, where he has studied with Horatio, but is ordered by the new king to remain at court.

The English church in the later sixteenth and seventeenth centuries was influenced by Luther not so much as by John Calvin (1509–64), whose theology put greater emphasis on the depravity of those persons whom God had decreed to be inherently unredeemable. Shakespeare makes no overt allusion in *Hamlet* to the Protestant Reformation, unless, as some scholars have argued, Hamlet's reference to "A certain convocation of politic worms" (4.3.20–21, TLN 2685–86) might have reminded theater audiences of the Diet of Worms in 1521, where Luther responded to the Church's charges of heresy (see extended note on p. 192); but Shakespeare's audiences might well have wondered what theological ideas Hamlet would have encountered at the University of Wittenberg. (The idea is anachronistic in any case, as *Hamlet* appears to be set in some bygone era, well before the Reformation.)

The seal of Wittenberg University, 1502.

Here in the cheer and comfort of our eye,
Our chiefest courtier, cousin, and our son.
QUEEN. Let not thy mother lose her prayers,[1] Hamlet.
I pray thee stay with us, go not to Wittenberg.
HAMLET. I shall in all my best[2] obey you, madam.   120
KING. Why, 'tis a loving and a fair reply.
Be as ourself[3] in Denmark.—Madam, come.
This gentle and unforced accord of Hamlet
Sits smiling to° my heart, in grace° whereof   *pleases / honor*
No jocund° health that Denmark[4] drinks today   *merry, joyful*   125
But the great cannon to the clouds shall tell,°   *sound, announce*
And the King's rouse[5] the heavens shall bruit again,[6]
Respeaking earthly thunder.[7] Come, away!
                                        Flourish. Exeunt all but Hamlet.
HAMLET. Oh, that this too too solid flesh would melt,
Thaw, and resolve° itself into a dew!   *dissolve*   130
Or that the Everlasting° had not fixed   *God*
His canon° 'gainst self-slaughter! Oh, God, God,   *divine law*
How weary, stale, flat, and unprofitable
Seem to me all the uses° of this world!   *customs, doings*
Fie on't, ah, fie! 'Tis an unweeded garden   135
That grows to seed; things rank and gross in nature[8]
Possess it merely.° That it should come to this!   *completely*
But two months dead—nay, not so much, not two!
So excellent a king, that was to this°   *compared to Claudius*
Hyperion[9] to a satyr,[10] so loving to my mother   140
That he might not beteem° the winds of heaven   *would not allow*
Visit her face too roughly. Heaven and earth,
Must I remember? Why, she would hang on him

---

1 Fail to achieve the thing she prays for.
2 To the best of my ability.
3 Enjoy the privileges and status of royalty. (The plural "ourself" indicates the royal plural; it means "myself, I as king.") The King invites Hamlet to enjoy the same privileges as the King himself.
4 The King of Denmark, Claudius.
5 Bout of drinking, ceremonial toast.
6 Loudly echo.
7 Echoing our cannon.
8 Things that are offensively vigorous in growth and coarse in their very natures.
9 Titan sun-god in Greek mythology. See Appendix A, "Apollo," p. 248.
10 Lecherous half-goat, half-human deity of classical mythology. See Appendix A, pp. 261–62.

As if increase of appetite had grown
145   By what it fed on.[1] And yet within a month—
Let me not think on't; frailty, thy name is woman!
A little month, or ere° those shoes were old   *even before*
With which she followed my poor father's body,
Like Niobe,[2] all tears, why, she, even she—
150   Oh, God, a beast that wants discourse of reason[3]
Would have mourned longer!—married with my uncle,
My father's brother, but no more like my father
Than I to Hercules.[4] Within a month,
Ere yet the salt of most unrighteous tears
155   Had left the flushing of her gallèd° eyes,   *inflamed, irritated*
She married. Oh, most wicked speed, to post°   *hasten*
With such dexterity to incestuous sheets![5]
It is not, nor it cannot come to good,
But break, my heart, for I must hold my tongue.

Enter Horatio, Marcellus, and Barnardo.
HORATIO. Hail to your lordship!
160   HAMLET.   I am glad to see you well.—
Horatio, or I do forget myself![6]
HORATIO. The same, my lord, and your poor servant ever.
HAMLET. Sir, my good friend, I'll change that name with you.[7]
And what make you from[8] Wittenberg, Horatio?—
165   Marcellus.
MARCELLUS. My good lord.

---

1   As if her desire and love for her husband were augmented by the intense pleasure of that love.
2   In Greek mythology, when Niobe boasted that her 14 children outnumbered
those of Leto, Leto's offspring Apollo and Artemis slew all of Niobe's children as
a punishment for her hubris, or pride. Despite being turned into a stone by Zeus,
Niobe never ceased her bitter tears, which flowed as a spring from the rock. See
Appendix A, pp. 258–59.
3   That lacks the ability to reason.
4   Hero of classical mythology noted for his twelve "labors," deeds requiring
"Herculean" strength. See Appendix A, pp. 253–54.
5   To marry one's deceased husband's brother was considered incest at this time.
See Appendices B, pp. 253–54 and D1, pp. 293–94.
6   I.e., forgetting you would be like forgetting my other self.
7   I will share and exchange mutually the name of "friend" with you, rather than
having you address me as your master. If anything, I am your servant.
8   What are you doing away from.

HAMLET. I am very glad to see you. [*To Barnardo*] Good even, sir.
    [*To Horatio*] But what, in faith, make you from Wittenberg?
·HORATIO. A truant disposition, good my lord.
HAMLET. I would not have your enemy say so,   170
    Nor shall you do my ear that violence
    To make it truster of your own report
    Against yourself.[1] I know you are no truant.
    But what is your affair in Elsinore?
    We'll teach you to drink deep ere you depart.   175
HORATIO. My lord, I came to see your father's funeral.
HAMLET. I prithee do not mock me, fellow student.
    I think it was to see my mother's wedding.
HORATIO. Indeed, my lord, it followed hard upon.°   *quickly afterwards*
HAMLET. Thrift, thrift, Horatio. The funeral baked meats   180
    Did coldly furnish forth the marriage tables.[2]
    Would I had met my dearest° foe in heaven   *most hated, bitterest*
    Ere I had ever seen that day, Horatio!
    My father—methinks I see my father.
HORATIO. Oh, where, my lord?
HAMLET.   In my mind's eye, Horatio.   185
HORATIO. I saw him once. 'A° was a goodly king.   *he*
HAMLET. 'A was a man, take him for all in all,
    I shall not look upon his like again.
HORATIO. My lord, I think I saw him yesternight.°   *last night*
HAMLET. Saw? Who?   190
HORATIO. My lord, the King your father.
HAMLET. The King my father?
HORATIO. Season your admiration[3] for a while
    With an attent° ear till I may deliver,   *attentive*
    Upon the witness of these gentlemen,   195
    This marvel to you.
HAMLET.   For God's love, let me hear!
HORATIO. Two nights together had these gentlemen,
    Marcellus and Barnardo, on their watch

---

1   Nor will I trust my own ears if they tell me you are calling yourself a truant, a
delinquent.
2   The food left uneaten from the funeral banquet, including meat pies and pas-
tries, provided cold leftovers for the marriage festivities.
3   Moderate your astonishment.

In the dead waste° and middle of the night *in the lifeless desolation*
200 Been thus encountered: a figure like your father
  Armed at all points,[1] exactly, cap-à-pie,° *from head to foot*
  Appears before them, and with solemn march ·
  Goes slow° and stately by them. Thrice he walked *slowly*
  By their oppressed and fear-surprisèd eyes[2]
205 Within his truncheon's[3] length, whilst they, distilled
  Almost to jelly with the act° of fear, *effect*
  Stand dumb and speak not to him. This to me
  In dreadful° secrecy impart they did, *full of dread, dread-inspired*
  And I with them the third night kept the watch,
210 Where, as they had delivered, both in time,
  Form of the thing, each word made true and good,
  The apparition comes. I knew your father.
  These hands are not more like.[4]

HAMLET.   But where was this?

MARCELLUS. My lord, upon the platform[5] where we watched.[6]

HAMLET. Did you not speak to it?

215 HORATIO.   My lord, I did,
  But answer made it none. Yet once methought
  It lifted up it head[7] and did address
  Itself to motion, like as it would speak;[8]
  But even° then the morning cock crew loud, *just*
220 And at the sound it shrunk in haste away
  And vanished from our sight.

HAMLET.   'Tis very strange.

HORATIO. As I do live, my honored lord, 'tis true,
  And we did think it writ down in our duty[9]
  To let you know of it.

---

1 Provided with weapons in every detail.
2 Eyes showing sudden surprise and fear.
3 A truncheon is a military officer's baton or staff, a sign of his office.
4 These two hands of mine are not more like each other than this apparition was like your father.
5 Battlements of the castle.
6 Stood watch.
7 Its head. ("It head" is the older, uninflected genitive form.)
8 Moved in such a way as to suggest that it was about to speak.
9 Prescribed in the duty we owe you.

HAMLET. Indeed, indeed, sirs, but this troubles me.   225
  Hold you the watch tonight?
ALL.[1]   We do, my lord.
HAMLET. Armed, say you?
ALL. Armed, my lord.
HAMLET. From top to toe?
ALL. My lord, from head to foot.   230
HAMLET. Then saw you not his face?
HORATIO. Oh, yes, my lord, he wore his beaver[2] up.
HAMLET. What looked he, frowningly?[3]
HORATIO. A countenance[4] more in sorrow than in anger.
HAMLET. Pale, or red?   235
HORATIO. Nay, very pale.
HAMLET. And fixed his eyes upon you?
HORATIO. Most constantly.
HAMLET. I would° I had been there.   *I wish*
HORATIO. It would have much amazed you.   240
HAMLET. Very like, very like.° Stayed it long?   *very likely*
HORATIO. While one with moderate haste might tell[5] a hundred.
BOTH.° Longer, longer.   *i.e., Marcellus and Barnardo*
HORATIO. Not when I saw 't.
HAMLET. His beard was grizzled, no?[6]   245
HORATIO. It was as I have seen it in his life,
  A sable silvered.°   *black sprinkled with silver-gray*
HAMLET.   I will watch° tonight.   *stand watch*
  Perchance 'twill walk again.
HORATIO.   I warr'nt° it will.   *guarantee*
HAMLET. If it assume my noble father's person,
  I'll speak to it, though hell itself should gape   250
  And bid me hold my peace.° I pray you all,   *be silent*
  If you have hitherto concealed this sight
  Let it be tenable° in your silence still,   *be held*

---

1   I.e., Marcellus, Barnardo, and Horatio.
2   Visor on the helmet.
3   How did he look? Frowningly? Did it appear that he was frowning?
4   An expression.
5   Count.
6   Gray or mingled with gray, was it not? (expecting an affirmative answer).

And whatsomever° else shall hap tonight,   *whatsoever*
255   Give it an understanding but no tongue;
I will requite° your loves. So, fare you well.   *repay*
Upon the platform 'twixt eleven and twelve
I'll visit you.
ALL.   Our duty to your honor.
                                          Exeunt [all but Hamlet].
HAMLET. Your loves, as mine to you.[1] Farewell.
260   My father's spirit—in arms! All is not well.
I doubt° some foul play. Would the night were come!   *suspect, fear*
Till then, sit still, my soul. Foul deeds will rise,
Though all the earth o'erwhelm them, to men's eyes.
                                                              Exit.

[1.3 POLONIUS'S APARTMENT IN THE CASTLE,
OR SOME PLACE NEARBY]

Enter Laertes, and Ophelia his sister.
LAERTES. My necessaries are embarked.[2] Farewell.
And sister, as° the winds give benefit   *whenever*
And convoy is assistant,[3] do not sleep
But let° me hear from you.   *do not sleep without letting*
OPHELIA.   Do you doubt that?
5   LAERTES. For Hamlet, and the trifling of his favor,[4]
Hold it a fashion and a toy in blood,[5]
A violet in the youth of primy nature,[6]
Forward,[7] not permanent, sweet, not lasting,
The perfume and suppliance of a minute,
No more.
OPHELIA.   No more but so?

---

1   I.e., I accept your "duty" as love, and I pledge my love to you in that same sense.
(Said as they leave.)
2   Loaded on board a sailing vessel.
3   And whenever means of transportation are available.
4   As for Hamlet and the attentions he pays you, which must be regarded as
trifling.
5   Consider it a passing fancy prompted by sexual attraction.
6   I.e., a natural impulse in the springtime of its vigor.
7   Insistent, early-blooming.

LAERTES. Think it no more. 10
For nature crescent does not grow alone
In thews and bulk, but as this temple waxes
The inward service of the mind and soul
Grows wide withal.[1] Perhaps he loves you now,
And now no soil nor cautel° doth besmirch   *stain or deceit* 15
The virtue of his will;[2] but you must fear,
His greatness weighed,[3] his will is not his own,
For he himself is subject to his birth.
He may not, as unvalued persons[4] do,
Carve for himself,[5] for on his choice depends 20
The safety and health of the whole state,
And therefore must his choice be circumscribed
Unto the voice and yielding of that body[6]
Whereof he is the head. Then if he says he loves you,
It fits your wisdom so far to believe it 25
As he in his particular act and place[7]
May give his saying deed,° which is no further   *may do as he promises*
Than the main voice of Denmark goes withal.[8]
Then weigh what loss your honor may sustain
If with too credent° ear you list[9] his songs,   *credulous, trusting* 30
Or lose your heart, or your chaste treasure open
To his unmastered importunity.[10]
Fear it, Ophelia, fear it, my dear sister,
And keep within the rear of your affection,
Out of the shot and danger of desire.[11] 35

---

1   For all living creatures (especially humans), as they mature, grow not in physical strength alone, but as the body ages the inner qualities of mind and soul develop also. ("Thews" are sinews, "inward service" is the inner life.)
2   The sincerity of his desires and intentions.
3   When his royal rank is taken into consideration.
4   Persons of ordinary social standing.
5   Help himself to the choicest morsel of the roast, i.e., choose for himself.
6   By the expressed opinion and consent of the body politic, the state.
7   In the particular circumstances to which he is restricted by his high station.
8   Than general opinion in Denmark will go along with.
9   Listen to.
10 To his uncontrolled urgency of desire.
11 I.e., don't let your passionate feelings lead you where you will be vulnerable to his amorous assaults.

The chariest° maid is prodigal enough   *most modest*
If she unmask her beauty to the moon.[1]
Virtue itself scapes° not calumnious° strokes.   *escapes / slanderous*
The canker galls the infants of the spring[2]

40   Too oft before their buttons be disclosed,°   *before their buds are open*
And in the morn and liquid dew of youth[3]
Contagious blastments[4] are most imminent.
Be wary, then; best safety lies in fear.
Youth to itself rebels, though none else near.[5]

45   OPHELIA. I shall the effect of this good lesson keep
As watchman to my heart.[6] But, good my brother,
Do not, as some ungracious[7] pastors do,
Show me the steep and thorny way to heaven
Whilst, like a puffed[8] and reckless libertine,

50   Himself the primrose path of dalliance treads,
And recks not his own rede.[9]

Enter Polonius.

LAERTES.   Oh, fear me not.[10]
I stay too long. But here my father comes.
A double blessing is a double grace;
Occasion smiles upon a second leave.[11]

55   POLONIUS. Yet here, Laertes? Aboard, aboard, for shame!
The wind sits in the shoulder of your sail,[12]
And you are stayed for. There, my blessing with thee,[13]

---

1   Is taking enough of a risk if she merely exposes herself to the chaste moon.
2   The cankerworm injures the budding flowers of springtime.
3   In the early time of life, a time that has the freshness and innocence of the dew-
sprinkled dawn.
4   Withering blasts of wind or frost.
5   Youth yields to the rebellion of the flesh without any outside promptings.
6   As guardian over my affections.
7   Ungodly, lacking in spiritual grace.
8   Bloated or swollen (presumably with the arrogance of youth).
9   And pays no heed to his own best advice.
10   Don't worry about me.
11   The goddess Occasion or Opportunity has smiled upon me by providing me
the chance to say goodbye to my father a second time and thereby receive from
him a second blessing.
12   I.e., you have a following wind now, so don't delay.
13   You are being waited for on board. There now, take my blessing.

And these few precepts in thy memory
See thou character.[1] Give thy thoughts no tongue,
Nor any unproportioned thought his act.[2]   60
Be thou familiar, but by no means vulgar.[3]
Those friends thou hast, and their adoption tried,[4]
Grapple them to thy soul with hoops of steel,[5]
But do not dull thy palm[6] with entertainment[7]
Of each new-hatched, unfledged[8] comrade. Beware   65
Of entrance to a quarrel, but, being in,
Bear't that th'opposèd[9] may beware of thee.
Give every man thine ear, but few thy voice.
Take each man's censure,[10] but reserve thy judgment.[11]
Costly thy habit° as thy purse can buy,   *clothing, dress* 70
But not expressed in fancy[12]—rich, not gaudy,
For the apparel oft proclaims the man,°   *we are what we wear*
And they in France of the best rank and station
Are of all most select and generous, chief in that.[13]
Neither a borrower nor a lender be,   75
For loan oft loses both itself and friend,
And borrowing dulleth edge of husbandry.°   *thrift*
This above all: to thine own self be true,
And it must follow as the night the day
Thou canst not then be false to any man.   80
Farewell. My blessing season this in thee![14]
LAERTES. Most humbly do I take my leave, my lord.

---

1 See to it that you inscribe.
2 And do not act upon any thought that is inadequately thought through or miscalculated.
3 Be sociable but not indiscriminate in your social dealings.
4 And their suitability as potential companions having been tested and screened.
5 With metal hoops such as would be used to hold together the sides of a barrel.
6 I.e., do not shake hands so often as to make the gesture essentially meaningless.
7 Greeting with a handshake.
8 Newly hatched in the nest and still unable to fly.
9 I.e., manage the business so that your adversary ...
10 Opinion, judgment.
11 Do not abandon your own opinion of what is said.
12 Extravagant fashion.
13 Are of all people the most refined in manners and in choosing what to wear.
14 May my blessing enable my advice to mature and ripen in your mind.

POLONIUS. The time invites you. Go. Your servants tend.[1]
LAERTES. Farewell, Ophelia, and remember well
85   What I have said to you.
OPHELIA. 'Tis in my memory locked,
    And you yourself shall keep the key of it.
LAERTES. Farewell.

                                    Exit Laertes.

POLONIUS. What is't, Ophelia, he hath said to you?
90 OPHELIA. So please you, something touching[2] the Lord Hamlet.
POLONIUS. Marry,[3] well bethought.[4]
    'Tis told me he hath very oft of late
    Given private time to you, and you yourself
    Have of your audience[5] been most free and bounteous.
95   If it be so—as so 'tis put on me,[6]
    And that in way of caution—I must tell you
    You do not understand yourself[7] so clearly
    As it behooves° my daughter and your honor.°   *befits / reputation*
    What is between you? Give me up the truth.
100 OPHELIA. He hath, my lord, of late made many tenders°   *offers*
    Of his affection to me.
POLONIUS. Affection? Pooh, you speak like a green[8] girl,
    Unsifted° in such perilous circumstance.   *untried*
    Do you believe his "tenders," as you call them?
105 OPHELIA. I do not know, my lord, what I should think.
POLONIUS. Marry, I'll teach you. Think yourself a baby
    That you have ta'en his tenders for true pay
    Which are not sterling.[9] Tender yourself more dearly,[10]
    Or—not to crack the wind of the poor phrase

---

1   Attend, are waiting.
2   Concerning.
3   I.e., by the Virgin Mary (a mild oath).
4   Appropriately thought of; I'm glad you mentioned that.
5   Hearing, attention.
6   Presented or suggested to me.
7   You don't appreciate your situation.
8   Inexperienced.
9   Lawful currency, with a play on the term "legal tender."
10 (1) Take better care of yourself; (2) hold out for a better bargain, i.e., marriage.

Running it thus[1]—you'll tender me a fool.[2]   110
OPHELIA. My lord, he hath importuned me with love
  In honorable fashion.
POLONIUS. Ay, fashion[3] you may call it. Go to, go to.[4]
OPHELIA. And hath given countenance[5] to his speech, my lord,
  With almost all the holy vows of heaven.   115
POLONIUS. Ay, springes to catch woodcocks.[6] I do know
  When the blood burns, how prodigal the soul
  Lends the tongue vows.[7] These blazes, daughter,
  Giving more light than heat, extinct in both
  Even in their promise as it is a-making,[8]   120
  You must not take° for fire. From this time, daughter,   *mistake*
  Be something° scanter of your maiden presence.   *somewhat*
  Set your entreatments at a higher rate
  Than a command to parley.[9] For° Lord Hamlet,   *as for*
  Believe so much in him[10] that he is young,   125
  And with a larger tether may he walk
  Than may be given you. In few,° Ophelia,   *in brief*
  Do not believe his vows, for they are brokers°   *go-betweens*
  Not of that dye which their investments show,[11]
  But mere implorators° of unholy suits,   *solicitors*   130
  Breathing° like sanctified and pious bawds[12]   *speaking*
  The better to beguile. This is for all:[13]

---

1 I.e., if I may use a metaphor from horsemanship, at the risk of running it so
hard that it is broken-winded.
2 (1) You'll make me look foolish, and yourself as well; (2) you'll present me with
a grandchild. (The word "fool" could be applied to babies, often endearingly.)
3 Mere form, conventional flattery. (Playing on Ophelia's "fashion" in the previous line in the more usual sense of "manner.")
4 I.e., what nonsense. (An expression of impatient dismissal.)
5 Authority, confirmation.
6 Traps to catch proverbially gullible birds.
7 When passionate desire rages, I know how prodigally the soul prompts the
tongue to promise anything to the desired person.
8 Lacking any real feeling or warmth of affection from the very first moment of
the promise-making.
9 Do not offer to surrender your chastity simply because he has requested a
meeting to discuss terms.
10 Believe this much concerning him.
11 Not truly of the color that their garments seem to show. (I.e., the vows are not
what they seem.)
12 Whores feigning innocence.
13 This is once for all; I don't want to have to say it again.

I would not, in plain terms, from this time forth
Have you so slander any moment leisure[1]
135 As to give words or talk with the Lord Hamlet.
Look to't, I charge you. Come your ways.°   *come along*
OPHELIA. I shall obey, my lord.

Exeunt.

[1.4 THE GUARD PLATFORM]

Enter Hamlet, Horatio, and Marcellus.
HAMLET. The air bites shrewdly;° it is very cold.   *keenly, sharply*
HORATIO. It is a nipping and an eager° air.   *biting, keen*
HAMLET. What hour now?
HORATIO. I think it lacks of° twelve.   *is just short of*
5 MARCELLUS. No, it is struck.
HORATIO. Indeed? I heard it not. It then draws near the season[2]
Wherein the spirit held his wont° to walk.   *has been accustomed*
A flourish of trumpets, and two pieces° goes off.   *i.e., of cannon, ordnance*
What does this mean, my lord?
HAMLET. The King doth wake[3] tonight and takes his rouse,[4]
10 Keeps wassail, and the swagg'ring upspring reels;[5]
And as he drains his drafts of Rhenish° down   *Rhine wine*
The kettledrum and trumpet thus bray out
The triumph of his pledge.[6]
HORATIO. Is it a custom?
15 HAMLET. Ay, marry, is't,
But to my mind, though I am native here
And to the manner born,[7] it is a custom
More honored in the breach than the observance.[8]

---

1 Have you abuse any moment's leisure (or any occasion).
2 Time.
3 Revels into the night.
4 Carouses.
5 Drinks many toasts and drunkenly reels his way through a lively German dance
called the "upspring."
6 Drums and trumpets raucously celebrate his draining the cup in his many
celebratory toasts.
7 Having a lifelong familiarity with this custom.
8 Better dispensed with than followed.

This heavy-headed revel east and west
Makes us traduced and taxed of other nations.[1]   20
They clepe° us drunkards, and with swinish phrase   *call*
Soil our addition,[2] and indeed it takes
From our achievements, though performed at height,[3]
The pith and marrow of our attribute.[4]
So, oft it chances in particular men,   25
That, for some vicious mole of nature in them,[5]
As in their birth,[6] wherein they are not guilty,
Since nature cannot choose his° origin,   *its*
By the o'ergrowth of some complexion,[7]
Oft breaking down the pales[8] and forts of reason,   30
Or by some habit that too much o'erleavens
The form of plausive manners,[9] that these men,
Carrying, I say, the stamp of one defect,
Being Nature's livery, or Fortune's star,
His virtues else,[10] be they as pure as grace,   35
As infinite as man may undergo,°   *sustain*
Shall in the general censure take corruption[11]
From that particular fault. The dram of evil
Doth all the noble substance often dout
To his own scandal.[12]

---

1   This drunken reveling causes us to be defamed and censored everywhere (east
and west) by all other nations.
2   And tarnish our reputation by calling us swine.
3   No matter how outstandingly performed.
4   The very essence of the reputation we should enjoy.
5   Because of some inborn flaw in them.
6   In the qualities bestowed on them by their parents and ancestors.
7   I.e., by one element of human nature gaining undue dominance over the
others.
8   Palisades, barrier fences, serving as a fortification.
9   I.e., that prompts excessive behavior, thereby corrupting what would otherwise be acceptable and pleasing manners (just as too much yeast causes excessive
swelling in the dough).
10   Such a person's virtues in other respects.
11   Shall in the court of public opinion acquire an unfavorable reputation.
12   I.e., the tiny amount (literally, one eighth of an ounce) of evil qualities often
blots or brings disrepute upon the noble substance of the whole. (To "dout" is to
extinguish, blot out.)

1.4.34:   FORTUNE (TLN 621.16)

The Roman goddess Fortuna or Fortune (Tyche to the Greeks), goddess of destiny or chance, is one of the most ancient of deities, able in her fickleness to give wealth or poverty, pleasure or misfortune, success or failure. In medieval iconography she is often represented as blindfolded, with a horn of plenty in her hands and a wheel whose turning represents the vicissitudes of fortune in all its inconsistency. There are many references to her in *Hamlet*. In this scene, the contrast of "Nature's livery" and "Fortune's star" reflects a familiar Renaissance debate as to the comparative importance in human life of that which is inborn and that which depends on fate. At 2.2.225–35 (TLN 1273–84), Hamlet engages Guildenstern and Rosencrantz in a playful debate about where a person can hope to rank in Fortune's favor, ending with a ribald joke that prompts Hamlet to observe, "she is a strumpet." His opinion is echoed by the First Player, in his recital about the fall of Troy, when he cries out against "strumpet Fortune" and beseeches the Olympian gods to take away her dreadful power (2.2.466–70, TLN 1533–37). The First Player similarly rails against "Fortune's state" (2.2.483, TLN 1552) for the goddess's role in the killing of King Priam and the resulting misery of his widow Hecuba. At 3.1.57–61 (TLN 1709–14), in the play's famous "To be, or not to be" soliloquy, Hamlet wonders whether "to suffer / The slings and arrows of outrageous fortune" (the word could be capitalized), or to end such sufferings by choosing "To die, to sleep." At 3.2.59–63 (TLN 1918–22), Hamlet warmly praises Horatio for his stoical resolve: he is "A man that Fortune's buffets and rewards / Hast ta'en with equal thanks"; Horatio is not "a pipe for Fortune's finger / To sound what stop she please." At 3.2.186–98 (TLN 2069–81), the Player King addresses his queen with a series of platitudes about love and fortune, another favorite Renaissance debating topic. At 4.4.53–54 (TLN 2743.44–45), Hamlet meditates wryly on the spectacle of a worldly prince like Fortinbras risking his life and the lives of his soldiers "To all that fortune, death, and danger dare, / Even for an eggshell." In all these instances, stoical resolve is seen as philosophy's best way of resisting the temptations offered by the fickle goddess Fortune.

Enter Ghost.

HORATIO.   Look, my lord, it comes!   40
HAMLET. Angels and ministers of grace defend us!
   Be thou a spirit of health or goblin damned,[1]
   Bring with thee airs from heaven or blasts[2] from hell,
   Be thy intents[3] wicked or charitable,
   Thou com'st in such a questionable shape   45
   That I will speak to thee. I'll call thee Hamlet,
   King, father, royal Dane. Oh, answer me!
   Let me not burst in ignorance, but tell
   Why thy canonized° bones, hearsèd[4] in death,   *consecrated*
   Have burst their cerements?[5] Why the sepulcher   50
   Wherein we saw thee quietly inurned[6]
   Hath oped his ponderous and marble jaws
   To cast thee up again? What may this mean
   That thou, dead corpse, again in complete steel°   *full armor*
   Revisits thus the glimpses of the moon,[7]   55
   Making night hideous, and we fools of nature[8]
   So horridly to shake our disposition[9]
   With thoughts beyond the reaches° of our souls?   *the capacities*
   Say, why is this? Wherefore? What should we do?
[The] Ghost beckons Hamlet.

HORATIO. It beckons you to go away with it,   60
   As if it some impartment[10] did desire
   To you alone.
MARCELLUS.   Look with what courteous action
   It wafts you to a more removèd ground.
   But do not go with it.
HORATIO.   No, by no means.

---

1   Whether you are a good angel or a demon.
2   Whether you bring gentle breezes from heaven or pestilent gusts.
3   Whether your intentions are.
4   Laid in a coffin.
5   Grave clothes.
6   Entombed, placed in an urn for ashes of the dead.
7   The sublunary world, all that is fitfully lit by pale moonlight.
8   We mere mortals, limited to natural knowledge and subject to nature.
9   To unsettle our mental composure so horrendously.
10 Communication, imparting of information.

65 HAMLET. It will not speak. Then I will follow it.

HORATIO. Do not, my lord.

HAMLET.   Why, what should be the fear?
  I do not set my life at a pin's fee,°   *the value of a pin*
  And for° my soul, what can it do to that,   *as for*
  Being a thing immortal as itself?

[*The Ghost beckons Hamlet.*]

70 It waves me forth again. I'll follow it.

HORATIO. What if it tempt you toward the flood,° my lord,   *sea*
  Or to the dreadful summit of the cliff
  That beetles o'er his base[1] into the sea,
  And there assume some other horrible form

75 Which might deprive your sovereignty of reason[2]
  And draw you into madness? Think of it:
  The very place puts toys of desperation,[3]
  Without more motive, into every brain
  That looks so many fathoms[4] to the sea

80 And hears it roar beneath.

[*The Ghost beckons Hamlet.*]

HAMLET. It wafts me still.—Go on, I'll follow thee.

MARCELLUS. You shall not go, my lord.

[*They attempt to restrain him.*]

HAMLET.   Hold off your hands!

HORATIO. Be ruled. You shall not go.

HAMLET.   My fate cries out[5]
  And makes each petty[6] artery in this body

85 As hardy as the Nemean lion's nerve.[7]

[*The Ghost beckons Hamlet.*]

  Still am I called. Unhand me, gentlemen!
  By heav'n, I'll make a ghost of him that lets° me.   *hinders*
  I say, away!—Go on, I'll follow thee.

---

1 That threateningly overhangs its base.
2 Take away from you the supremacy of reason over passion.
3 Imaginings of desperate acts, such as suicide.
4 Units of depth measurement at sea of about six feet.
5 My destiny summons me.
6 Even the most insignificant.
7 As a sinew of the huge lion (from Nemea, near Corinth in Greece) slain by
Hercules in the first of his 12 labors. See Appendix A, pp. 256–57.

Exeunt Ghost and Hamlet.

HORATIO. He waxes desperate with imagination.

MARCELLUS. Let's follow. 'Tis not fit thus to obey him.   90

HORATIO. Have after.° To what issue[1] will this come?   *let's go after him*

MARCELLUS. Something is rotten in the state of Denmark.

HORATIO. Heaven will direct it.[2]

MARCELLUS.   Nay, let's follow him.

Exeunt.

[1.5]

Enter Ghost and Hamlet.[3]

HAMLET. Whither wilt thou lead me? Speak. I'll go no further.

GHOST. Mark me.

HAMLET.   I will.

GHOST.   My hour is almost come

   When I to sulf'rous and tormenting flames

   Must render up myself.

HAMLET.   Alas, poor ghost!

GHOST. Pity me not, but lend thy serious hearing   5

   To what I shall unfold.

HAMLET. Speak. I am bound[4] to hear.

GHOST. So art thou to revenge, when thou shalt hear.

HAMLET. What?

GHOST. I am thy father's spirit,   10

   Doomed for a certain term to walk the night,

   And for the day confined to fast° in fires,   *to do penance by fasting*

   Till the foul crimes° done in my days of nature[5]   *sins*

---

1 Outcome.

2 I.e., heaven will determine the ultimate "issue" or outcome.

3 The scene is virtually continuous, though the stage is momentarily bare, and
we are to understand that the Ghost and Hamlet have moved to a new location on
the battlements.

4 (1) Destined, ready; (2) obligated, duty-bound. The Ghost replies to the second
of these meanings.

5 In my days on earth as a mortal.

Are burnt and purged[1] away. But that° I am forbid   *were it not that*
15 To tell the secrets of my prison house,
I could a tale unfold whose lightest word
Would harrow up[2] thy soul, freeze thy young blood,
Make thy two eyes like stars start from their spheres,[3]
Thy knotted and combinèd locks[4] to part,
20 And each particular hair to stand on end
Like quills upon the fretful° porpentine.[5]   *peevish*
But this eternal blazon[6] must not be
To ears of flesh and blood. List, Hamlet, oh, list:[7]
If thou didst ever thy dear father love—
25 HAMLET. O God!
GHOST. Revenge his foul and most unnatural murder.
HAMLET. Murder?
GHOST. Murder most foul, as in the best it is,[8]
But this most foul, strange, and unnatural.
30 HAMLET. Haste me to know't, that I with wings as swift
As meditation or the thoughts of love
May sweep to my revenge.
GHOST.   I find thee apt,
And duller shouldst thou be than the fat[9] weed
That rots itself in ease on Lethe[10] wharf
35 Wouldst thou not° stir in this. Now, Hamlet, hear: *if you would not*
'Tis given out° that, sleeping in my orchard,[11]   *the official story goes*

---

1 In Roman Catholic doctrine, Purgatory (not actually mentioned by name in this play) is an intermediate state after death for the purging of sins. If an individual has died in God's grace but has committed sins not yet pardoned (owing, as in this present instance, to a sudden death leaving no time for confessing those sins to a priest), the soul can make satisfaction in Purgatory for those sins and thus become fit for heaven.
2 Lacerate, uproot.
3 Eye-sockets, compared here to the crystalline spheres or orbits in which, according to Ptolemaic astronomy, the heavenly bodies moved around the earth.
4 Your neatly combed and properly arranged hair.
5 Shakespeare's usual spelling of "porcupine."
6 Revelation of the secrets of the supernatural world.
7 Listen.
8 Murder is foul even under the best of circumstances.
9 Lethargic, bloated.
10 The river of forgetfulness in Hades. See Appendix A, p. 255.
11 My garden.

A serpent stung me. So the whole ear of Denmark
Is by a forgèd process° of my death   *fabricated account*
Rankly abused.° But know, thou noble youth,   *grossly deceived*
The serpent that did sting thy father's life   40
Now wears his crown.
HAMLET. Oh, my prophetic soul! My uncle?
GHOST. Ay, that incestuous, that adulterate beast,
   With witchcraft of his wits, with traitorous gifts[1]—
   Oh, wicked wit and gifts, that have the power   45
So to seduce!—won to his shameful lust
The will of my most seeming virtuous queen.
Oh, Hamlet, what a falling off was there!

---

1   (1) With perfidious natural qualities; (2) with seductive presents.

1.5.43:   "AY, THAT INCESTUOUS,
      THAT ADULTERATE BEAST" (TLN 729)

The charge of murder against Claudius is coupled with the accusation
of incest and adultery. Later in the same scene, the Ghost insists that
Hamlet not allow "the royal bed of Denmark" to be "A couch for luxury
[i.e., lechery] and damnèd incest" (1.5.82–83, TLN 767–68). But how complicit was Gertrude in his crimes? At 3.4.29–30 (TLN 2409–10), Hamlet
indirectly questions her as to whether she could do such a thing "As kill
a king, and marry with his brother." Her answer, "As kill a king?" may
suggest to him that she is at least not guilty of that. Once Hamlet Senior
is dead, to be sure, Gertrude's marriage to Claudius is, technically, not
adultery, but the audience is left to wonder whether an adulterous relationship may have existed before the murder. While the Ghost insists
that Claudius's intent was adulterous, he instructs Hamlet to "leave her
[Gertrude] to heaven / And to those thorns that in her bosom lodge
/ To prick and sting her" (1.5.86–88, TLN 771–73), suggesting that the
Ghost is willing to give her the benefit of the doubt. The play leaves the
question unanswered, even if Hamlet's reconciliation with his mother
at the end may imply that he agrees with his dead father about her and
forgives her. See also Appendix D1, pp. 293–94.

From me, whose love was of that dignity

50 That it went hand in hand even with the vow°   *with the very vow*
I made to her in marriage, and to decline
Upon a wretch whose natural gifts were poor
To[1] those of mine. But virtue, as it never will be moved,
Though lewdness court it in a shape of heaven,

55 So lust, though to a radiant angel linked,
Will sate itself in a celestial bed
And prey on garbage.[2]
But soft,[3] methinks I scent the morning's air.[4]
Brief let me be. Sleeping within my orchard,

60 My custom always of the afternoon,
Upon my secure hour,[5] thy uncle stole
With juice of cursèd hebona in a vial,
And in the porches of my ears[6] did pour
The leperous distillment,[7] whose effect

65 Holds such an enmity with blood of man
That swift as quicksilver° it courses through   *mercury*
The natural gates and alleys of the body,
And with a sudden vigor it doth posset
And curd[8] like eager° droppings into milk   *sour, acid*

70 The thin and wholesome blood; so did it mine,
And a most instant tetter[9] barked about,
Most lazarlike° with vile and loathsome crust   *leper-like*
All my smooth body.
Thus was I sleeping by a brother's hand

75 Of life, of crown, of queen at once dispatched,°   *deprived*

---

1   Compared with.
2   I.e., similarly, a thoroughly lustful man, though married to a woman of angelic beauty and virtue, will refuse to be satisfied with that and turn instead to filthy desire elsewhere.
3   Wait a minute, hold on.
4   The Ghost here confirms the tradition that Horatio has reported at 1.1.155–62 (TLN 148–55): ghosts who visit the world of the living at night are supposed to return to their confines by dawn.
5   At a time when I was normally free from worries and able to relax my guard.
6   I.e., in the entranceways into my head.
7   A distillation causing a leprosy-like disfigurement.
8   Thicken and curdle (causing the blood to clot like sour cream).
9   Eruption of scabs or blisters.

"WITH JUICE OF CURSÈD
HEBONA IN A VIAL" (TLN 747)

The Ghost describes in exquisite detail how he was poisoned by his brother. In other Renaissance plays as well, by Thomas Middleton and others, we encounter such ingenious devices as (in John Webster's *The White Devil*, 1612) a painted portrait smeared invisibly with poison so that Isabella, long-suffering wife of the Duke of Bracciano, will die when she kisses a portrait of him in an act of devotion.

The Italians, in the Renaissance, were credited with having devised ingenious means of murder through poisoning; however, not much is known about the hebona that is mentioned in *Hamlet*. It may be related to henbane or black henbane or stinking nightshade, *Hyoscayamus niger*, a poisonous plant used sometimes in combination with mandrake and deadly nightshade. Probably "hen" originally meant "death." In Christopher Marlowe's *The Jew of Malta* (c. 1590), the title character Barabas refers to "the juice of hebon," along with the draft of poison that killed Alexander, the "Borgia's wine" that poisoned a pope, "the blood of Hydra, Lerna's bane," "poisons of the Styygian pool," and other dire concoctions.

Der Kronenräuber, literally, the crown-robber. The event alluded to here in Act 1, Scene 5, "Claudio Murders His Brother, King Hamlet, By Pouring Poison into His Ear as He Lies Sleeping in the Garden," is actually staged later in Act 3, Scene 2. By Johann Heinrich Lips, 1806.

Cut off even in the blossoms of my sin,[1]
Unhousled, disappointed, unaneled,[2]
No reck'ning made,[3] but sent to my account
With all my imperfections on my head.
80 Oh, horrible, oh, horrible, most horrible!
If thou hast nature[4] in thee, bear it not.
Let not the royal bed of Denmark be
A couch for luxury° and damnèd incest.   *lechery*
But howsomever thou pursues this act,
85 Taint not thy mind, nor let thy soul contrive
Against thy mother aught;° leave her to heaven   *in any way*
And to those thorns that in her bosom lodge
To prick and sting her. Fare thee well at once.
The glow-worm shows the matin° to be near   *morning*
90 And 'gins to pale his[5] uneffectual fire.
Adieu, adieu, Hamlet! Remember me.

                                                         Exit.

HAMLET. O all you host of heaven! O earth! What else?
And shall I couple° hell? Oh, fie! Hold, hold,[6] my heart,   *add*
· And you, my sinews,° grow not instant old,   *tendons, muscles*
95 But bear me stiffly° up. Remember thee?   *strongly, vigorously*
Ay, thou poor ghost, whiles memory holds a seat
In this distracted globe.[7] Remember thee?
Yea, from the table° of my memory   *wax writing tablet*
I'll wipe away all trivial fond° records,   *foolish*
100 All saws of books, all forms, all pressures past[8]
That youth and observation copied there,[9]

---

1 When my sins were at their height.
2 Without having partaken of the sacrament of the Mass, unprepared because of
not having made deathbed confession and not having received absolution, and not
anointed with the holy oil of Extreme Unction.
3 No settling of spiritual accounts, no making restitution for sins.
4 I.e., the natural feelings of a son for his father.
5 Begins to pale its.
6 Hold fast; do not panic; do not waver.
7 As long as memory continues to function in my distracted head (with perhaps
a glance at the Globe Theatre, where these lines are being spoken).
8 All wise sayings copied from books, all shapes or images drawn on the tablet of
my memory, all past impressions.
9 That I observed and noted down when I was young.

And thy commandment all alone shall live
Within the book and volume° of my brain,   *voluminous book*
Unmixed with baser matter. Yes, yes, by heaven.
Oh, most pernicious woman!   105
Oh, villain, villain, smiling damnèd villain!
My tables, my tables—meet° it is I set it down   *fitting*
That one may smile, and smile, and be a villain.
At least I am sure it may be so in Denmark.
So, uncle, there you are.[1] Now to my word.[2]   110
It is "Adieu, adieu, remember me."
I have sworn't.

Enter Horatio and Marcellus [calling first from within].
HORATIO. My lord, my lord!
MARCELLUS. Lord Hamlet!
HORATIO. Heavens secure him![3]   115
HAMLET. So be it.
MARCELLUS. Illo, ho, ho, my lord![4]
HAMLET. Hillo, ho, ho, boy, come, bird, come![5]
MARCELLUS. How is't, my noble lord?
HORATIO. What news, my lord?   120
HAMLET. Oh, wonderful!
HORATIO. Good my lord, tell it.
HAMLET. No, you'll reveal it.
HORATIO. Not I, my lord, by heaven.
MARCELLUS. Nor I, my lord.   125
HAMLET. How say you then, would heart of man once[6] think it—
    But you'll be secret?
BOTH.   Ay, by heaven, my lord.
HAMLET. There's ne'er a villain dwelling in all Denmark

---

1 I.e., I've noted that down (literally or metaphorically).
2 Now to the business of fulfilling what I have promised.
3 May heaven keep him safe!
4 Marcellus is hallooing to Hamlet, seeking still to find him. Hamlet has not yet spoken to them to assure them he is safe.
5 Hamlet halloos in reply, as though he were calling out to a hawk or falcon, commanding it to return to its master.
6 Ever.

But he's an arrant knave.[1]

130 HORATIO. There needs no ghost, my lord, come from the grave
To tell us this.

HAMLET.   Why, right, you are i'th' right.
And so, without more circumstance° at all   *elaboration*
I hold it fit that we shake hands and part:
You as your business and desires shall point you
135 (For every man hath business and desire,
Such as it is), and for my own poor part,
Look you, I'll go pray.

HORATIO. These are but wild and whirling words, my lord.

HAMLET. I am sorry they offend you—heartily,
Yes, faith, heartily.

140 HORATIO.   There's no offense,[2] my lord.

HAMLET. Yes, by Saint Patrick,[3] but there is, Horatio,
And much offense too. Touching[4] this vision here,
It is an honest° ghost, that let me tell you.   *genuine and truthful*
For° your desire to know what is between us,   *as for, regarding*
145 O'ermaster it as you may. And now, good friends,
As you are friends, scholars, and soldiers,
Give me one poor request.

HORATIO. What is't, my lord? We will.

HAMLET. Never make known what you have seen tonight.

150 BOTH. My lord, we will not.

HAMLET. Nay, but swear't.

HORATIO. In faith, my lord, not I.[5]

MARCELLUS. Nor I, my lord, in faith.

---

1 Hamlet seems about ready to tell them what he has learned from the Ghost, but then jestingly turns the matter aside with a self-evident truism: there's no villain in Denmark who is not a thoroughgoing villain.

2 Horatio here means "There was no offense in what you just said; no need to apologize." Hamlet then changes the meaning of the word to apply to Claudius's crime: "There certainly is a great offense, against all human decency and law."

3 The keeper of Purgatory, according to tradition.

4 Concerning, regarding.

5 Horatio insists that he will not tell anyone what they have seen this night. In the next speech, Marcellus vows also to keep the secret. They are not refusing to swear; in fact, they both seemingly take the view that they have sworn already by what they just said "in faith." But Hamlet insists that they now swear by his sword, an especially solemn oath since the sword hilt can be held so as to form a crucifix. Hamlet may hold it that way.

HAMLET. Upon my sword.
[*He holds out his sword.*]
MARCELLUS. We have sworn, my lord, already.   155
HAMLET. Indeed, upon my sword, indeed.
Ghost cries under the stage.
GHOST. Swear.

1.5.141:   "YES, BY SAINT PATRICK" (TLN 829)

This fifth-century Christian missionary and bishop was, according
to popular Irish legend, the keeper
of Purgatory. Station Island (or
perhaps Saints Island) in Lough
Derg, County Donegal, was long
venerated as the site where Christ
had revealed to Saint Patrick a
cave or pit in the ground named
Purgatory, which the Saint could
then show to Irish folk of waver-
ing faith to demonstrate the truth
of Christian teaching about the
joys of heaven and the torments
of hell. This place became a pilgrimage site. Perhaps Hamlet's
expression is meant to remind
the audience of Purgatory, since
that idea is so prominent earlier
in the scene; but Saint Patrick
was also, in more general terms, a
very popular figure associated with
England as well as Ireland. This is
the only instance in all his writings

Saint Patrice, Mattheus Borrekens,
1625–70.

that Shakespeare invokes the saint's name in an oath; "Friar Patrick's
cell" is incidentally mentioned thrice as a place of meeting (in Italy, presumably) in *The Two Gentlemen of Verona*.

HAMLET. Ha, ha, boy, say'st thou so? Art thou there,
    truepenny?[1]—
  Come on, you hear this fellow in the cellarage.
  Consent to swear.
160 HORATIO.   Propose the oath, my lord.
HAMLET. Never to speak of this that you have seen.
  Swear by my sword.
GHOST. Swear.
HAMLET. Hic et ubique?[2] Then we'll shift our ground.[3]
[*He moves them to another spot.*]
165   Come hither, gentlemen,
    And lay your hands again upon my sword.
  Never to speak of this that you have heard
  Swear by my sword.
GHOST. Swear by his sword.
170 HAMLET. Well said, old mole. Canst work i'th' earth so fast?
  A worthy pioneer![4]—Once more remove,[5] good friends.
[*They move once more.*]
HORATIO. Oh, day and night, but this is wondrous strange.
HAMLET. And therefore as a stranger give it welcome.
  There are more things in heaven and earth, Horatio,
175 Than are dreamt of in your philosophy.[6] But come,
  Here as before: never, so help you mercy,°   *as you hope for God's mercy*
  How strange or odd some'er° I bear myself   *however strangely or oddly*
  (As I perchance hereafter shall think meet°   *appropriate, fit*
  To put an antic disposition on),[7]
180 That you at such times seeing me never shall,
  With arms encumbered° thus, or this headshake,[8]   *folded*
  Or by pronouncing of some doubtful° phrase   *ambiguous*
  As, "Well, well, we know," or "We could an if we would,"[9]

---

1 Honest fellow, as trustworthy as the penny.
2 Here and everywhere (Latin).
3 Change where we are standing for another spot.
4 A foot soldier who dug tunnels and trenches used in warfare.
5 Let us move.
6 In this "natural philosophy" (i.e., science) that people talk about.
7 To assume the wild and erratic behavior of a madman.
8 Shaking my head thus.
9 We could if we wanted to.

Or "If we list[1] to speak," or "There be, an if they might,"[2]
Or such ambiguous giving out,[3] to note°   *indicate* 185
That you know aught° of me. This not to do,   *anything*
So grace and mercy at your most need help you,[4]
Swear.
GHOST. Swear.
[*They swear.*]
HAMLET. Rest, rest, perturbèd spirit.—So, gentlemen,   190
With all my love I do commend me to you,°   *I give you my best wishes*
And what so poor a man as Hamlet is
May do t'express his love and friending[5] to you,
God willing, shall not lack.[6] Let us go in together,
And still° your fingers on your lips, I pray.   *always, continually* 195
The time is out of joint.[7] Oh, cursèd spite,
That ever I was born to set it right!
[*They wait for him to leave first.*]
Nay, come, let's go together.

                                            Exeunt.

[2.1 POLONIUS'S APARTMENT, AS IN 1.3]

Enter old Polonius, with his man [Reynaldo] or two.
POLONIUS. Give him[8] this money, and these notes, Reynaldo.
[*He gives money and papers.*]
REYNALDO. I will, my lord.
POLONIUS. You shall do marv'lous[9] wisely, good Reynaldo,
Before you visit him, to make inquire°   *to inquire*
Of his behavior.
REYNALDO.   My lord, I did intend it.   5
POLONIUS. Marry, well said, very well said. Look you, sir,

---

1 If we chose.
2 There are those (namely, ourselves) who could talk if they chose to do so.
3 Utterance, pronouncement.
4 As you hope for God's grace and mercy at your hour of greatest spiritual need.
5 Friendliness, friendship.
6 Will not be lacking or left undone.
7 Disjointed, lacking coherence.
8 Laertes (as confirmed in lines 6 ff.)
9 Marvelously.

Inquire me[1] first what Danskers° are in Paris,   *Danes*
And how,[2] and who, what means,[3] and where they keep,[4]
What company, at what expense; and finding
10 By this encompassment and drift of question[5]
That they do know my son, come you more nearer
Than your particular demands will touch it.[6]
Take you,[7] as 'twere, some distant knowledge of him,
As thus: "I know his father, and his friends,
15 And in part him." Do you mark this, Reynaldo?
REYNALDO. Ay, very well, my lord.
POLONIUS. "And in part him. But," you may say, "not well,
But if 't be he I mean, he's very wild,
Addicted so and so," and there put on him°   *impute to him*
20 What forgeries[8] you please—marry, none so rank°   *gross*
As may dishonor him, take heed of that,
But, sir, such wanton,° wild, and usual slips   *unrestrained*
As are companions noted and most known
To youth and liberty.
25 REYNALDO. As gaming,° my lord?   *gambling*
POLONIUS. Ay, or drinking, fencing, swearing,
Quarreling, drabbing°—you may go so far.   *whoring*
REYNALDO. My lord, that would dishonor him.
POLONIUS. Faith, no, as you may season it in the charge.[9]
30 You must not put another scandal on him
That he is open to incontinency;[10]
That's not my meaning. But breathe[11] his faults so quaintly[12]

---

1 Inquire on my behalf.
2 How they live.
3 What wealth they have.
4 Dwell, frequent.
5 By this roundabout way of asking questions.
6 Finding out more this way than you would by making pointed inquiries.
7 Assume, pretend.
8 Invented tales.
9 Well, that would depend on how well you would temper or mitigate the accusation.
10 Chronic sexual overindulgence.
11 Name, utter.
12 Artfully, subtly.

That they may seem the taints of liberty,[1]
The flash and outbreak of a fiery mind,
A savageness in unreclaimèd blood,   35
Of general assault.[2]
REYNALDO. But, my good lord—
POLONIUS. Wherefore should you do this?
REYNALDO. Ay, my lord, I would know that.
POLONIUS. Marry sir, here's my drift,   40
And I believe it is a fetch of warrant.°   *a justifiable stratagem*
You laying these slight sullies[3] on my son
As 'twere a thing a little soiled i'th' working,[4]
Mark you, your party in converse,[5] him you would sound,[6]
Having ever seen in the prenominate crimes   45
The youth you breathe of guilty,[7] be assured
He closes with you in this consequence:[8]
"Good sir" (or so), or "friend," or "gentleman,"
According to the phrase and the addition[9]
Of man and country.
REYNALDO.   Very good, my lord.   50
POLONIUS. And then, sir, does 'a this, 'a does—what was I about
    to say?
By the mass,[10] I was about to say something.
Where did I leave?°   *leave off*
REYNALDO.   At "closes in the consequence."
At "friend," or so, and "gentleman."
POLONIUS. At "closes in the consequence." Ay, marry, 55
He closes with you thus: "I know the gentleman,
I saw him yesterday"—or t'other day,

---

1 Faults arising from too much free living.
2 A wildness in untamed youth that afflicts most young men.
3 Stains, blemishes.
4 In the handling.
5 The person you are conversing with.
6 Sound out.
7 If he has ever detected the young man you are asking about to be guilty of the offenses we have just enumerated.
8 He will take you into his confidence in the following way.
9 The title or form of address.
10 By the Holy Sacrament (a strong oath).

Or then, or then—"with such and such, and as you say,
There was 'a gaming, there o'ertook in's rouse,[1]
60   There falling out° at tennis," or perchance   *quarreling*
"I saw him enter such a house of sale,"°   *whorehouse*
Videlicet,° a brothel, or so forth. See you now,   *namely (Latin)*
Your bait of falsehood takes this carp° of truth,   *a fish*
And thus do we of wisdom and of reach,[2]
65   With windlasses[3] and with assays of bias,[4]
By indirections find directions out;[5]
So by my former lecture[6] and advice
Shall you my son. You have me,° have you not?   *understand me*
REYNALDO. My lord, I have.
POLONIUS.   God b'wi' ye, fare ye well.[7]
70 REYNALDO. Good my lord.
POLONIUS. Observe his inclination in yourself.[8]
REYNALDO. I shall, my lord.
POLONIUS. And let him ply his music.
REYNALDO. Well, my lord.

Exit Reynaldo.

Enter Ophelia.
75 POLONIUS. Farewell.—How now, Ophelia, what's the matter?
OPHELIA. Alas, my lord, I have been so affrighted!
POLONIUS. With what, i'th' name of God?
OPHELIA. My lord, as I was sewing in my chamber,
Lord Hamlet, with his doublet all unbraced,[9]
80   No hat upon his head, his stockings fouled,°   *dirty and untidy*

---

1   There he was gambling in that place, or overcome by drink.
2   Capacity, wide understanding.
3   I.e., by circuitous paths (literally, a hunter's roundabout circuit to head off pursued animals).
4   Indirect courses (resembling the curved path or "bias" of the bowling ball that is weighted to one side).
5   By these indirect means find out what is actually going on.
6   By the instructions I've just given you.
7   God be with you; farewell.
8   Take a personal interest in observing Laertes's habits; judge his behavior from the perspective of your knowledge of your own inclinations.
9   Man's close-fitting jacket all unfastened.

Ungartered, and down-gyvèd to his ankle,[1]
Pale as his shirt, his knees knocking each other,
And with a look so piteous in purport°   *in what it expressed*
As if he had been loosèd out of hell
To speak of horrors, he comes before me.   85
POLONIUS. Mad for thy love?
OPHELIA.   My lord, I do not know,
But truly I do fear it.
POLONIUS.   What said he?
OPHELIA. He took me by the wrist, and held me hard.
Then goes he to the length of all his arm,
And with his other hand thus o'er his brow   90
He falls to such perusal of my face
As 'a° would draw it. Long stayed he so.   *as if he*
At last, a little shaking of mine arm,
And thrice his head thus waving up and down,
He raised a sigh so piteous and profound   95
That it did seem to shatter all his bulk°   *body*
And end his being. That done, he lets me go,
And with his head over his shoulder turned
He seemed to find his way without his eyes,
For out o' doors he went without their help,   100
And to the last bended their light on me.
POLONIUS. Come, go with me. I will go seek the King.
This is the very ecstasy° of love,   *madness*
Whose violent property fordoes itself[2]
And leads the will to desperate° undertakings *suicidal, self-destructive* 105
As oft as any passion under heaven
That does afflict our natures. I am sorry.
What, have you given him any hard words of late?
OPHELIA. No, my good lord, but as you did command
I did repel his letters, and denied   110
His access to me.
POLONIUS.   That hath made him mad.

---

1   Having fallen down around his ankles, like a prisoner's "gyves" or shackles.
2   Whose violent nature is self-destructive.

I am sorry that with better heed[1] and judgment
I had not quoted° him. I feared he did but trifle   *observed*
And meant to wrack[2] thee; but beshrew my jealousy![3]
115   By heaven, it is as proper to our age
To cast beyond ourselves in our opinions[4]
As it is common for the younger sort
To lack discretion. Come, go we to the King.
This must be known,[5] which, being kept close, might move
120   More grief to hide than hate to utter love.[6]
Come.

                                           Exeunt.

[2.2 THE CASTLE]

Flourish. Enter King, Queen, Rosencrantz, and Guildenstern, with others.
KING. Welcome, dear Rosencrantz and Guildenstern.
Moreover that[7] we much did long to see you,
The need we have to use you did provoke
Our hasty sending.° Something have you heard   *sending for you*
5   Of Hamlet's transformation—so I call it,
Since not° th'exterior nor the inward man   *since neither*
Resembles that° it was. What it should be,   *what*
More than his father's death, that thus hath put him
So much from th'understanding of himself,
10   I cannot dream of. I entreat you both
That, being of° so young days brought up with him,   *from*
And since so neighbored to his youth and humor,[8]
That you vouchsafe your rest[9] here in our court
Some little time, so by your companies°   *companionship*

---

1   Attentiveness, care.
2   Ruin, seduce.
3   A plague on my suspicious nature!
4   It is as natural for old men to miscalculate through an excess of caution.
5   Must be made known to the King.
6   Which, being kept secret, might cause more unhappiness by such concealment than the hatred that might result from a well-intended telling of the truth.
7   Besides the fact that.
8   And since you were so well bonded to him in youthful ways.
9   That you will consent to stay.

To draw him on to pleasures, and to gather,   15
So much as from occasions you may glean,[1]
Whether aught to us unknown afflicts him thus
That, opened,° lies within our remedy.   *being revealed*
QUEEN. Good gentlemen, he hath much talked of you,
   And sure I am two men there is not living   20
   To whom he more adheres. If it will please you
   To show us so much gentry° and good will   *courtesy*
   As to expend your time with us awhile
   For the supply and profit of our hope,[2]
   Your visitation shall receive such thanks   25
   As fits a king's remembrance.[3]
ROSENCRANTZ.   Both your majesties
   Might, by the sovereign power you have of us,°   *over us*
   Put your dread pleasures[4] more into command
   Than to entreaty.
GUILDENSTERN.   But we both obey,
   And here give up ourselves in the full bent[5]   30
   To lay our service freely at your feet
   To be commanded.
KING. Thanks, Rosencrantz, and gentle Guildenstern.
QUEEN. Thanks, Guildenstern, and gentle Rosencrantz.
   And I beseech you instantly to visit   35
   My too-much-changèd son.—Go, some of you,
   And bring these gentlemen where Hamlet is.
GUILDENSTERN. Heavens make our presence and our practices[6]
   Pleasant and helpful to him!
QUEEN.   Ay, amen.
   Exeunt Rosencrantz and Guildenstern [and other Courtiers].

Enter Polonius.

---

1   As much as you may gather or infer from such opportunities.
2   In order to aid us in furthering what we hope for.
3   As would be a fitting royal reward for your service.
4   Your reverend wishes.
5   To the utmost extent of which we are capable (a metaphor from drawing the
bow in archery).
6   Doings.

40 POLONIUS. Th'ambassadors from Norway, my good lord,
      Are joyfully returned.
    KING. Thou still° hast been the father of good news.   *always*
    POLONIUS. Have I, my lord? Assure you, my good liege,¹
      I hold my duty as I hold my soul,
45   Both to my God and to my gracious king;
      And I do think—or else this brain of mine
      Hunts not the trail of policy° so sure   *statecraft*
      As it hath used to do²—that I have found
      The very cause of Hamlet's lunacy.
50 KING. Oh, speak of that! That do I long to hear.
    POLONIUS. Give first admittance to th'ambassadors.
      My news shall be the fruit° to that great feast.   *the dessert*
    KING. Thyself do grace to them,³ and bring them in.
      [*Polonius goes to bring in the ambassadors.*]
      He tells me, my sweet Queen, that he hath found
55   The head° and source of all your son's distemper.   *origin*
    QUEEN. I doubt⁴ it is no other but the main:
      His father's death, and our o'erhasty marriage.

    Enter Polonius, Voltemand, and Cornelius.
    KING. Well, we shall sift him.⁵—Welcome, my good friends.
      Say, Voltemand, what from our brother Norway?⁶
60 VOLTEMAND. Most fair return of greetings and desires.°   *good wishes*
      Upon our first,⁷ he sent out to suppress
      His nephew's levies,⁸ which to him appeared
      To be a preparation 'gainst the Polack,⁹
      But, better looked into, he truly found

---

1   One who is entitled to feudal allegiance and service.
2   As it has customarily done.
3   Honor them ceremoniously (with a suggestion of a "grace" said before a meal,
continuing the metaphor of the previous line).
4   Fear, suspect.
5   Question Polonius.
6   My fellow monarch, the King of Norway.
7   At our first presentation of our mission.
8   Young Fortinbras's raising of troops.
9   The King of Poland (and his army).

It was[1] against your highness; whereat grieved   65
That so his sickness, age, and impotence°   *weakness*
Was falsely borne in hand,[2] sends out arrests°   *orders to desist*
On Fortinbras, which he in brief obeys,
Receives rebuke from Norway, and, in fine,°   *in conclusion*
Makes vow before his uncle never more   70
To give th'assay of arms[3] against your majesty.
Whereon old Norway, overcome with joy,
Gives him three thousand crowns in annual fee[4]
And his commission to employ those soldiers
So levied (as before) against the Polack,   75
With an entreaty herein further shown
[*Giving a letter to the King*]
That it might please you to give quiet pass[5]
Through your dominions for his enterprise
On such regards of safety and allowance[6]
As therein[7] are set down.
KING.   It likes° us well,   *pleases* 80
And at our more considered[8] time we'll read,
Answer, and think upon this business.
Meantime, we thank you for your well-took labor.
Go to your rest. At night we'll feast together.
Most welcome home!
                                        Exeunt Ambassadors.
POLONIUS.   This business is well ended.   85
My liege and madam, to expostulate°   *expound*
What majesty should be, what duty is,
Why day is day, night night, and time is time,
Were nothing but to waste night, day, and time.

---

1 He found that it was in fact.
2 Was taken advantage of.
3 To make trial of military might.
4 3,000 gold coins in income, payment.
5 Safe and uninterrupted passage.
6 With such consideration for Denmark's safety and for the permission granted
to Fortinbras.
7 In the document we have just delivered to you.
8 Suitable for deliberation.

90   Therefore, since brevity is the soul of wit,[1]
      And tediousness the limbs and outward flourishes,[2]
      I will be brief. Your noble son is mad.
      Mad call I it, for to define true madness,
      What is't but to be nothing else but mad?
      But let that go.

---

1   Since brevity is essential to sound reasoning and argument.
2   And since long-windedness can add nothing but decorative rhetorical flourishes.

2.2.115-18:   ASTRONOMY AND COSMOLOGY
                (TLN 1144-47)

Renaissance poets, including Shakespeare and Milton, used the Ptolemaic earth-centered universe as the basis for their imaginings about heavenly bodies, even though the hypothesis of a solar system had been advanced by Copernicus in 1543. That idea was not supported by experimental evidence until the discoveries of Galileo in the early seventeenth century, and even then the idea was acutely controversial and condemned by the Catholic Church. Ptolemaic astronomy is the basis for Hamlet's love verse to Ophelia, when he writes, "Doubt thou the stars are fire, / Doubt that the sun doth move, / Doubt truth to be a liar, / But never doubt I love (2.2.115-18)." To doubt that the sun moves about the earth, he seems to say, is an impossibility equivalent to doubting my love for you. The idea that the stars are fire is also Ptolemaic.

Ptolemy was a Greco-Egyptian astronomer and astrologer of Alexandria, Egypt, in the second century CE, whose geocentric model of the universe prevailed as the orthodox view until well into the Renaissance. In his scheme, the sun, moon, planets, and stars all circled around the earth in their assigned orbits. Difficulties with the system, such as the occasional retrograde movement, especially of the outer planets Mars, Jupiter, and Saturn, were rationalized by the imposition of epicycles on the cyclical movements of these heavenly bodies. Claudius, at 4.7.16 (TLN 3023), compares his dependency on Gertrude to "the star" that "moves not but in his sphere." Hamlet ironically expresses his

QUEEN.	More matter with less art.[1]	95

POLONIUS. Madam, I swear I use no art at all.
    That he is mad, 'tis true. 'Tis true 'tis pity,
    And pity 'tis 'tis true—a foolish figure,°   *figure of speech*
    But farewell it, for I will use no art.
    Mad let us grant him, then. And now remains   100
    That we find out the cause of this effect,
    Or rather say the cause of this defect,

---

1   Give us more substance with less artfulness.

From *Harmonia Macrocosmica*, Andreas Cellarius, 1660.

amazement at the hyperbole of Laertes, who "Conjures the wand'ring stars [i.e., the planets], and makes them stand" (5.1.231, TLN 3451), i.e., remain stationary in their celestial paths.

For this effect defective comes by cause.[1]
Thus it remains, and the remainder thus.[2]
105   Perpend.°   *consider this*
I have a daughter—have whilst she is mine[3]—
Who in her duty and obedience, mark,
Hath given me this. Now gather and surmise.[4]
[*He reads from*] *the letter.* "To the celestial and my soul's idol, the most
110   beautified Ophelia." That's an ill phrase, a vile phrase; "beautified"
is a vile phrase. But you shall hear. "These in her excellent white
bosom, these," etc.[5]
QUEEN. Came this from Hamlet to her?
POLONIUS. Good madam, stay[6] awhile, I will be faithful.[7]
[*He reads the*] *letter.*
115   "'Doubt thou the stars are fire,[8]
        Doubt that the sun doth move,[9]
    Doubt truth to be a liar,
        But never doubt I love.'
    O dear Ophelia, I am ill at these numbers.[10] I have not art to
120   reckon[11] my groans. But that I love thee best, oh, most best,
    believe it. Adieu.
    Thine evermore, most dear lady, whilst this machine is to him,
                                                            Hamlet."

---

1   For this defective behavior in Hamlet must have a cause.
2   That pretty much sums up the situation, and leaves us to figure out what to make of it, what to do.
3   Who is legally mine until she marries.
4   Think about this and draw your own conclusions. ("Gather" may also suggest "gather around me.")
5   I.e., "These words are addressed to the spotlessly white bosom of the one I love." (Young ladies would often keep such love letters in their blouses, next to their hearts.) The "etc." could be a part of the letter, or, more plausibly, Polonius's way of summarizing what he chooses not to read.
6   Hold on, be patient.
7   I will do as I said I would.
8   Suspect or question the undoubted truth that the stars are fire (sooner than doubt my love for you).
9   (This "undoubted truth" seems postulated on the traditional Ptolemaic cosmology with the earth at the center of the universe and the sun being one of the celestial bodies that moves about it.)
10 I lack the skill needed to write verses like these, and am too lovesick to do so.
11 (1) Count, enumerate; (2) number metrically, scan.

This in obedience hath my daughter shown me,
And, more above, hath his solicitings,   125
As they fell out, by time, by means, and place,
All given to mine ear.[1]
KING. But how hath she received his love?
POLONIUS. What do you think of me?
KING. As of a man faithful and honorable.   130
POLONIUS. I would fain[2] prove so. But what might you think,
When I had seen this hot love on the wing—
As I perceived it (I must tell you that)
Before my daughter told me—what might you,
Or my dear majesty your queen here, think   135
If I had played the desk or table-book,[3]
Or given my heart a winking, mute and dumb,[4]
Or looked upon this love with idle sight,[5]
What might you think? No, I went round[6] to work,
And my young mistress thus I did bespeak:°   address   140
"Lord Hamlet is a prince out of thy star.[7]
This must not be." And then I precepts° gave her   orders
That she should lock herself from his resort,[8]
Admit no messengers, receive no tokens.
Which done, she took the fruits of my advice,   145
And he, repulsèd, a short tale to make,
Fell into a sadness, then into a fast,
Thence to a watch,° thence into a weakness,   sleepless state
Thence to a lightness,[9] and by this declension[10]
Into the madness wherein now he raves,   150
And all we mourn for.

---

1   And moreover she has let me know when, by what means, and where his
solicitings occurred ("fell out").
2   Gladly, willingly.
3   I.e., if I had noted all this in my memory-book but had done nothing about it;
or, if I had acted as go-between.
4   Or if I had deliberately shut my eyes to what my heart suspected.
5   Complacently or uncomprehendingly.
6   Directly, energetically.
7   Above your sphere or social station.
8   From his having access to her.
9   Lightheadedness.
10 Decline, deterioration (playing also with the grammatical sense of declension).

KING. [*To Queen*] Do you think 'tis this?

QUEEN. It may be, very like.°   *very likely*

POLONIUS. Hath there been such a time—I'd fain know that—

155   That I have positively said "'Tis so"

When it proved otherwise?

KING.   Not that I know.

POLONIUS. Take this from this,[1] if this be otherwise.

If circumstances lead me, I will find

Where truth is hid, though it were hid indeed

Within the center.[2]

160 KING.   How may we try° it further?   *test*

POLONIUS. You know sometimes he walks four hours together

Here in the lobby.[3]

QUEEN.   So he does indeed.

POLONIUS. At such a time, I'll loose[4] my daughter to him.

Be you and I behind an arras° then;   *wall-hanging, tapestry*

165   Mark the encounter. If he love her not,

And be not from his reason fall'n thereon,°   *on that account*

Let me be no assistant for a state

But keep a farm and carters.°   *cart drivers*

KING.   We will try it.

Enter Hamlet reading on a book.

QUEEN. But look where sadly the poor wretch comes reading.

170 POLONIUS. Away, I do beseech you both, away.

I'll board him presently.[5] Oh, give me leave.[6]—

                    Exeunt King and Queen.

How does my good Lord Hamlet?

HAMLET. Well, God-a-mercy.°   *God have mercy (i.e., thank you)*

POLONIUS. Do you know me, my lord?

---

1   I.e., cut off this head from my shoulders (or something similar, signaled by a gesture that Polonius makes; perhaps, "Take from me this chain of office that I wear around my neck").

2   Center of the earth, traditionally regarded as wholly inaccessible.

3   Corridor or waiting-room.

4   Let loose (as if she were a caged animal about to be mated).

5   Accost him immediately.

6   Leave this to me; leave me alone to handle this.

HAMLET. Excellent, excellent well. You're a fishmonger.¹ 175
POLONIUS. Not I, my lord.
HAMLET. Then I would you were so honest a man.
POLONIUS. Honest, my lord?
HAMLET. Ay, sir, to be honest, as this world goes, is to be one man
picked out of ten thousand. 180
POLONIUS. That's very true, my lord.
HAMLET. For if the sun breed maggots in a dead dog, being a good
kissing carrion²—Have you a daughter?
POLONIUS. I have, my lord.
HAMLET. Let her not walk i'th' sun.³ Conception⁴ is a blessing, but 185
as your daughter may conceive, friend, look to't.⁵
POLONIUS. [Aside] How say you by that? Still harping on⁶ my daugh-
ter. Yet he knew me not at first. 'A said I was a fishmonger. 'A is far
gone, far gone. And truly, in my youth I suffered much extremity
for love, very near this. I'll speak to him again.—What do you 190
read, my lord?
HAMLET. Words, words, words.
POLONIUS. What is the matter,⁷ my lord?
HAMLET. Between who?
POLONIUS. I mean the matter that you read, my lord. 195
HAMLET. Slanders sir; for the satirical rogue says here that old men
have gray beards, that their faces are wrinkled, their eyes purging
thick amber and plumtree gum,⁸ and that they have a plentiful
lack of wit,⁹ together with most weak hams¹⁰—all which, sir,
though I most powerfully and potently believe, yet I hold it not 200

---

1 Fish merchant.
2 Being a suitable piece of flesh for such kissing.
3 (1) In public; (2) into the sunshine of Hamlet's princely favors (continuing the pun on sun/son in the previous lines).
4 (1) Understanding; (2) conceiving a child.
5 Take care, be wary.
6 Dwelling obsessively on.
7 What is the substance of what you are reading? (But Hamlet deliberately misunderstands, answering as if Polonius had asked, "What is the quarrel between the people you are talking about?")
8 Their eyes are dropping thick, moist discharges like the sticky resins from various trees.
9 Understanding.
10 Exceedingly weak thighs.

honesty[1] to have it thus set down; for you yourself, sir, shall grow old as I am, if, like a crab, you could go backward.

POLONIUS. [*Aside*] Though this be madness, yet there is method in't.—Will you walk out of the air, my lord?

205 HAMLET. Into my grave.

POLONIUS. [*Aside*] Indeed, that's out of the air. How pregnant[2] sometimes his replies are! A happiness[3] that often madness hits on, which reason and sanity could not so prosperously[4] be delivered of. I will leave him, and suddenly contrive the means

210 of meeting between him and my daughter.—My honorable lord, I will most humbly take my leave of you.

HAMLET. You cannot, sir, take from me anything that I will more willingly part withal[5]—except my life, except my life, except my life.

Enter Guildenstern and Rosencrantz.

215 POLONIUS. Fare you well, my lord.

HAMLET. These tedious old fools!

POLONIUS. [*To Rosencrantz and Guildenstern*] You go to seek the Lord Hamlet? There he is.

ROSENCRANTZ. [*To Polonius*] God save you, sir.

[*Exit Polonius.*]

220 GUILDENSTERN. My honored lord!

ROSENCRANTZ. My most dear lord!

HAMLET. My excellent good friends! How dost thou, Guildenstern? Ah, Rosencrantz! Good lads, how do ye both?

ROSENCRANTZ. As the indifferent[6] children of the earth.

225 GUILDENSTERN. Happy[7] in that we are not over-happy. On Fortune's cap we are not the very button.[8]

HAMLET. Nor the soles of her shoe?

ROSENCRANTZ. Neither, my lord.

---

1 Decency, honorable behavior.
2 Cogent, full of meaning.
3 Aptness, felicity of expression.
4 Successfully, effectively.
5 With.
6 Ordinary, neither extremely fortunate nor unfortunate.
7 Fortunate.
8 Presumably, Fortune's cap has a button at its very top.

HAMLET. Then you live about her waist, or in the middle of her favors.[1] 230

GUILDENSTERN. Faith,[2] her privates[3] we.

HAMLET. In the secret parts of Fortune? Oh, most true, she is a strumpet.[4] What's the news?

ROSENCRANTZ. None, my lord, but that the world's grown honest.

HAMLET. Then is doomsday near.[5] But your news is not true. Let 235
me question more in particular. What have you, my good friends, deserved at the hands of Fortune that she sends you to prison hither?

GUILDENSTERN. Prison, my lord?

HAMLET. Denmark's a prison. 240

ROSENCRANTZ. Then is the world one.

HAMLET. A goodly one, in which there are many confines,[6] wards, and dungeons, Denmark being one o'th' worst.

ROSENCRANTZ. We think not so, my lord.

HAMLET. Why, then 'tis none to you, for there is nothing either good 245
or bad but thinking makes it so. To me it is a prison.

ROSENCRANTZ. Why, then your ambition makes it one. 'Tis too narrow for your mind.

HAMLET. Oh, God, I could be bounded in a nutshell and count myself a king of infinite space, were it not that I have bad dreams. 250

GUILDENSTERN. Which dreams indeed are ambition, for the very substance of the ambitious is merely the shadow of a dream.[7]

HAMLET. A dream itself is but a shadow.

ROSENCRANTZ. Truly, and I hold ambition of so airy and light a quality that it is but a shadow's shadow. 255

---

1 In her genital area.

2 In good faith (a mild oath).

3 (1) Sexual members; (2) ordinary foot-soldiers; (3) informal friends and counselors, without official title.

4 Whore. (Fortune was proverbially fickle in bestowing her favors.)

5 See Appendix B, p. 270.

6 Enclosures, places of confinement.

7 The goal of ambition is without substance, being nothing more than the unreal image of something that is itself mere illusion. (Rosencrantz repeats this idea in his next speech.)

Hamlet quips that the idea of the world growing honest is so radical as to be apocalyptic, a sure sign that the end is near. The widespread belief that doomsday was imminent was based substantially on the Book of Revelation, traditionally the last book of the New Testament, envisaging the final destruction of the world as a time of final reckoning when God's ultimate purposes are to be revealed. A sense of apocalyptic disaster hangs over the play, as it does in *King Lear*. Horatio speaks of the assassination of Julius Caesar as a time when the moon was "sick almost to doomsday with eclipse" (1.1.124, TLN 124.13). Hamlet invokes an image of apocalypse when he arraigns his mother for her infidelity to her first marriage: "Heaven's face doth glow / O'er this solidity and compound mass / With tristful visage, as against the doom" (3.4.49–51, TLN 2431–33), suggesting that the "visage" of heaven glows reproachfully in red-hot anger against the seemingly solid earth that is about to experience the Day of Doom. On a lighter note, the First Gravedigger poses a riddle that speaks of graves as houses that last "till doomsday" (5.1.52, TLN 3249).

Day of Judgment, Hans Memling, c. 1470.

HAMLET. Then are our beggars bodies, and our monarchs and out-
stretched heroes the beggars' shadows.[1] Shall we to th'court? For,
by my fay,[2] I cannot reason.

BOTH. We'll wait upon[3] you.

HAMLET. No such matter.[4] I will not sort[5] you with the rest of my   260
servants, for, to speak to you like an honest man, I am most
dreadfully attended. But, in the beaten way[6] of friendship, what
make you[7] at Elsinore?

ROSENCRANTZ. To visit you, my lord, no other occasion.

HAMLET. Beggar that I am, I am even poor in thanks, but I thank   265
you; and sure, dear friends, my thanks are too dear a halfpenny.[8]
Were you not sent for? Is it your own inclining? Is it a free[9]
visitation? Come, come, deal justly with me. Come, come, nay,
speak.

GUILDENSTERN. What should we say, my lord?   270

HAMLET. Why, anything—but to th' purpose.[10] You were sent for,
and there is a kind of confession in your looks which your
modesties have not craft enough to color.[11] I know the good King
and Queen have sent for you.

ROSENCRANTZ. To what end, my lord?   275

HAMLET. That you must teach me. But let me conjure[12] you, by the
rights of our fellowship, by the consonancy of our youth,[13] by the

---

1 In that case, ordinary beggars must be more substantial, in that they lack ambition, whereas our monarchs and others, whom we make to seem greater than they
really are by our adulation of them, are in fact only the unsubstantial shadows cast
by our beggars.
2 Faith.
3 Accompany, attend.
4 Certainly not. (Hamlet interprets their "wait upon" as meaning "provide
menial service." He will not treat his boyhood friends this way.)
5 Class, categorize.
6 In the well-trodden path.
7 What are you doing.
8 A mere halfpenny, a coin of little value, would be too much to pay for my poor
thanks. (Hamlet may suggest that his power to assist friends is very limited.)
9 Voluntary.
10 Say anything you like, but let's get to the main point.
11 Disguise.
12 Solemnly entreat.
13 By the close friendship of our younger days and of our ages.

obligation of our ever-preserved love, and by what more dear a
better proposer could charge you withal,[1] be even[2] and direct
280 with me whether you were sent for or no.
ROSENCRANTZ. [Aside to Guildenstern] What say you?
HAMLET. [Aside] Nay, then, I have an eye of you.[3]—If you love me,
hold not off.[4]
GUILDENSTERN. My lord, we were sent for.
285 HAMLET. I will tell you why; so shall my anticipation prevent your
discovery,[5] and your secrecy to the King and Queen molt no feath-
er.[6] I have of late, but wherefore I know not, lost all my mirth,
forgone all custom of exercise; and indeed it goes so heavily with
my disposition[7] that this goodly frame,[8] the earth, seems to me
290 a sterile promontory. This most excellent canopy the air, look you,
this brave o'erhanging firmament,[9] this majestical roof fretted[10]

---

1 By whatever more earnest entreaty a more skillful proposer might urge.
2 Be straightforward.
3 I have my eye on you.
4 Don't hold back.
5 In that way, my speaking first will spare you the embarrassment of confessing
the truth.
6 I.e., will lose none of its seeming integrity.
7 It weighs so heavily on my spirits.
8 Structure, substance.
9 This splendid heavenly canopy hanging over us.
10 Adorned, inlaid.

2.2.297:   QUINTESSENCE (TLN 1355)

Hamlet seems to be using the word in its modern sense of a perfect
example of some quality or class of things. In medieval philosophy,
"quintessence" (literally "fifth essence") was a distillation of the traditional four elements of earth, air, fire, and water. In cosmic terms
quintessence was ether, the supposed essence out of which the heavenly
bodies were made. These ideas go back to Aristotle, who saw ether as
permeating all creation. The medical authority Galen, who lived in the
second century CE, was widely associated with the theory of the four
"humors," which corresponded to the four elements, down to the time
of the Renaissance; see extended note on p. 140.

with golden fire, why, it appears no other thing to me than a foul
and pestilent congregation[1] of vapors. What a piece of work is
a man! How noble in reason, how infinite in faculties, in form
and moving[2] how express[3] and admirable! In action, how like an   295
angel! In apprehension,[4] how like a god; the beauty of the world;
the paragon of animals. And yet to me what is this quintessence
of dust?[5] Man delights not me, no, nor woman neither, though
by your smiling you seem to say so.

ROSENCRANTZ. My lord, there was no such stuff in my thoughts.   300

HAMLET. Why did you laugh, then, when I said man delights not
me?

ROSENCRANTZ. To think, my lord, if you delight not in man, what
lenten entertainment[6] the players shall receive from you. We
coted[7] them on the way, and hither are they coming to offer you   305
service.

HAMLET. He that plays the King shall be welcome; his majesty
shall have tribute of me.[8] The Adventurous Knight shall use his
foil and target,[9] the Lover shall not sigh gratis, the Humorous
Man shall end his part in peace,[10] the Clown shall make those   310
laugh whose lungs are tickled o'th' sear,[11] and the Lady shall say
her mind freely, or the blank verse shall halt for't.[12] What players
are they?

---

1 Mass, assemblage.
2 In shape and motion.
3 Well framed; expressive.
4 In the power of comprehending.
5 See extended note on p. 122.
6 Meager reception (appropriate to Lent, the forty days of penitence and fasting
from Ash Wednesday to Easter).
7 Overtook and passed.
8 (1) Payment; (2) homage, praise from me.
9 His sword and shield.
10 The eccentric character, displaying the dominance in him of a particular "humor" (obsession, whim, fancy), will have full license to speak without
interruption.
11 I.e., the Clown will make those laugh who are predisposed to laugh. (A sear is
part of a gun-lock; those whose lungs are "tickled o'th' sear" have a hair-trigger
response and are apt to laugh readily.)
12 The boy actor playing the female parts will be allowed to speak without interruption also, or the blank verse will limp.

This description of a public controversy involving adult actors and juvenile acting companies occurs only in F1; Q1 gives a shortened version and Q2 omits the passage entirely. It evidently alludes to a theatrical rivalry that took place in the years around 1599–1600 that is often called "The War of the Theaters" or "the Poetomachia"—the Poets' War. Rosencrantz, in response to Hamlet's insistent questions, describes how troupes of boy actors presenting sharply satirical plays have become much in fashion. It has reached the point, indeed, that no playwright can hope to see his plays acted unless he joins in the fray.

The juvenile acting companies had been closed by the authorities throughout most of the 1590s because of their penchant for satire that often took aim at matters of national and international politics, London shopkeepers and their wives, Puritans, busybody public officials, hangers-on at court, sheriffs and other officers of the law, and much else. When one such group known as Paul's Boys and another known as the Children of the Chapel were allowed to resume performances in 1599–1600, the volleying of insults and criticisms quickly became intense. As this passage in *Hamlet* suggests, the boys and the adult actors tended to line up on opposite sides of many issues. The debate was further heightened and made colorful by some notable dramatists. Ben Jonson's *Poetaster*, performed at the Blackfriars Theatre in 1601 by a troupe misleadingly called "the Children of Her Majesty's Chapel," lampooned the playwrights John Marston and Thomas Dekker. Dekker soon replied with a satirical portrait of Jonson in *Satiromastix*, acted by the adult Chamberlain's Men in conjunction with Paul's Boys. Marston had offered an affront to the adult companies in his *Histriomastix, or the Player Whipped*, performed by Paul's Boys (c. 1599), and had attacked Jonson in *Jack Drum's Entertainment* (1600). Marston and Dekker purported to see lampoons of themselves in the characters Hedon and Anaides in Jonson's *Cynthia's Revels* (1600), acted by the so-called Children of the Chapel at the Blackfriars Theater. Whether Shakespeare took part in the fray is much debated. The adult actor Will Kemp, depicted in an anonymous play called *The Return from Parnassus, Part II*, acted at Cambridge some time around 1601–02, asserts that "our fellow Shakespeare puts them [i.e., the London playwrights] all down [i.e., criticizes them publicly]," and among the rest has given

Satiro--maſtix.

OR

The vntruſſing of the Humo-
rous Poet.

As it hath bin preſented publikely,
by the Right Honorable, the Lord Cham-
berlaine his Seruants; and priuately, by the
Children of Paules.

By *Thomas Dekker.*

Non recito cuiquam niſi Amicis idq; coactus.

LONDON,

Printed for *Edward VVhite*, and are to bee
ſolde at his ſhop, neere the little North doore of Paules
Church, at the ſigne of the Gun. 1602.

Satiromatrix by Thomas Dekker, title page, 1602.

Jonson "a purge that made him beray his credit." Was this possibly in reference to *Troilus and Cressida*, or *Twelfth Night*? For a lively account of all this, see Bednarz, p. 303.

ROSENCRANTZ. Even those you were wont to take such delight in,[1]
315   the tragedians[2] of the city.

HAMLET. How chances it they travel?[3] Their residence[4] both in
reputation and profit was better both ways.

ROSENCRANTZ. I think their inhibition comes by the means of the
late innovation.[5]

320 HAMLET. Do they hold the same estimation[6] they did when I was
in the city? Are they so followed?

ROSENCRANTZ. No, indeed, they are not.

HAMLET. How comes it? Do they grow rusty?

ROSENCRANTZ. Nay, their endeavor keeps in the wonted pace.[7] But
325   there is, sir, an eyrie of children, little eyases,[8] that cry out on the
top of question,[9] and are most tyrannically[10] clapped for't. These
are now the fashion, and so berattle the common stages[11]—so
they call them—that many wearing rapiers are afraid of goose
quills[12] and dare scarce come thither.

330 HAMLET. What, are they children? Who maintains 'em? How are
they escoted?[13] Will they pursue the quality no longer than they
can sing?[14] Will they not say afterwards, if they should grow
themselves to common players[15]—as it is most like if their means
are not better[16]—their writers do them wrong to make them
335   exclaim against their own succession?[17]

---

1 You were accustomed to take such delight in.
2 Actors (of comedy or tragedy).
3 I.e., tour the provinces.
4 Remaining in the city, not on tour.
5 I think their finding it necessary to travel comes as a result of restraints being
placed upon the adult actors in the wake of recent disturbances.
6 Esteem, reputation.
7 Continues at the accustomed level.
8 A nest full of chicks, of young hawks (here signifying the boy actors).
9 Who shout more shrilly than their competitors.
10 Vehemently, outrageously.
11 Make such noisy clamor against the adult acting companies.
12 That many gentlemen fear being satirized in the juvenile companies' plays.
13 Maintained, provided for.
14 I.e., will they pursue acting as a profession no longer when their voices break at
adolescence?
15 If they should mature into adult actors for the "public" stage.
16 Which is most likely if they can find no better way to support themselves.
17 To induce them to satirize their own future profession.

ROSENCRANTZ. Faith, there has been much to-do[1] on both sides, and the nation[2] holds it no sin to tarre[3] them to controversy. There was for a while no money bid for argument unless the poet and the player went to cuffs in the question.[4]

HAMLET. Is't possible? 340

GUILDENSTERN. Oh, there has been much throwing about of brains.[5]

HAMLET. Do the boys carry it away?[6]

ROSENCRANTZ. Ay, that they do, my lord, Hercules and his load too.[7] 345

HAMLET. It is not very strange, for my uncle is King of Denmark, and those that would make mows[8] at him while my father lived give twenty, forty, fifty, a hundred ducats[9] apiece for his picture in little.[10] 'Sblood,[11] there is something in this more than natural, if philosophy could find it out. 350

Flourish for the players.[12]

GUILDENSTERN. There are the players.

HAMLET. Gentlemen, you are welcome to Elsinore. Your hands,[13] come. Th'appurtenance of welcome is fashion and ceremony.[14] Let me comply with you in this garb, lest my extent to the players—which, I tell you, must show fairly outward—should more 355

---

1 Ado.
2 The city populace.
3 To goad, incite (as in inciting dogs to attack a chained bear).
4 I.e., for a while, no money was offered to a playwright unless his play took part in the sharp controversy between the satirical writers for the juvenile companies and the dramatists who wrote for the adult companies.
5 Lively exchanges in the battle of wits.
6 Win the day.
7 See Appendix A, pp. 253–54.
8 Faces, grimaces.
9 Gold coins.
10 For his portrait in miniature.
11 By God's (Christ's) blood. (An oath.)
12 I.e., a fanfare announcing the arrival of the actors at Elsinore Castle. They do not enter on stage until line 398 (TLN 1466).
13 Give me your hands.
14 Ceremonious actions and gestures are appropriate when one is welcoming visitors.

appear like entertainment than yours.[1] You are welcome. But my uncle-father[2] and aunt-mother[3] are deceived.

GUILDENSTERN. In what, my dear lord?

HAMLET. I am but mad north-north-west;[4] when the wind is south-
360 erly, I know a hawk from a handsaw.[5]

Enter Polonius.

POLONIUS. Well be[6] with you, gentlemen.

HAMLET. Hark you, Guildenstern, and you too, at each ear a hearer: that great baby you see there is not yet out of his swaddling clouts.[7]

365 ROSENCRANTZ. Haply[8] he is the second time come to them, for they say an old man is twice a child.

HAMLET. I will prophesy he comes to tell me of the players. Mark it.—You say right, sir, o'Monday morning, 'twas then indeed.[9]

POLONIUS. My lord, I have news to tell you.

370 HAMLET. My lord, I have news to tell you. When Roscius was an actor in Rome[10]—

POLONIUS. The actors are come hither, my lord.

HAMLET. Buzz, buzz.[11]

POLONIUS. Upon my honor—

375 HAMLET. Then came each actor on his ass.

---

1 Let me comply with ceremonious custom by shaking hands with you now, lest my extending a welcome to the actors—which, I tell you, must necessarily display all the customary signs of a courtesy—should appear more cordial than the welcome I have just extended to you.

2 Both uncle and stepfather.

3 Both mother and now aunt (by the marriage which Hamlet considers incestuous).

4 Mad only a small degree from true north, i.e., not very mad; or, mad only when the wind blows from that direction.

5 I.e., only a mad person would be unable to distinguish a hawk from a handsaw, and I have no trouble distinguishing. (Or "handsaw" might be intended for "hern-shaw," a heron.)

6 May all be well (a conventional greeting).

7 Clothes in which a baby is wrapped to keep it safe and still.

8 Perhaps.

9 (Hamlet pretends to be in conversation with his friends.)

10 Quintus Roscius Gallus, the famous Roman actor, lived c. 126–62 BCE.

11 An interjection, here conveying Hamlet's contempt for Polonius's telling the already stale news of the actors' arrival.

POLONIUS. The best actors in the world, either for tragedy, comedy, history, pastoral, pastoral-comical, historical-pastoral, tragical-historical, tragical-comical-historical-pastoral, scene individable, or poem unlimited.[1] Seneca[2] cannot be too heavy nor Plautus[3] too light. For the law of writ and the liberty,[4] these[5] are the only   380
   men.

HAMLET. O Jephthah, judge of Israel,[6] what a treasure hadst thou?

POLONIUS. What a treasure had he, my lord?

HAMLET. Why,
   "One fair daughter and no more,   385
   The which he lovèd passing well."[7]

POLONIUS. [Aside] Still on my daughter.

HAMLET. Am I not i'th' right, old Jephthah?

POLONIUS. If you call me Jephthah, my lord, I have a daughter that
   I love passing well.   390

HAMLET. Nay, that follows not.[8]

POLONIUS. What follows then, my lord?[9]

HAMLET. Why,
   "As by lot, God wot,°   *as by chance, God knows*
   and then you know,   395
   It came to pass, as most like it was°—"   *as was most likely*

---

1 I.e., plays without scene breaks and unrestrained by rules, hence all-inclusive or unclassifiable—an absurdly catchall conclusion to Polonius's ponderous list of dramatic categories.
2 Lucius Annaeus Seneca, known as Seneca the Younger (c. 3 BCE–65 CE), the most widely read of Latin writers of tragedy. See Appendix A, pp. 262–63.
3 Titus Maccius Plautus (c. 254–184 BCE), the most popular of Latin writers of comedy. See Appendix A, p. 260.
4 For plays written according to the classical rules as well as for those that disregard these conventions.
5 I.e., these actors, or possibly Seneca and Plautus.
6 Old Testament patriarch (Judges 11:30–40) who vowed that, if God granted him victory over the Ammonites in battle, he would sacrifice the first living thing he saw when he returned home; the first thing he saw turned out to be his daughter and only child. See Appendix B, pp. 270–71.
7 Surpassingly well. (Hamlet quotes from a ballad about Jephthah and his daughter.)
8 I.e., (1) just because you resemble Jephthah in having a daughter does not logically demonstrate that you love her; (2) you haven't quoted the next line of the ballad.
9 Polonius asks, what does follow logically? But Hamlet answers as if Polonius had asked, what are the next lines of the ballad?

the first row of the pious chanson will show you more,[1] for look
where my abridgment comes.[2]

Enter four or five Players.

HAMLET. You are welcome, masters,[3] welcome all.—I am glad to
see thee well. Welcome, good friends.—Oh, my old friend! Thy
face is valanced[4] since I saw thee last. Com'st thou to beard[5] me
in Denmark?—What, my young lady[6] and mistress![7] By'r Lady,[8]
your ladyship is nearer heaven[9] than when I saw you last, by the
altitude of a chopine.[10] Pray God your voice, like a piece of uncur-
rent gold,[11] be not cracked within the ring.[12]—Masters, you are
all welcome. We'll e'en to't, like French falconers:[13] fly at anything
we see. We'll have a speech straight.[14] Come, give us a taste of your
quality.[15] Come, a passionate speech.

FIRST PLAYER. What speech, my good lord?

HAMLET. I heard thee speak me[16] a speech once, but it was[17] never
acted, or, if it was, not above once; for the play, I remember,
pleased not the million, 'twas caviare to the general.[18] But it was,

---

1 The first line or stanza of this pious ballad will tell you more.
2 Look, the actors are coming who will cut short what I was about to say, and
who will provide entertainments or diversions.
3 Good sirs. (Said to social inferiors.)
4 I.e., fringed with beard.
5 Confront, challenge, defy (with obvious pun on the player's beard).
6 The boy actor, to whom the female roles are assigned.
7 Hamlet addresses the boy actor with playful and courtly hyperbole as if he/she,
now coming to age as a young adult, were a woman to be admired and courted.
(With no necessary suggestion of the modern sense of "sexual partner.")
8 By Our Lady (the Virgin Mary). (A mild oath.)
9 (1) You are taller; (2) you are older, and thus nearer death.
10 High platform shoe of Italian fashion.
11 Gold coin not legal because it is cracked or chipped inside the ring enclosing
the image of the sovereign. Shaving or chipping gold coins was a common form of
cheating.
12 I.e., the young male's voice having lost its soprano range suitable for acting
female parts.
13 We'll go at it like those Frenchmen who are avid falconers, not discriminating
as to what they loose their birds to fly at.
14 At once.
15 Your skill in acting.
16 Speak for me or to me.
17 But the play containing this speech was.
18 I.e., it was a delicacy not generally appreciated by unsophisticated tastes.

as I received it, and others whose judgments in such matters
cried in the top of mine,[1] an excellent play, well digested in the
scenes,[2] set down with as much modesty as cunning.[3] I remem-   415
ber one said there were no sallets[4] in the lines to make the matter
savory, nor no matter in the phrase that might indict[5] the author
of affectation, but called it an honest method, as wholesome as
sweet, and by very much more handsome than fine.[6] One speech
in't I chiefly loved: 'twas Aeneas' tale to Dido,[7] and thereabout   420
of it[8] especially where he speaks of Priam's slaughter.[9] If it live
in your memory, begin at this line—let me see, let me see—
The rugged Pyrrhus,[10] like th'Hyrcanian beast[11]—
'Tis not so, it begins with Pyrrhus.

The rugged Pyrrhus, he whose sable arms,°	*black armor*	425
Black as his purpose, did the night resemble		
When he lay couchèd in the ominous horse,[12]		
Hath now this dread and black complexion smeared		
With heraldry more dismal.[13] Head to foot		
Now is he total gules,[14] horridly tricked°	*smeared, decorated*	430
With blood of fathers, mothers, daughters, sons,		
Baked and empasted with the parching streets[15]		
That lend a tyrannous° and damnèd light	*cruel, fierce*	

1 Others whose judgment and good taste exceeded mine.
2 Well organized in orderly fashion into scenes.
3 Written with as much restraint as skill.
4 I.e., there were no spicy bits, improprieties. (Literally, salads.)
5 Accuse.
6 And much more gracefully natural in proportion than artfully ornamented.
7 The story of the fall of Troy, as told by Aeneas to Dido in Book 1 of Virgil's
Aeneid. See Appendix A, pp. 265–66.
8 That part of it.
9 The slaying of Priam, King of Troy, by Pyrrhus, as Troy fell to the Greeks.
10 The savage Pyrrhus, also known as Neoptolemus, was the son of Achilles, and
was thus another son (like Hamlet or Laertes or Fortinbras) seeking to avenge his
father's death.
11 Tiger from Hyrcania, a wild region near the Caspian Sea. See Appendix A, p. 255.
12 Lay concealed in the fateful wooden Trojan horse, hidden inside of which thirty
Greek warriors deceitfully gained access to the citadel of Troy. See Appendix A, p. 264.
13 I.e., with the blood that Pyrrhus has smeared on his already dark and terrifying
appearance.
14 Totally red, as if in heraldic colors.
15 Roasted and encrusted into a thick paste by the parching heat of the streets and
burning houses.

To their vile murders.[1] Roasted in wrath and fire,
435 And thus o'ersizèd[2] with coagulate° gore, *congealed*
With eyes like carbuncles,[3] the hellish Pyrrhus
Old grandsire Priam seeks.
So proceed you.
POLONIUS. 'Fore God, my Lord, well spoken, with good accent and
440 good discretion.
FIRST PLAYER. Anon° he finds him, *soon*
Striking too short at Greeks. His antique° sword, *ancient, long-used*
Rebellious to his arm, lies where it falls,
Repugnant to command.[4] Unequal matched,[5]
445 Pyrrhus at Priam drives, in rage strikes wide,
But with the whiff and wind of his fell° sword *cruel, fierce*
Th'unnervèd father[6] falls. Then senseless Ilium,[7]
Seeming to feel this blow, with flaming top
Stoops to his base,[8] and with a hideous crash
450 Takes prisoner Pyrrhus' ear; for lo! his sword,
Which was declining° on the milky° head *descending / white-haired*
Of reverend[9] Priam, seemed i'th' air to stick.
So as a painted° tyrant Pyrrhus stood, *motionless, as in a painting*
And, like a neutral to his will and matter,[10]
455 Did nothing.
But as we often see against° some storm *just before*
A silence in the heavens, the rack° stand still, *mass of clouds*
The bold winds speechless, and the orb° below *globe, earth*
As hush as death, anon the dreadful thunder
460 Doth rend the region,[11] so, after Pyrrhus' pause,

---

1 I.e., to the vile murders of "fathers, mothers, daughters, sons" mentioned three lines earlier.
2 Covered with size (a glutinous substance applied to canvases to make them ready for painting); also suggesting "larger than life size."
3 Large, fiery-red gems, thought to emit their own light.
4 Resistant to Priam's bidding.
5 They being unequally matched.
6 The strengthless old man (and father of many sons).
7 Then the citadel of Troy, unble to express itself.
8 Comes crashing down to its base.
9 Worthy of deep respect.
10 And, as though suspended between intent and fulfillment.
11 Tears asunder the sky.

A rousèd vengeance sets him new a-work,
And never did the Cyclops'[1] hammers fall
On Mars his[2] armor forged for proof eterne[3]
With less remorse° than Pyrrhus' bleeding[4] sword   *pity*
Now falls on Priam.   465
Out,[5] out, thou strumpet Fortune![6] All you gods
In general synod° take away her power,   *assembly*
Break all the spokes and fellies[7] from her wheel,
And bowl the round nave[8] down the hill of heaven[9]
As low as to the fiends!   470

POLONIUS. This is too long.

HAMLET. It shall to the barber's with your beard.—Prithee, say on.
    He's for a jig,[10] or a tale of bawdry, or he sleeps. Say on. Come to
    Hecuba.[11]

FIRST PLAYER. But who, oh, who, had seen[12] the moblèd[13] queen—   475

HAMLET. The moblèd queen!

POLONIUS. That's good. "Moblèd queen" is good.

FIRST PLAYER. Run barefoot up and down, threat'ning the flames
    With bisson rheum,[14] a clout° upon that head   *cloth*
    Where late° the diadem° stood, and, for a robe,   *lately / crown*   480
    About her lank and all-o'erteemèd loins[15]

---

1 The Cyclopes were primordial one-eyed giants of Greek mythology who served
as armor-makers in Hephaestus's (Roman Vulcan's) smithy. The next line here
presumes that they were the makers of armor for Ares (Roman Mars), the god of
war. See Appendix A, pp. 249–50.

2 On Mars's. See Appendix A, pp. 255–56.

3 To provide eternal protection against assault.

4 I.e., covered with the blood of previous assaults, and anticipating the blood
that is about to be shed.

5 An expression of outrage or fury.

6 The whorish goddess of Chance.

7 The curved pieces of wood forming the exterior rim of a wheel, to which the
spokes are attached.

8 Wheel hub (all that would be left on a wheel if its spokes and fellies were
broken).

9 Down from Mount Olympus, home of the gods in Greek mythology.

10 Comic entertainment with dance, often performed at the end of a play.

11 Wife of Priam and Queen of Troy. See Appendix A, pp. 252–53.

12 But anyone, alas, who might have seen.

13 Veiled, muffled.

14 I.e., weeping so with blinding tears that she seemed almost capable of extin-
guishing the flames of burning Troy.

15 Withered loins, utterly worn out with child-bearing.

A blanket in th'alarm of fear caught up—
Who this had seen,[1] with tongue in venom steeped
'Gainst Fortune's state would treason have pronounced;[2]
485   But if° the gods themselves did see her then,   *but even if*
When she saw Pyrrhus make malicious sport
In mincing with his sword her husband's limbs,
The instant burst of clamor that she made,
Unless things mortal move them not at all,
490   Would have made milch the burning eyes of heaven[3]
And passion[4] in the gods.

POLONIUS. Look whe'er[5] he has not turned his color, and has tears
in's eyes.—Prithee, no more.

HAMLET. 'Tis well. I'll have thee speak out the rest of this soon. [*To*
495   *Polonius*] Good my lord, will you see the players well bestowed?[6]
Do ye hear, let them be well used,[7] for they are the abstracts and
brief chronicles of the time.[8] After your death you were better
have a bad epitaph[9] than their ill report while you live.

POLONIUS. My lord, I will use them according to their desert.

500 HAMLET. God's bodykins,[10] man, much better. Use every man after
his desert and who should scape whipping? Use them after[11] your
own honor and dignity; the less they deserve, the more merit is
in your bounty. Take them in.

POLONIUS. Come, sirs.

                                     Exit Polonius.

505 HAMLET. Follow him, friends. We'll hear a play tomorrow. [*Aside to
the First Player*] Dost thou hear me, old friend, can you play "The
Murder of Gonzago"?

[FIRST] PLAYER. Ay, my lord.

---

1 Whoever had seen this.
2 Would have protested treasonously against Fortune's fickle rule.
3 Would have caused the sun and other heavenly bodies to weep. ("Milch" means
"milky," in this case moist with tears.)
4 And would have provoked compassionate pity.
5 Whether.
6 Lodged.
7 Well treated.
8 Actors give us summaries and brief histories of the age in which we live.
9 I.e., you would do better to be remembered as a bad person.
10 By God's (Christ's) dear little body. (An oath.)
11 According to.

HAMLET. We'll ha't[1] tomorrow night. You could for a need[2] study[3] a speech of some dozen or sixteen lines, which I would 510 set down and insert in't, could you not?

[FIRST] PLAYER. Ay, my lord.

HAMLET. Very well. Follow that lord, and look you mock him not.

                  Exeunt Players.

My good friends, I'll leave you till night. You are welcome to Elsinore. 515

ROSENCRANTZ. Good my lord.[4]

HAMLET. Ay, so, God b'wi' you.

              Exeunt [Rosencrantz and Guildenstern].
              Now I am alone.

Oh, what a rogue and peasant slave am I!
Is it not monstrous that this player here,
But° in a fiction, in a dream of passion,   *merely* 520
Could force his soul so to his whole conceit[5]
That from her working all his visage wanned,[6]
Tears in his eyes, distraction in's aspect,°   *in his look*
A broken voice, and his whole function suiting
With forms to his conceit?[7] And all for nothing?   525
For Hecuba?
What's Hecuba to him, or he to Hecuba,
That he should weep for her? What would he do
Had he the motive and the cue for passion
That I have? He would drown the stage with tears,   530
And cleave the general ear° with horrid[8] speech, *everybody's ear*
Make mad the guilty, and appal the free,[9]

---

1 Have it performed.
2 As required and necessary.
3 Learn, memorize.
4 Rosencrantz politely bids Hamlet farewell, understanding that he has asked them to leave.
5 Could bring his innermost being so entirely into accord with his conception of the role he is playing.
6 That as a result of, or in response to, his soul's activity, his face turned entirely pale.
7 And all his bodily gestures perfectly suited to what he was imagining.
8 Horror-causing.
9 Horrify the innocent. ("Appal" conveys the literal sense of "make pale.")

2.2.506–07:   "THE MURDER OF GONZAGO"
(TLN 1577–78)

The play-within-the-play, which Hamlet later calls "The Mousetrap" (3.2.221, TLN 2105), has a number of precedents and analogs on the Elizabethan stage. Prominent among them is Thomas Kyd's *The Spanish Tragedy* (c. 1586–90). In its climactic final scene, Don Hieronimo, the beleaguered protagonist and ultimate revenger of the play, adopts a guise of madness (like Hamlet) and persuades his enemies to enact roles with him in a tragedy to be performed for the King of Spain. The villains agree to the plan, in order to humor the presumably mad Hieronimo. As the play-within-the-play proceeds, the deaths are actual—a kind of "snuff" drama. The King, witness to this tragedy, learns too late that the kingdom is now deprived of three people: the King's brother, the crown prince, and his intended bride.

Other Shakespeare plays-within-plays include "Pyramus and Thisbe" in Act 5 of *A Midsummer Night's Dream*, and the pageant of the Nine Worthies in Act 5 of *Love's Labor's Lost*. *The Tempest* features a brief masque devised by Prospero and Ariel to celebrate the forthcoming nuptials of Ferdinand and Miranda. In a sense, too, *The Taming of the Shrew* is itself a play-within-a-play devised to trick a beggar-tinker named Christopher Sly into thinking (in the play's Induction) that he is a well-born person who has awakened from a long sleep and is now lying in bed in a Lord's house with many servants in attendance and even a wife; the Induction is thus a frame plot. Other Elizabethan examples include Francis Beaumont's *The Knight of the Burning Pestle* (c. 1608), which stages a series of comic adventures in the life of Rafe, an apprentice, performed for Rafe's shopkeeper master and his wife. Ben Jonson's *Bartholomew Fair* (1614) ends with a hilarious puppet-show spoof of the mythical love story of Hero and Leander, transposed from ancient Greece to contemporary London. The Puritan Zeal of the Land Busy, part of the onstage audience, insists on interrupting and denouncing a display he regards as idolatrous and profane.

See Arthur Brown, "The Play within a Play: An Elizabethan Dramatic Device," *Essays and Studies* 13 (1960), 36–48; and Dieter Mehl, "Zur Entwicklung des 'Play within a Play' im elisabethanischen Drama," *Shakespeare Jahrbuch* 97 (1961), 134–52.

The Spanish Tragedie:
OR,
Hieronimo is mad againe.

Containing the lamentable end of *Don Horatio*, and
Belimperia; with the pittifull death of *Hieronimo*.

Newly corrected, amended, and enlarged with new
Additions of the *Painters* part, and others, as
it hath of late been diuers times acted.

LONDON,
Printed by W. White, for I. White and T. Langley,
and are to be fold at their Shop ouer againft the
Sarazens head without New-gate. 1615.

The *Spanish Tragedy* (c. 1586–90) by Thomas Kyd, title page of the 1615 edition.

Confound the ignorant,[1] and amaze° indeed   *stun, bewilder*
The very faculties of eyes and ears. Yet I,
535   A dull and muddy-mettled° rascal, peak°   *dull-spirited / mope*
Like John-a-dreams, unpregnant of my cause,[2]
And can say nothing; no, not for a king
Upon whose property° and most dear life   *person and identity as king*
A damned defeat[3] was made. Am I a coward?
540   Who calls me villain? Breaks my pate across?[4]
Plucks off my beard[5] and blows it in my face?
Tweaks me by th' nose? Gives me the lie i'th' throat[6]
As deep as to the lungs? Who does me this,°   *does this to me*
Ha? 'Swounds,[7] I should take it;[8] for it cannot be
545   But I am pigeon-livered,[9] and lack gall
To make oppression bitter,[10] or ere this
I should ha' fatted all the region kites[11]
With this slave's offal.[12] Bloody, bawdy° villain!   *lewd, immoral*
Remorseless, treacherous, lecherous, kindless[13] villain!
550   Oh, vengeance!
Why, what an ass am I! This is most brave,[14]
That I, the son of a dear father murdered,
Prompted to my revenge by heaven and hell,
Must like a whore unpack my heart with words,
555   And fall a-cursing like a very drab,°   *whore*

---

1   Dumbfound those who know nothing of the crime that has been committed.
2   Like an idle dreamer, not quickened into action by my cause.
3   A murderous and damnable act.
4   Slaps me across the face (a profound insult). "Pate" means "head."
5   Yanks at my beard. Another deep insult, questioning the manliness of the one thus insulted. The beard could hardly be yanked entirely off, but the yank would be accompanied by a sharp slap to the face.
6   Calls me an out-and-out liar (again, an especially insulting gesture).
7   By his (Christ's) wounds. (A strong oath.)
8   I.e., take it lying down, offering no response.
9   It cannot be otherwise than that I am a coward. (Pigeons' livers were thought to secrete no gall, thus making them mild and disinclined to anger.)
10   And lack the spirit of anger needed to make my oppression bitter to me and thereby make me dangerous to my enemy.
11   All the kites (birds of prey) of the air.
12   This wretch's entrails.
13   Unnatural, lacking in affection for one's kind.
14   Fine, admirable (said sarcastically).

A scullion.° Fie upon't, foh! About,[1] my brain!   *kitchen servant*
Hum, I have heard
That guilty creatures sitting at a play
Have by the very cunning° of the scene   *artfulness, skill*
Been struck so to the soul that presently°   *at once*   560
They have proclaimed their malefactions;°   *evil deeds, crime*
For murder, though it have no tongue, will speak
With most miraculous organ. I'll have these players
Play something like the murder of my father
Before mine uncle. I'll observe his looks;   565
I'll tent him to the quick.[2] If 'a but blench[3]
I know my course. The spirit that I have seen
May be the devil, and the devil hath power
T'assume a pleasing shape; yea, and perhaps,
Out of my weakness and my melancholy,   570
As he is very potent with such spirits,
Abuses° me to damn me. I'll have grounds   *deludes, deceives*
More relative[4] than this. The play's the thing
Wherein I'll catch the conscience of the King.

                                                              Exit.

                              [3.1]

Enter King, Queen, Polonius, Ophelia, Rosencrantz, Guildenstern, and
Lords.
KING. And can you by no drift of circumstance[5]
   Get from him why he puts on this confusion,
   Grating so harshly all his days of quiet
   With turbulent and dangerous lunacy?
ROSENCRANTZ. He does confess he feels himself distracted,   5
   But from what cause, 'a will by no means speak.
GUILDENSTERN. Nor do we find him forward to be sounded,[6]

---

1 Go about it, get to work.
2 I'll probe his wound (i.e., his conscience) to its core.
3 If he merely flinches or turns pale.
4 Relevant, convincing.
5 Can you not, by means of roundabout inquiry.
6 Willing to be probed and questioned.

But with a crafty madness keeps aloof
When we would bring him on to some confession
10   Of his true state.
QUEEN. Did he receive you well?
ROSENCRANTZ. Most like a gentleman.
GUILDENSTERN. But with much forcing of his disposition.[1]
ROSENCRANTZ. Niggard of question,[2] but of our demands[3]
15   Most free in his reply.

---

1 Inclination, mood.
2 Laconic, reluctant to initiate talk.
3 In response to our questions.

2.2.570; 3.1.161–62:   MELANCHOLY AND
THE FOUR HUMORS (TLN 1641, 1821–22)

Hamlet regards himself as suffering from melancholy, and later Claudius speaks of "something in his soul / O'er which his melancholy sits on brood" (3.1.161–62, TLN 1821–22). Melancholy was a favorite subject of learned writers in the English Renaissance. Prominent among them was Robert Burton (1577–1640), whose *Anatomy of Melancholy* was first published in 1621. Burton used melancholy as a concept through which he could marshal an awesome amount of scholarly and scientific learning to analyze the entire range of human emotion and thought.

Hippocratic medicine, as formulated especially by Galen of Pergamon (130–200 CE), proposed that the human body contained four essential "humors": blood, yellow bile, black bile, and phlegm. The right balance of these four was essential to maintaining good health. An overbalance of one of these individual humors would produce a temperament that was (respectively) sanguine, or choleric, or melancholic, or phlegmatic. The sanguine temperament was hot and moist, choleric hot and dry, melancholic cold and dry, phlegmatic cold and moist. These humors and temperaments also had correspondence to the four elements in natural science: sanguine was associated with air, choleric with fire, melancholic with earth, and phlegmatic with water.

A sanguine person tended to be lively, carefree, easygoing, talkative, outgoing, sociable; a choleric person might be impulsive, aggressive,

QUEEN. Did you assay him to[1] any pastime?
ROSENCRANTZ. Madam, it so fell out[2] that certain players
    We o'erraught[3] on the way. Of these we told him,
    And there did seem in him a kind of joy
    To hear of it. They are about the court,[4]   20
    And, as I think, they have already order
    This night to play before him.

---

1   Endeavor to persuade him to try.
2   Happened.
3   Overtook, passed.
4   Have arrived and are present here in the court.

angry, restless, touchy, excitable; a melancholic person might be unsociable, reserved, pessimistic, moody, despondent, depressed, anxious, rigid; a phlegmatic person tended to be controlled, passive, careful, thoughtful, even-tempered. Sanguine and choleric both tended to be extroverted, melancholic and phlegmatic introverted. Sanguine was associated with springtime and infancy, choleric with summer and youth, melancholic with autumn and full maturity, phlegmatic with winter and old age. The heart predominated in the sanguine, the liver or gall bladder in the choleric, the spleen in the melancholic, and the brain in the phlegmatic.

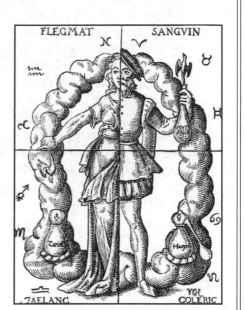

From *Quinta Essentia*,
Leonhart Thurneisser, 1574.

Medical practice for centuries relied on purging the body to rid it of humoral imbalance, by bleeding or by inducing vomiting or evacuation of the bowels—treatments that sometimes proved fatal.

POLONIUS.   'Tis most true,
   And he beseeched me to entreat your majesties
   To hear and see the matter.
25 KING. With all my heart, and it doth much content me
   To hear him so inclined. Good gentlemen,
   Give him a further edge,° and drive his purpose on   *incitement*
   To these delights.
   ROSENCRANTZ. We shall, my lord.
              Exeunt Rosencrantz and Guildenstern [and Lords].
   KING.   Sweet Gertrude, leave us too,
30 For we have closely¹ sent for Hamlet hither,
   That he, as 'twere by accident, may here
   Affront° Ophelia.   *confront, encounter*
   Her father and myself, lawful espials,°   *justifiable spies*
   Will so bestow ourselves that, seeing unseen,
35 We may of their encounter frankly judge,
   And gather by him, as he is behaved,°   *by his behavior*
   If't be th'affliction of his love or no
   That thus he suffers for.
   QUEEN.   I shall obey you.
   And for your part, Ophelia, I do wish
40 That your good beauties be the happy cause
   Of Hamlet's wildness. So shall I hope your virtues
   Will bring him to his wonted way again,
   To both your honors.
   OPHELIA.   Madam, I wish it may.
                             [Exit Queen.]
   POLONIUS. Ophelia, walk you here.—Gracious,² so please you,
45 We will bestow ourselves. [*To Ophelia, as he gives her a book*] Read
      on this book,³
   That show of such an exercise° may color⁴   *religious exercise*
   Your loneliness. We are oft to blame in this,
   'Tis too much proved,⁵ that with devotion's visage

---

1 Privately and with secret intent.
2 Your Grace (addressed to the King).
3 Presumably a book of devotion.
4 Give a plausible appearance to, justify.
5 It is too often shown to be the case and too often practiced.

And pious action we do sugar o'er
The devil himself.

KING. [*Aside*]　　　　Oh, 'tis too true!　　　　　　　　　　50
How smart° a lash that speech doth give my conscience!　*stinging*
The harlot's cheek, beautied with plast'ring art,[1]
Is not more ugly to the thing that helps it[2]
Than is my deed to my most painted word.
Oh, heavy burden!　　　　　　　　　　　　　　　　　　55

Enter Hamlet.

POLONIUS. I hear him coming. Let's withdraw, my lord.
[*The King and Polonius conceal themselves.*]
HAMLET. To be, or not to be, that is the question,
　Whether 'tis nobler in the mind to suffer
　The slings[3] and arrows of outrageous fortune,
　Or to take arms against a sea of troubles,　　　　　　60
　And by opposing end them. To die, to sleep—
　No more[4]—and by a sleep to say we end
　The heartache and the thousand natural shocks
　That flesh is heir to; 'tis a consummation
　Devoutly to be wished. To die, to sleep;　　　　　　　65
　To sleep, perchance to dream. Ay, there's the rub,[5]
　For in that sleep of death what dreams may come
　When we have shuffled off this mortal coil[6]
　Must give us pause. There's the respect°　　*consideration*
　That makes calamity of so long life.[7]　　　　　　　　70
　For who would bear the whips and scorns of time,
　Th'oppressor's wrong, the proud man's contumely,[8]

1　Beautified by means of cosmetics.
2　In comparison with or in response to the cosmetic that gives the cheek its false beauty.
3　Devices for propelling several kinds of missiles toward an enemy.
4　I.e., death is nothing more than a prolonged sleep.
5　Impediment, difficulty. (Literally, an obstacle in the path of the ball in the game of bowls.)
6　Cast off our mortal flesh and the turmoil of existence.
7　(1) That allows calamity to last so long; (2) that makes long life a calamity in itself.
8　The insolent abuse meted out by those of superior social rank.

The pangs of disprized° love, the law's delay,   *scorned, undervalued*
The insolence of office,° and the spurns[1]   *officialdom*
75   That patient merit of th'unworthy takes,[2]
When he himself might his quietus make[3]
With a bare bodkin?[4] Who would these fardels[5] bear,
To grunt and sweat under a weary life,
But that the dread of something after death,
80   The undiscovered country from whose bourn°   *boundary, border*
No traveler returns, puzzles the will,
And makes us rather bear those ills we have
Than fly to others that we know not of.
Thus conscience[6] does make cowards of us all,
85   And thus the native hue of resolution
Is sicklied o'er with the pale cast of thought,[7]
And enterprises of great pith and moment[8]
With this regard their currents turn awry[9]
And lose the name of action. Soft you now,[10]
90   The fair Ophelia!—Nymph, in thy orisons
Be all my sins remembered.

OPHELIA.   Good my lord,
How does your honor for this many a day?

HAMLET. I humbly thank you, well, well, well.

OPHELIA. My lord, I have remembrances of yours
95   That I have longèd long to redeliver.
I pray you now receive them.

HAMLET. No, not I. I never gave you aught.

---

1   Insults; literally, kicks.
2   That patient, deserving people must endure at the hands of unworthy persons.
3   Might settle his accounts (at the end of his life). A quietus was an affirmation that a bill had been paid, marked "Quietus est," laid to rest.
4   With nothing more than an unsheathed dagger.
5   Such burdens.
6   (1) Introspection, consciousness; (2) moral promptings, attuned to fear of divine punishment after death for sins committed while one is alive.
7   And thus the natural ruddiness of one's complexion that signals manliness is made to look weak and sickly with the white-faced pallor that accompanies too much introspection.
8   Of high seriousness and momentous significance.
9   With this consideration lose their sense of direction and turn askew.
10   I.e., wait a minute (said as Hamlet sees Ophelia).

3.1.90–91: "NYMPH, IN THY ORISONS / BE ALL MY SINS REMEMBERED" (TLN 1743–44)

When Hamlet asks Ophelia to pray for him in his sinful state, he is affirming the concept of original sin, a central doctrine of medieval Christianity. It held that all humans, after the expulsion of Adam and Eve from the Garden of Eden, were inveterately sinful and thus wholly in need of God's mercy through the sacrifice of his son Jesus Christ. Hamlet alludes to this idea later in the scene when he says angrily, "We are arrant knaves, all; believe none of us" (3.1.126–27, TLN

The Expulsion from Paradise, Giuseppe Cesari, c. 1600–10.

1784)—"we" meaning all males or even all humans. The Queen refers to "sin's true nature" as it speaks to her "sick soul" (4.5.17, TLN 2762). Earlier, the Ghost describes how, by being murdered, he was "Cut off even in the blossoms of my sin" (1.5.76, TLN 761).

The concept of original sin, first introduced in the second century CE, was further developed by St. Augustine (354–430) on the basis especially of Paul's epistles to the Romans (5:12–21) and 1 Corinthians (15:22). Other important exponents of the concept include Tertullian (c. 155–c. 240), St. Ambrose (340–97), Martin Luther (1483–1546), and John Calvin (1509–64).

OPHELIA. My honored lord, you know right well you did,
And with them words of so sweet breath composed
100   As made these things more rich. Their perfume lost,
Take these again, for to the noble mind
Rich gifts wax° poor when givers prove unkind,   *grow*
There, my lord.
[*She offers Hamlet the remembrances.*]
HAMLET. Ha, ha! Are you honest?[1]
105 OPHELIA. My lord?
HAMLET. Are you fair?°   *beautiful*
OPHELIA. What means your lordship?
HAMLET. That if you be honest and fair, your honesty should admit
no discourse to your beauty.[2]
110 OPHELIA. Could beauty, my lord, have better commerce[3] than with
honesty?
HAMLET. Ay, truly, for the power of beauty will sooner transform
honesty from what it is to a bawd than the force of honesty can
translate beauty into his likeness.[4] This was sometime a paradox,[5]
115 but now the time gives it proof. I did love you once.
OPHELIA. Indeed, my lord, you made me believe so.
HAMLET. You should not have believed me, for virtue cannot so
inoculate our old stock but we shall relish of it.[6] I loved you not.
OPHELIA. I was the more deceived.
120 HAMLET. Get thee to a nunnery.[7] Why wouldst thou be a breeder of
sinners? I am myself indifferent honest,[8] but yet I could accuse
me[9] of such things that it were better my mother had not borne
me: I am very proud, revengeful, ambitious, with more offenses
at my beck[10] than I have thoughts to put them in, imagination to

---

1 (1) chaste; (2) truthful.
2 You should be chastely wary of any dealings with your beauty (since a beautiful
woman is too often in danger of being seduced).
3 Dealings.
4 Its (honesty's) likeness.
5 Formerly a seeming absurdity, a conundrum.
6 Virtue cannot be grafted onto our inherently sinful nature without our retain-
ing some taste or trace of the old stock, i.e., Original Sin.
7 Convent (perhaps too with the suggestion of a brothel, since Hamlet is openly
skeptical of the idea that beauty and chastity can coexist in women).
8 Reasonably virtuous.
9 Accuse myself.
10 Command.

give them shape, or time to act them in. What should such fellows 125
as I do crawling between heaven and earth? We are arrant[1] knaves,
all; believe none of us.[2] Go thy ways to a nunnery. Where's your
father?

OPHELIA. At home, my lord.

HAMLET. Let the doors be shut upon him, that he may play the fool 130
nowhere but in's own house. Farewell.

OPHELIA. Oh, help him, you sweet heavens!

HAMLET. If thou dost marry, I'll give thee this plague for thy dowry:
be thou as chaste as ice, as pure as snow, thou shalt not escape
calumny.[3] Get thee to a nunnery. Go, farewell. Or if thou wilt 135
needs marry, marry a fool, for wise men know well enough what
monsters you make of them.[4] To a nunnery go, and quickly too.
Farewell.

OPHELIA. O heavenly powers, restore him!

HAMLET. I have heard of your paintings too, well enough. God hath 140
given you one face, and you make yourselves another. You jig, you

---

1 Downright.
2 See Appendix B, p. 271.
3 Slander.
4 For wise men know all too well how you women, by cheating on your husbands
in marriage, turn them into cuckolds with imaginary horns on their foreheads as a
sign of their shame.

3.1.140:   "I HAVE HEARD OF
        YOUR PAINTINGS TOO" (TLN 1798)

Shakespeare frequently echoes a common complaint in the literature of
his day against cosmetics. Such "paintings," as Hamlet avers, are used by
women to disguise their true appearance with artifice. Claudius, secretly
tormented with guilt for what he has done, earlier soliloquizes that "The
harlot's cheek, beautified with plast'ring art, / Is not more ugly to the
thing that helps it / Than is my deed to my most painted word" (3.1.51–53,
TLN 1703–05). Similarly, as Hamlet continues here, women "nickname
God's creatures," imposing false names on the beasts and fowl created
and named by God in his great act of creation described in Genesis 1
and 2.

amble, and you lisp,[1] and nickname God's creatures,[2] and make
your wantonness your ignorance.[3] Go to,[4] I'll no more on't;[5] it
hath made me mad. I say we will have no more marriages. Those
145 that are married already, all but one,[6] shall live; the rest shall keep
as they are. To a nunnery, go.

                 Exit.

OPHELIA. Oh, what a noble mind is here o'erthrown!
 The courtier's, soldier's, scholar's, eye, tongue, sword,[7]
 Th'expectancy and rose° of the fair state, *the hope and ornament*
150 The glass of fashion and the mold of form,[8]
 Th'observed of all observers,[9] quite, quite down,
 And I, of ladies most deject and wretched,
 That sucked the honey of his music[10] vows,
 Now see that noble and most sovereign reason[11]
155 Like sweet bells jangled out of tune and harsh,
 That unmatched form and feature of blown youth[12]
 Blasted with ecstasy.° Oh, woe is me *blighted with madness*
 T'have seen what I have seen, see what I see!

Enter King and Polonius [stepping forward from concealment].
KING. Love? His affections° do not that way tend, *emotions, feelings*
160 Nor what he spake, though it lacked form a little,
 Was not like madness. There's something in his soul

---

1 You dance about, you swing your hips suggestively when you walk, you speak
with an affected voice.
2 See Appendix B, p. 271.
3 And you excuse your bad behavior on the grounds that you don't know any
better.
4 An expression of impatience.
5 I won't have any more of this.
6 Presumably, all but the King. (Whether Hamlet says this in the knowledge that
the King is listening is a matter of interpretation.)
7 I.e., the courtier's tongue in speaking eloquently, the soldier's sword, and
the scholar's eye in seeking truth. (Or perhaps "eye" goes with the courtier and
"tongue" with the scholar.)
8 The mirror of true self-fashioning and the model of courtly decorum.
9 The admired center of attention in the court.
10 Sweetly and harmoniously uttered.
11 I.e., reason as properly the sovereign or ruler over the emotions and the senses.
12 Of youth in its full blossoming.

O'er which his melancholy sits on brood,[1]
And I do doubt the hatch and the disclose[2]
Will be some danger; which to prevent,
I have in quick determination   165
Thus set it down:[3] he shall with speed to England
For the demand of our neglected tribute.
Haply the seas, and countries different,
With variable objects,[4] shall expel
This something-settled° matter in his heart,   *somewhat fixated* 170
Whereon his brains still° beating puts him thus   *continually*
From fashion of himself.[5] What think you on't?
POLONIUS. It shall do well. But yet do I believe
The origin and commencement of his grief
Sprung from neglected love.—How now, Ophelia?   175
You need not tell us what Lord Hamlet said,
We heard it all.—My lord, do as you please,
But if you hold it fit, after the play
Let his queen-mother all alone entreat him
To show his grief. Let her be round° with him,   *blunt*   180
And I'll be placed (so please you) in the ear
Of all their conference. If she find him not,[6]
To England send him, or confine him where
Your wisdom best shall think.
KING.   It shall be so;
Madness in great ones must not unwatched go.   185
                                                           Exeunt.

---

1 Sits like a bird on a nest, about to "hatch" mischief (in the next line).
2 And I do fear that the fulfillment and the discovery (like the hatching of a chick as it emerges from its shell).
3 Thus resolved the matter and put it in writing.
4 Various sights and surroundings to divert him.
5 Out of his normal mode of behavior.
6 If she is unable to discover what is troubling him.

[3.2]

Enter Hamlet, and two or three of the Players.

HAMLET. Speak the speech, I pray you, as I pronounced it to you,
trippingly on the tongue; but if you mouth[1] it, as many of your
players[2] do, I had as lief[3] the town crier[4] had spoke my lines. Nor
do not saw the air too much with your hand, thus, but use all gen-
5   tly; for in the very torrent, tempest, and, as I may say, whirlwind
of your passion, you must acquire and beget[5] a temperance that
may give it smoothness. Oh, it offends me to the soul to hear
a robustious[6] periwig-pated[7] fellow tear a passion to tatters,
to very rags, to split the ears of the groundlings,[8] who for the
10 most part are capable of[9] nothing but inexplicable dumb-shows
and noise.[10] I would have such a fellow whipped for o'erdoing
Termagant. It out-Herods Herod.[11] Pray you avoid it.

PLAYER. I warrant[12] your honor.

HAMLET. Be not too tame, neither, but let your own discretion be
15 your tutor. Suit the action to the word, the word to the action,
with this special observance, that you o'erstep not the modesty of
nature.[13] For anything so o'erdone is from the purpose[14] of playing,
whose end, both at the first and now, was and is to hold as 'twere
the mirror up to nature, to show virtue her own feature, scorn
20 her own image,[15] and the very age and body of the time his form

---

1   Declaim, speak exaggeratedly.
2   Actors nowadays, the actors that people talk about.
3   I'd just as soon, be just as willing.
4   Person assigned the responsibility of loudly proclaiming public announcements in the streets.
5   Cultivate and nurture.
6   Boisterous, bombastic.
7   Wig-wearing.
8   Spectators who paid the lowest price of admission (usually a penny) and who
stood in the yard around the raised platform stage.
9   Able to understand.
10 Noisy spectacles (as differentiated from complex and intellectually demanding
drama).
11 See extended note on p. 151.
12 Assure.
13 Natural restraint and moderation.
14 Contrary to the purpose.
15 To show human nature an image of itself and to scornful persons a picture of
what they look like.

3.2.12:   TERMAGANT AND HEROD
                 (TLN 1861–62)

Hamlet cites both Termagant and Herod as instances of overacting.
Termagant was a supposed Mohammedan deity who, though not
actually found in extant English medieval drama, became a byword for
tyrannical bluster. In medieval texts, Termagant is often paired with
Mahound or Mohammed, both of whom could be boisterously comic in
their ranting against and persecution of Christians. Herod was a King
of Judea infamous for ordering the "Slaughter of the Innocents," the
massacre of all male children in his kingdom as a means of destroying
the child that, wise men told him, was "born King of the Jews" (Matthew
2:2)—namely, Christ. This Herod was a figure of comic bluster in many
depictions of the Christmas story in medieval religious drama. The boy
Shakespeare might have seen biblical plays near Stratford, even though
the great cycles were being closed down by the Protestant authorities.
Certainly these comic characters were familiar in the culture of the time,
as a way of ridiculing figures of demonic power such as the Antichrist
or Satan himself.

The Massacre of the Innocents, attributed to Andrea di Bartolo and Bartolo di Fredi, c. 1380.

and pressure.[1] Now this overdone, or come tardy off,[2] though it make the unskillful laugh, cannot but make the judicious grieve, the censure of the which one must in your allowance[3] o'erweigh a whole theater of others. Oh, there be players that I have seen
25 play, and heard others praise, and that highly, not to speak it profanely, that, neither having th'accent of Christians nor the gait of Christian, pagan, nor no man,[4] have so strutted and bellowed that I have thought some of nature's journeymen[5] had made men, and not made them well, they imitated humanity so abominably.
30 PLAYER. I hope we have reformed that indifferently[6] with us, sir.
HAMLET. Oh, reform it altogether. And let those that play your clowns speak no more than is set down for them; for there be of them[7] that will themselves laugh, to set on[8] some quantity of barren[9] spectators to laugh too, though in the meantime some
35 necessary question of the play be then to be considered. That's villainous, and shows a most pitiful ambition in the fool that uses it. Go make you ready.

Exit Players.

Enter Polonius, Rosencrantz, and Guildenstern.
[*To Polonius*] How now, my lord, will the King hear this piece of work?
40 POLONIUS. And the Queen too, and that presently.°   at once
HAMLET. Bid the players make haste.

Exit Polonius.

Will you two help to hasten them?
ROSENCRANTZ AND GUILDENSTERN. We will, my lord.

Exeunt [Rosencrantz and Guildenstern].

HAMLET. What ho, Horatio!

---

1   And the present state of affairs a likeness of itself. ("His form" means "its form.")
2   Done lamely.
3   The critical judgment of even one of whom must, in your scale of values.
4   I.e., I hope I will not be speaking profanely if I venture so far as to condemn such bad actors as neither Christian, pagan, or any other part of the human race.
5   Nature's untalented hired assistants.
6   Tolerably, moderately well.
7   Some among them.
8   Incite.
9   Devoid of wit or judgment.

Enter Horatio.

HORATIO. Here, sweet lord, at your service.   45

HAMLET. Horatio, thou art e'en as just a man[1]
  As e'er my conversation coped withal.[2]

HORATIO. Oh, my dear lord—

HAMLET.   Nay, do not think I flatter,
  For what advancement may I hope from thee
  That no revenue hast but thy good spirits   50
  To feed and clothe thee? Why should the poor be flattered?
  No, let the candied° tongue lick absurd pomp   *sugary, flattering*
  And crook the pregnant° hinges of the knee   *compliant*
  Where thrift may follow fawning.[3] Dost thou hear?
  Since my dear soul was mistress of her choice   55
  And could of men distinguish her election,
  Sh'hath sealed thee for herself,[4] for thou hast been
  As one in suff'ring all that suffers nothing,[5]
  A man that Fortune's buffets and rewards
  Hast ta'en with equal thanks; and blest are those   60
  Whose blood and judgment[6] are so well commingled
  That they are not a pipe for Fortune's finger
  To sound what stop[7] she please. Give me that man
  That is not passion's slave, and I will wear him
  In my heart's core, ay, in my heart of heart,   65
  As I do thee.—Something too much of this.[8]—
  There is a play tonight before the King.
  One scene of it comes near the circumstance
  Which I have told thee of my father's death.
  I prithee, when thou see'st that act afoot,   70
  Even with the very comment of thy soul[9]

---

1 Absolutely as judicious, honorable, and trustworthy a man.
2 As I have ever encountered in my experience with people.
3 Wherever profit may accrue from abject flattery.
4 And could make discriminating choices among men, she (my soul) has marked you as her own, as though putting a legal seal on you to ensure possession.
5 On this passage in general, see Appendix A, "Stoicism," p. 263.
6 Passion and reason.
7 Hole in a recorder or similar wind instrument for controlling pitch.
8 I.e., I've already said too much on this subject. (Hamlet obliquely apologizes to Horatio for having expressed so deeply and personally his affection and admiration.)
9 With your utmost powers of concentration.

Observe my uncle. If his occulted° guilt   *hidden*
Do not itself unkennel[1] in one speech,[2]
It is a damnèd ghost that we have seen,
75   And my imaginations are as foul
As Vulcan's stithy.[3] Give him heedful note,°   *careful observation*
For I mine eyes will rivet to his face,
And after we will both our judgments join
In censure of his seeming.[4]
HORATIO.   Well, my lord,
80   If 'a steal aught the whilst[5] this play is playing
And scape detecting, I will pay the theft.[6]

Enter King, Queen, Polonius, Ophelia, Rosencrantz, Guildenstern, and other lords attendant with his Guard carrying torches. Danish march. Sound a flourish.

HAMLET. They are coming to the play. I must be idle.[7] Get you a place.

KING. How fares our cousin Hamlet?[8]

85 HAMLET. Excellent, i'faith, of the chameleon's dish; I eat the air, promise-crammed.[9] You cannot feed capons[10] so.

KING. I have nothing with this answer, Hamlet. These words are not mine.[11]

---

1   Reveal itself (as a fox might be flushed from its lair).
2   Presumably Hamlet here refers to the speech that he has asked the First Player to memorize and insert into the upcoming performance of "The Murder of Gongazo." See 3.1.509–11 (TLN 1580–82) above.
3   The workshop of Vulcan, blacksmith-god of fire (and husband of Venus); stiths are anvils. See Appendix A, pp. 266–67.
4   In judgment of his appearance and behavior.
5   If he gets away with anything while.
6   And escapes being detected, I will pay for what has been stolen, i.e, make amends for my inadequate observation of the King.
7   (1) Be unoccupied; (2) resume my mad guise.
8   How are things with you, my kinsman Hamlet? (But Hamlet, in his reply, plays on "fares" in the sense of "dines.")
9   (1) I am feeding on air, like the chameleon (which was fabled to feed thus); (2) I am feeding myself with thoughts about succeeding to the Danish crown, having been given nothing but empty promises of succession. (Hamlet is "heir" apparent; the word sounds like "air.")
10 (1) Castrated roosters, often crammed with feed to make them succulent for the dinner table; (2) fools.
11 Your words do not respond to what I asked and thus are meaningless to me.

HAMLET. No, nor mine now.[1] [*To Polonius*] My lord, you played
    once i'th' university, you say?   90

POLONIUS. That I did, my lord, and was accounted a good actor.

HAMLET. And what did you enact?

POLONIUS. I did enact Julius Caesar. I was killed i'th' Capitol.
    Brutus killed me.

HAMLET. It was a brute[2] part[3] of him to kill so capital a calf[4] there.— 95
    Be the players ready?

ROSENCRANTZ. Ay, my lord, they stay upon your patience.[5]

QUEEN. Come hither, my dear Hamlet, sit by me.

HAMLET. No, good mother, here's mettle[6] more attractive.

POLONIUS. [*To the King*] Oho, do you mark that?   100

HAMLET. [*To Ophelia, as he reclines at her feet*] Lady, shall I lie in your
    lap?[7]

OPHELIA. No, my lord.

HAMLET. I mean, my head upon your lap.

OPHELIA. Ay, my lord.   105

HAMLET. Do you think I meant country matters?[8]

OPHELIA. I think nothing, my lord.

HAMLET. That's a fair thought to lie between maids' legs.

OPHELIA. What is, my lord?

HAMLET. Nothing.[9]   110

OPHELIA. You are merry, my lord.

HAMLET. Who, I?

OPHELIA. Ay, my lord.

---

1 I.e., now that I have sent these words out from me, they are no longer a part of
who I am.

2 The word plays on "Brutus," the name of one of the chief conspirators against
Caesar (and also of Brutus's great ancestor, Lucius Junius Brutus) and also a syn-
onym in Latin for "stupid." See Appendix A, pp. 248–49.

3 (1) Action; (2) role in a play.

4 I.e., so outstanding a fool.

5 They await instructions from you as to when to begin.

6 (1) Mettle, disposition, temperament; (2) metal, possessing attractive qualities
(much as a magnet attracts iron).

7 May I lie with my head in your lap (but with a pointed sexual suggestion that
Hamlet continues; see next two notes).

8 Rustic goings-on. (The obscene punning here on "cunt" continues in "nothing"; see next note.)

9 (1) The oval figure of zero, suggesting a woman's vagina; (2) no "thing," no
penis. ("Thing" is a common euphemism in this sense.)

HAMLET. Oh, God, your only jig-maker.[1] What should a man do
115   but be merry? For look you how cheerfully my mother looks, and
my father died within's[2] two hours.

OPHELIA. Nay, 'tis twice two months, my lord.

HAMLET. So long? Nay, then, let the devil wear black, for I'll have
a suit of sables.[3] Oh, heavens! Die two months ago, and not for-
120   gotten yet? Then there's hope a great man's memory may outlive
his life half a year. But, by'r Lady, 'a must build churches then, or
else shall 'a suffer not thinking on,[4] with the hobby-horse, whose
epitaph is, "For oh, for oh, the hobby-horse is forgot."

Hautboys play. The dumb-show enters.

Enter [Players as] a King and Queen very lovingly; the Queen embracing
him. She kneels and makes show of protestation unto him. He takes her
up, and declines his head upon her neck. Lays him down upon a bank of
flowers. She, seeing him asleep, leaves him. Anon comes in a fellow, takes
off his crown, kisses it, pours poison in the King's ears, and exits. The
Queen returns, finds the King dead, and makes passionate action. The
Poisoner, with some two or three mutes,[5] comes in again, seeming to
lament with her. The dead body is carried away. The Poisoner woos the
Queen with gifts. She seems loath and unwilling awhile, but in the end
accepts his love.

Exeunt [Players].

OPHELIA. What means this, my lord?

125   HAMLET. Marry, this is miching mallico.[6] It means mischief.

OPHELIA. Belike[7] this show imports the argument[8] of the play.

---

1   I.e., if you talk of being merry, let me tell you that I'm the very best singer and
dancer of jigs (that is, of pointless vulgar merriment) you could hope to find. (Said
sardonically.)

2   Within these.

3   I.e., if mourning for my dead father has ceased after only two months, then
the devil can wear mourning black for all I care, while I shift to the dark fur of the
sable, outwardly suitable for remembrance of the dead but in fact quite soft and
luxurious. (Ophelia's "twice two months" is plausible, but in his reply Hamlet
persists in shortening the interval.)

4   Or else he must endure being wholly forgotten.

5   Silent actors, with no spoken lines.

6   This is stealthy mischief.

7   Probably, perhaps.

8   Signifies the plot.

Enter [a Player as] Prologue.

HAMLET. We shall know by this fellow. The players cannot keep counsel;[1] they'll tell all.

OPHELIA. Will 'a tell us what this show meant?

---

1 Keep a secret.

3.2.123:   "FOR OH, FOR OH,
     THE HOBBY-HORSE IS FORGOT" (TLN 1989)

The hobby-horse, made of wickerwork or other light material, was shaped in the figure of a horse and fastened around the waist of one of the performers in a Morris dance, a popular English folk dance executed by choreographed dancers carrying sticks, swords, and handkerchiefs, and wearing bells attached to their shins. Hamlet quotes from a lost ballad that turns up also in *Love's Labor's Lost*, 3.1.37–38. The idea here seems to be a lament for the disappearance of such folk customs, in much the way that the memory of Hamlet's father seems to have been quickly forgotten.

The Thames at Richmond, with the Old Royal Palace, Flemish, early seventeenth century. One of the dancers standing in a row is outfitted with a horse-like contraption fastened around his waist.

130 HAMLET. Ay, or any show that you will show him. Be not you[1]
     ashamed to show, he'll not shame to tell you what it means.
OPHELIA. You are naught,[2] you are naught. I'll mark[3] the play.
PROLOGUE.
     For us and for our tragedy,
     Here stooping to your clemency,[4]
135 We beg your hearing patiently.

                                                        [*Exit.*]

HAMLET. Is this a prologue, or the posy of a ring?[5]
OPHELIA. 'Tis brief, my lord.
HAMLET. As woman's love.

Enter [two Players as] King and his Queen.
PLAYER KING. Full thirty times hath Phoebus' cart gone round
140 Neptune's salt wash and Tellus' orbèd ground,[6]
     And thirty dozen moons with borrowed sheen[7]
     About the world have times twelve thirties[8] been
     Since love our hearts and Hymen[9] did our hands
     Unite commutual[10] in most sacred bands.°   bonds
145 PLAYER QUEEN. So many journeys may the sun and moon
     Make us again count o'er ere love be done!
     But woe is me, you are so sick of late,
     So far from cheer and from your former state,
     That I distrust you.° Yet though I distrust,   am anxious about you
150 Discomfort you, my lord, it nothing must.[11]

---

1 Provided you are not.
2 Naughty, indecent. (Ophelia sees all too clearly the offensive thrust of Hamlet's
talk about her not being ashamed to show all.)
3 Pay attention to.
4 Bowing to you, merciful and generous patrons.
5 Brief verse motto inscribed inside a ring.
6 Thirty times the sun-god's chariot has circled the sea and the earth, the realms
respectively of the gods Neptune and Tellus. (Although the sun also appears to
circle the earth each day, it will have completed its yearly cycle thirty times.) See
Appendix A, pp. 257 and 263–64.
7 With light reflected from the sun.
8 The moon has circled the world for thirty years—the length of time that the
King and Queen have been married. (Each year comprises a span of twelve lunar
cycles.)
9 God of marriage. See Appendix A, p. 254.
10 Mutually, reciprocally.
11 It must not distress you at all, my lord.

For women fear too much, even as they love,[1]
And women's fear and love holds quantity;[2]
In neither aught, or in extremity.[3]
Now what my love is, proof° hath made you know,   *experience*
And as my love is sized, my fear is so.[4]   155
Where love is great, the littlest° doubts are fear;   *even the littlest*
Where little fears grow great, great love grows there.
PLAYER KING. Faith, I must leave thee, love, and shortly too;
  My operant powers their functions leave to do.[5]
  And thou shalt live in this fair world behind,°   *after I am gone* 160
  Honored, beloved; and haply one as kind
  For husband shalt thou[6]—
PLAYER QUEEN.   Oh, confound the rest!
  Such love must needs be treason in my breast.
  In second husband let me be accurst!
  None[7] wed the second but who° killed the first.   *except she who* 165
HAMLET. Wormwood, wormwood.[8]
PLAYER QUEEN. The instances that second marriage move[9]
  Are base respects of thrift,[10] but none of love.
  A second time I kill my husband dead
  When second husband kisses me in bed.   170
PLAYER KING. I do believe you think what now you speak,
  But what we do determine, oft we break.
  Purpose is but the slave to memory,[11]
  Of violent birth, but poor validity,[12]
  Which now like fruit unripe sticks on the tree,   175

---

1 Women are apt to be extreme in their loving, and are fearful to the same excessive extent.
2 Are equal in proportions to each other.
3 Either women feel no anxiety if they do not love at all, or, if they love extremely, they are prone to extreme anxiety.
4 And just as my love is great in quantity, my fear of losing you is proportionately huge.
5 My vital faculties are ceasing to perform their functions.
6 The Player Queen interrupts before he can complete the rhyme with the word "find."
7 (1) Let no wife; (2) no wife does.
8 I.e., how bitter! (Wormwood is a bitter-tasting plant.)
9 The reasons that motivate a second marriage.
10 Are ignoble considerations of financial need and security.
11 Our good intentions are too often subject to forgetfulness.
12 Rashly conceived at first and lacking in staying power.

But fall unshaken when they mellow be.[1]
Most necessary 'tis that we forget
To pay ourselves what to ourselves is debt.[2]
What to ourselves in passion we propose,
180 The passion ending, doth the purpose lose.
The violence of either grief or joy
Their own enacture with themselves destroy.[3]
Where joy most revels, grief doth most lament;
Grief joys, joy grieves, on slender accident.[4]
185 This world is not for aye,[5] nor 'tis not strange
That even our loves should with our fortunes change;
For 'tis a question left us yet to prove[6]
Whether love lead fortune, or else fortune love.
The great man down, you mark his favorites flies;[7]
190 The poor advanced makes friends of enemies;[8]
And hitherto doth love on fortune tend,[9]
For who not needs shall never lack a friend,[10]
And who in want a hollow friend doth try
Directly seasons him his enemy.[11]
195 But orderly to end where I begun,[12]

---

1 I.e., the promises of fidelity we make are immature, like unripe fruit; when they ripen with time, they are so ready to fall that they do so even without shaking of the tree.
2 It's inevitable and even in a sense necessary that in time we neglect to fulfill the obligations that we have imposed on ourselves.
3 Violent extremes of both grief and joy engender their own destruction in the very act of manifesting themselves.
4 Grief turns to joy and joy to grief on the slightest occasion.
5 The world will not endure forever.
6 Yet to be demonstrated.
7 When a great man falls in fortune, you will note that those who bask in his favor abandon him.
8 When one of humble station is promoted, you'll see his former enemies now becoming his friends.
9 Up to this point in the argument, and to this extent, love plays a subservient role to fortune.
10 Anyone who is so well off as to have no need of wealth or friend will be sure to have friends in any case.
11 Whereas anyone who needfully tests the generosity of an insincere friend is sure to turn that seeming friend into one who is hostile and unwilling to help.
12 Began. ("Begun" is acceptable usage in early modern English.)

Our wills and fates do so contrary run[1]
That our devices still[2] are overthrown;
Our thoughts are ours, their ends none of our own.[3]
So, think[4] thou wilt no second husband wed,
But die thy thoughts[5] when thy first lord is dead.   200
PLAYER QUEEN. Nor earth to me give[6] food, nor heaven light,
    Sport and repose lock from me day and night,[7]
    To desperation turn my trust and hope,
    An anchor's cheer in prison be my scope![8]
    Each opposite that blanks the face of joy   205
    Meet what I would have well, and it destroy![9]
    Both here and hence pursue me lasting strife,[10]
    If once a widow, ever I be wife!
HAMLET. If she should break it now![11]
PLAYER KING. 'Tis deeply sworn. Sweet, leave me here awhile.   210
    My spirits grow dull, and fain° I would beguile   *gladly*
    The tedious day with sleep.
PLAYER QUEEN.   Sleep rock thy brain,
    And never come mischance between us twain!
[*The Player King*] *sleeps.*

                                        Exit [*Player Queen*].

HAMLET. Madam, how like you this play?
QUEEN. The lady doth protest too much,[12] methinks.   215
HAMLET. Oh, but she'll keep her word.
KING. Have you heard the argument?[13] Is there no offense[14] in't?

---

1 What we wish for ourselves and what in fact happens to us go in such contrary
directions.
2 Our intentions continually.
3 No matter what we intend, the results go astray.
4 I.e., (1) so, go ahead and think, or, (2) so, even if you think now that.
5 Either (1) your thoughts will die, or (2) let them die.
6 Neither let earth give me.
7 May I be barred from recreation by day and from repose at night.
8 May an anchorite's (religious hermit's) fare be the extent of my sustenance.
9 May every adverse thing that causes the face of joy to turn blank or pale
encounter and destroy everything that I wish to see prosper!
10 May eternal punishment pursue me in this life and the next.
11 I.e., after the vows that she has sworn.
12 Offers too many promises and protestations.
13 Plot.
14 Something that might offend one's sensibilities.

HAMLET. No, no, they do but jest,[1] poison in jest. No offense[2]
i'th' world.

220 KING. What do you call the play?

HAMLET. "The Mousetrap."[3] Marry, how? Tropically.[4] This play is
the image of a murder done in Vienna. Gonzago is the Duke's[5]
name, his wife Baptista. You shall see anon. 'Tis a knavish piece
of work, but what of that? Your majesty and we that have free[6]

225 souls, it touches[7] us not. Let the galled jade wince, our withers
are unwrung.[8]

Enter Lucianus.

This is one Lucianus, nephew to the King.

OPHELIA. You are as good as a chorus,[9] my lord.

HAMLET. I could interpret between you and your love if I could see

230 the puppets dallying.[10]

OPHELIA. You are keen,[11] my lord, you are keen.

HAMLET. It would cost you a groaning to take off mine edge.[12]

OPHELIA. Still better and worse.[13]

---

1 Make believe.

2 Crime.

3 Hamlet's nickname here for "The Murder of Gonzago" hints to the audience
at his plan to use the play to "catch the conscience of the King" (2.2.574, TLN 1645).
See extended note on p. 136.

4 How, indeed? Figuratively, as a "trope" or figure of speech, playing on words.

5 I.e., the King's.

6 Guiltless, unfettered.

7 Concerns, threatens.

8 Let the chafed horse wince and kick at being galled by its saddle or harness; our
horse is not rubbed sore between its shoulder blades. (I.e., only the guilty will be
made uncomfortable by this story.)

9 You serve as well as the actor whose function is to introduce forthcoming
action on stage (as in *Henry V*, *Romeo and Juliet*, *Pericles*, and *The Winter's Tale*).

10 Hamlet imagines for himself the role of interpreter or chorus for a puppet
show, with the suggestion too of being a go-between in an affair. "Dallying" continues the sexual suggestion, as do Hamlet's quips in the following lines (see notes
that follow).

11 Sharp, bitterly satirical. (But see next note for Hamlet's wordplay.)

12 It would cost you a pregnancy to satiate the keenness of my sexual appetite.

13 I.e., witty as always, albeit incorrigibly smutty. (These exchanges are said as
playful banter, not as overt barbs.)

HAMLET. So you mis-take your husbands.[1]—Begin, murderer.
    Pox,[2] leave thy damnable faces[3] and begin. Come, the croak- 235
    ing raven doth bellow for revenge.
LUCIANUS. Thoughts black, hands apt, drugs fit, and time
        agreeing,
    Confederate season, else no creature seeing,[4]
    Thou mixture rank,[5] of midnight weeds collected,
    With Hecate's ban[6] thrice blasted,° thrice infected,   *blighted* 240
    Thy natural magic and dire property°   *baleful power or quality*
    On wholesome life usurp immediately.
Pours the poison in his ears.

                                            [Exit.]
HAMLET. 'A poisons him i'th' garden for his estate. His name's
    Gonzago. The story is extant, and written in very choice Italian.
    You shall see anon how the murderer gets the love of Gonzago's 245
    wife.
OPHELIA. The King rises.
HAMLET. What, frighted with false fire?
QUEEN. How fares my lord?
POLONIUS. Give o'er the play.   250
KING. Give me some light. Away!
THE COURTIERS. Lights, lights, lights!
                        Exeunt all but Hamlet and Horatio.
HAMLET. "Why, let the strucken deer go weep,
    The heart ungallèd° play,   *unafflicted*
    For some must watch° while some must sleep;   *stay awake* 255

---

1   I.e., that's just the way you women take other men who are not your husbands
into your beds.
2   An exclamation of impatience, referring literally to the pock-marks caused by
syphilis and other diseases.
3   Leave off your deplorable and devilish grimaces.
4   A complicit or conspiring time, providing darkness so that no one will discover
the crime.
5   Foul, offensive.
6   The curse invoked by Hecate, goddess of witchcraft. See Appendix A, p. 252.

Thus runs the world away."[1]
Would not this,[2] sir, and a forest of feathers[3]—if the rest of
my fortunes turn Turk with me[4]—with two provincial roses[5]
on my razed[6] shoes, get me a fellowship in a cry of players,[7]
260   sir?

HORATIO. Half a share.

HAMLET. A whole one, I.
"For thou dost know, O Damon[8] dear,
   This realm dismantled was
265   Of Jove himself, and now reigns here
   A very, very—pajock."[9]

HORATIO. You might have rhymed.

HAMLET. O good Horatio, I'll take the Ghost's word for a thousand
   pound. Didst perceive?

270 HORATIO. Very well, my lord.

HAMLET. Upon the talk of the poisoning?

HORATIO. I did very well note him.

---

1 That is the way of the world. (These four lines appear to be from an unknown
ballad, alluding to the folk tradition of the wounded deer that retires from
company to weep in solitude as it dies.)
2 I.e., the play I have just presented and contributed some lines to.
3 I.e., and an abundance of extravagantly plumed headgear worn by the actors.
4 Even if good fortune should desert me. (To "turn Turk" is to renounce
Christianity in favor of the Muslim religion.) Hamlet jestingly asks if his newly
proven skill in theatrical matters might offer him a means of livelihood if his
fortunes turn otherwise against him.
5 Two large rosettes of ribbon, worn decoratively over shoelaces and named for
the region of Provence in southern France.
6 Decoratively slashed.
7 Get me a membership in an acting company. (A "cry" is a pack.)
8 The steadfast friend of Pythias in the story as dramatized in Richard Edwards's
Damon and Pythias, c. 1564–65, and derived from the often-told tale as found
in Aristoxenus (fl. 335 BCE), Cicero (*De Officiis* 3.45), Diodorus Siculus (10.4),
Valerius Maximus (first century CE), Castiglione (*The Courtier*, translated into
English by Sir Thomas Hoby, 1561), and others, here appropriate to the friendship
of Hamlet and Horatio. See Appendix A, p. 250.
9 This realm has been divested of its greatness by Jove (see Appendix A, p. 255)
himself, leaving the kingdom in the charge of a vain pretender to virtue and
authority. ("Pajock," meaning "peacock" or "patchcock," provides a ludicrous
substitution for the word that would rhyme with "was" in line 264, presumably
"ass." This stanza, like that at lines 253–56 above, appears to be adapted from some
unknown ballad.)

Enter Rosencrantz and Guildenstern.

HAMLET. Aha, come, some music! Come, the recorders.[1]
  For if the King like not the comedy,
  Why, then belike° he likes it not, pardie.[2]   *perhaps* 275
  Come, some music.

GUILDENSTERN. Good my lord, vouchsafe[3] me a word with you.

HAMLET. Sir a whole history.°   *story, account*

GUILDENSTERN. The King, sir—

HAMLET. Ay, sir, what of him?   280

GUILDENSTERN. Is in his retirement[4] marvelous distempered.[5]

HAMLET. With drink,[6] sir?

GUILDENSTERN. No, my lord, rather with choler.[7]

HAMLET. Your wisdom should show itself more richer[8] to signify
  this to his doctor, for, for me to put him to his purgation would   285
  perhaps plunge him into far more choler.[9]

GUILDENSTERN. Good my lord, put your discourse into some
  frame,[10] and start not[11] so wildly from my affair.[12]

HAMLET. I am tame sir. Pronounce.°   *say what you have to say*

GUILDENSTERN. The Queen your mother, in most great affliction   290
  of spirit, hath sent me to you.

HAMLET. You are welcome.

---

1 Wind instruments characterized by a conical tube, a whistle mouthpiece, and eight finger holes; related to the flute.
2 Indeed, pardieu (i.e., by God [French]).
3 Grant.
4 His withdrawal to his private chambers.
5 Out of temper.
6 Hamlet deliberately takes Guildenstern's "out of temper" to mean "drunk," supposing the four "humors" in the King's body to have been thrown out of balance by excessive drinking.
7 Instead of that, with anger.
8 More rich in wisdom. (The double comparative is allowable in early modern usage.)
9 Hamlet's sarcastic reply interprets "choler" in terms of humors theory, which saw "choler" as an excess of yellow bile producing indigestion as well as anger, and requiring purgation, usually bloodletting—with the ominous suggestion of Hamlet's letting out some of the King's blood. "Purgation" also suggests the spiritual cleaning through confession that the King is greatly in need of, with also the legal sense of clearing of guilt for a crime committed.
10 Coherent order.
11 Do not shy away like a nervous horse.
12 From the matter I need to discuss with you.

GUILDENSTERN. Nay, good my lord, this courtesy is not of the right breed.[1] If it shall please you to make me a wholesome[2] answer, I
295   will do your mother's commandment. If not, your pardon[3] and my return shall be the end of my business.

HAMLET. Sir, I cannot.

GUILDENSTERN. What, my lord?

HAMLET. Make you a wholesome answer; my wit's diseased. But,
300   sir, such answer as I can make, you shall command, or rather, as you say, my mother.[4] Therefore no more, but to the matter. My mother, you say.

ROSENCRANTZ. Then thus she says: your behavior hath struck her into amazement and admiration.[5]
305 HAMLET. Oh, wonderful son, that can so 'stonish a mother! But is there no sequel at the heels of this mother's admiration? Impart.[6]

ROSENCRANTZ. She desires to speak with you in her closet[7] ere you go to bed.

HAMLET. We shall obey, were she ten times our mother. Have you
310   any further trade with us?

ROSENCRANTZ. My lord, you once did love me.

HAMLET. So I do still, by these pickers and stealers.[8]

ROSENCRANTZ. Good my lord, what is your cause of distemper?[9] You do surely bar the door upon your own liberty[10] if you deny
315   your griefs to[11] your friend.

---

1 (1) Kind; (2) breeding, manners. (Guildenstern's point is that Hamlet's "You are welcome," while seemingly polite, sounds sarcastic and not addressed to the issue at hand.)
2 Healthy, sane.
3 Your permission for me to depart.
4 Instead, it is my mother's command you are uttering, not your own.
5 Bewilderment.
6 Speak, say something.
7 Private chamber.
8 I.e., by these hands. In the Catechism in the Anglican Book of Common Prayer, the person who is being prepared for Confirmation must vow "to keep my hands from picking and stealing."
9 The cause of your disorder.
10 I.e., upon your own freedom to act as you choose (with the threatening suggestion that as an "insane" person he may be locked up).
11 Refuse to share your unhappiness with.

HAMLET. Sir, I lack advancement.[1]

ROSENCRANTZ. How can that be, when you have the voice of the
King himself for your succession in Denmark?

---

1 Opportunity for advancement to higher station (such as the kingship).

3.2.313–18: ELECTIVE MONARCHY
(TLN 2207–12)

The Denmark of this play appears to follow the pattern of an elective
monarchy, in which, on the death of a king, a successor is chosen by a
select group of electors. The Holy Roman Empire in the late Middle
Ages and early modern period used this practice; so does the Papacy of
today. Though the electors in *Hamlet* are never named, Hamlet seems
to refer clearly to such a practice when he complains to Horatio that
the hated uncle, Claudius, has "Popped in between th'election and my
hopes" (5.2.65, TLN 3569). As son of his dead royal father, Hamlet justly
resents the fact that he has been supplanted while he was out of the
kingdom; nor is he mollified to hear Claudius name him "the most
immediate to our throne" (1.2.109, TLN 291). Thus, even though the
Danish throne appears to be elective, the idea of inherited rule seems to
have had some considerable weight in deliberations on the succession.

Here, Rosencrantz and Guildenstern wonder if Hamlet's erratic
behavior has been induced by his disappointment over the succession.
The two compliant courtiers evidently cannot understand how a royal
person who once enjoyed the title of crown prince and was presumed
heir to the former King Hamlet might now be impatient with waiting
for the death of his uncle before being permitted to mount the throne.

At the end of the play, as Hamlet lies dying, he prophesies that
"th'election lights / On Fortinbras" (5.2.335–36, TLN 3844–45). "He
has my dying voice," Hamlet adds, and his announcement presumably
has some final authority. Who could venture to challenge Hamlet's
royal edict? Especially since no living alternative presents itself. This is
Hamlet's one act as king, if, as we can suppose, the kingship passes from
Claudius to him for a flickering moment.

Enter the Players, with recorders.

HAMLET. Ay, sir, but "while the grass grows"[1]—the proverb is some-
320   thing[2] musty.—Oh, the recorders. Let me see one. [*He takes a*
recorder.] To withdraw[3] with you, why do you go about to recover
the wind of me,[4] as if you would drive me into a toil?

GUILDENSTERN. Oh, my lord, if my duty be too bold, my love is too
unmannerly.[5]

325   HAMLET. I do not well understand that.[6] Will you play upon this
pipe?

GUILDENSTERN. My lord, I cannot.

HAMLET. I pray you.

GUILDENSTERN. Believe me, I cannot.

330   HAMLET. I do beseech you.

GUILDENSTERN. I know no touch of it, my lord.

HAMLET. It is as easy as lying. Govern these ventages[7] with your
fingers and thumb, give it breath with your mouth, and it will
discourse most eloquent music. Look you, these are the stops.

335   GUILDENSTERN. But these cannot I command to any utt'rance of
harmony. I have not the skill.

HAMLET. Why, look you now, how unworthy a thing you make of
me! You would play upon me, you would seem to know my stops,
you would pluck out the heart of my mystery,[8] you would sound
340   me[9] from my lowest note to the top of my compass,[10] and there is

---

1   The whole proverb reads "While the grass grows, the horse (steed) starves"
(Dent G423). Hamlet implies that his hopes of succeeding to the throne are
delayed and distant at best, despite the King's having named him "most immediate to our throne" at 1.2.109 (TLN 291).

2   Somewhat.

3   Speak privately.

4   To get to my windward side (just as a hunter would position himself in such a
way that the hunted game, scenting danger, would then be driven in the opposite
direction and thus into the "toil" or net).

5   If I am being bold in an unmannerly fashion, it is my affection for you that
prompts me to be so.

6   Hamlet sounds skeptical of Guildenstern's protestations of love.

7   Finger holes, the "stops" on the recorder.

8   (1) Secret; (2) skill in one of the craft guilds, as practiced for example by
musicians.

9   (1) Fathom me to the depths of my mystery; (2) cause me to emit a sound.

10 Limit or range.

much music, excellent voice in this little organ,[1] yet cannot you make it speak. 'Sblood, do you think I am easier to be played on than a pipe? Call me what instrument you will, though you can fret me,[2] you cannot play upon me.[3]

Enter Polonius.

[*To Polonius, as he enters*] God bless you, sir.   345

POLONIUS. My lord, the Queen would speak with you, and presently.[4]

HAMLET. Do you see yonder cloud that's almost in shape of a camel?

POLONIUS. By th' mass,[5] and 'tis like a camel indeed.

HAMLET. Methinks it is like a weasel.   350

POLONIUS. It is backed like a weasel.

HAMLET. Or like a whale.

POLONIUS. Very like a whale.

HAMLET. Then I will come to my mother by and by.[6] [*Aside*] They fool me to the top of my bent.[7] [*Aloud*] I will come by and by.   355

POLONIUS. I will say so.

                                                                                             Exit.

HAMLET. "By and by" is easily said.—Leave me, friends.

                              [*Exeunt Rosencrantz and Guildenstern.*]

'Tis now the very witching time[8] of night,
When churchyards yawn,[9] and hell itself breathes out
Contagion to this world. Now could I drink hot blood,   360
And do such bitter business as the day
Would quake to look on. Soft, now to my mother.
O heart, lose not thy nature!° Let not ever   *natural feeling*

---

1 Musical instrument (playing too on the idea of a human organ).
2 (1) Can irritate me; (2) can press down on my "frets" or ridges on the finger-board of a stringed instrument to guide the fingers in playing various notes.
3 I.e., get me to play or dance to your tune.
4 I.e., and she means right now.
5 By the Holy Sacrament. (A strong oath.)
6 At once.
7 They humor me to the limit of my endurance.
8 A time for witchcraft, when spells are cast and evil is abroad.
9 Gape to let forth their grisly contents.

The soul of Nero¹ enter this firm° bosom   *resolved*
365   Let me be cruel, not unnatural;
I will speak daggers to her, but use none.
My tongue and soul in this be hypocrites:
How in my words somever she be shent,
To give them seals never my soul consent!²

Exit.

[3.3]

Enter King, Rosencrantz, and Guildenstern.
KING. I like him° not, nor stands it safe with us   *i.e., his behavior*
To let his madness range.° Therefore prepare you.   *roam freely*
I your commission will forthwith dispatch,³
And he to England shall along with you.
5   The terms of our estate may not endure
Hazard so dangerous as doth hourly grow
Out of his lunacies.⁴
GUILDENSTERN.   We will ourselves provide.⁵
Most holy and religious fear⁶ it is
To keep those many many bodies⁷ safe
10   That live and feed upon your majesty.
ROSENCRANTZ. The single and peculiar life⁸ is bound
With all the strength and armor of the mind
To keep itself from noyance,° but much more   *harm*

---

1   Despotic and emotionally unbalanced Roman emperor (37–68 CE) who had his
mother Agrippina put to death. The accusations that she had plotted against her
paternal uncle and second husband Claudius to enable her son Nero to succeed
to the throne, and that she had had an incestuous affair with her brother Caligula,
suggest intriguing parallels to the story of Hamlet. See Appendix A, pp. 257–58.
2   However much my words may rebuke her, let not my soul ever consent to ratify
those words with violence. ("Somever" means "soever.")
3   Prepare, cause to be drawn up.
4   A person in my exalted position cannot afford to put up with such hazardous
threats as seem hourly to be erupting out of Hamlet's feverish brain.
5   We will prepare ourselves.
6   Sacred concern and wise caution.
7   I.e., subjects, the members of the "body politic." The King's life must be protected because he is the embodiment of the body politic.
8   Any individual and private life.

That spirit° upon whose weal[1] depends and rests   *royal person*
The lives of many. The cease° of majesty   *cessation*   15
Dies not alone, but like a gulf° doth draw   *whirlpool*
What's near it with it. It is a massy° wheel   *massive*
Fixed on the summit of the highest mount,
To whose huge spokes ten thousand lesser things
Are mortised and adjoined,[2] which, when it falls,[3]   20
Each small annexment, petty consequence,[4]
Attends[5] the boist'rous° ruin. Never alone   *tumultuous*
Did the king sigh, but with a general groan.
KING. Arm you, I pray you, to[6] this speedy voyage,
For we will fetters put upon this fear   25
Which now goes too free-footed.
ROSENCRANTZ AND GUILDENSTERN. We will haste us.
                    Exeunt gentlemen [Rosencrantz and Guildenstern].

Enter Polonius.
POLONIUS. My lord, he's going to his mother's closet.
    Behind the arras I'll convey myself
    To hear the process.° I'll warrant she'll tax him home.[7]   *proceedings*
    And, as you said—and wisely was it said—   30
    'Tis meet° that some more audience than a mother,   *fitting*
    Since nature makes them partial,[8] should o'erhear
    The speech of vantage.[9] Fare you well, my liege.[10]
    I'll call upon you ere you go to bed,
    And tell you what I know.
KING.   Thanks, dear my lord.   35
                    Exit [Polonius].

---

1   Well-being.
2   Are fastened as if by inserting a tenon, or projecting member at the end of a
timber, into a groove or slot in an adjoining timber called the mortise.
3   Descends, like the wheel of Fortune.
4   I.e., each lesser person or thing serving and dependent on the King.
5   Takes part in, accompanies.
6   Prepare yourselves, I urge you, for.
7   Reprove him severely.
8   Since their nearness of blood might render them less likely than a third person
to see the business objectively.
9   (1) From an advantageous position, or, (2) in addition.
10 Liege lord, feudal superior to whom allegiance is due.

Oh, my offense is rank! It smells to heaven.
It hath the primal eldest curse[1] upon't,
A brother's murder. Pray can I not,
Though inclination be as sharp as will;[2]
40   My stronger guilt defeats my strong intent,
And like a man to double business bound[3]
I stand in pause where I shall first begin,
And both neglect. What if this cursèd hand
Were thicker than itself with brother's blood,[4]
45   Is there not rain enough in the sweet heavens
To wash it white as snow?[5] Whereto serves mercy
But to confront the visage of offense?[6]
And what's in prayer but this twofold force,
To be forestallèd ere we come to fall,
50   Or pardoned being down?[7] Then I'll look up.
My fault is past.[8] But, oh, what form of prayer
Can serve my turn? "Forgive me my foul murder"?
That cannot be, since I am still possessed
Of those effects for which I did the murder:
55   My crown, mine own ambition, and my queen.
May one be pardoned and retain th'offense?[9]
In the corrupted currents of this world,
Offense's gilded hand[10] may shove by justice,
And oft 'tis seen the wicked prize[11] itself

---

1   The curse of Cain, whose murder of his brother Abel was the first such crime (Genesis 4). See Appendix B, p. 270.
2   Even though my desire (to seek forgiveness in prayer) is as strong as my determination to do so (or as my will to sin).
3   Like a person who is simultaneously obliged to undertake two tasks that are mutually incompatible. (The King wishes he could seek forgiveness while still holding onto the guilty rewards of his crime.)
4   Were covered with a layer of a brother's blood thicker than the hand itself.
5   See Appendix B, pp. 271–72.
6   What function does mercy serve other than to confront sin face to face?
7   To be prevented from sinning, or pardoned once we have sinned.
8   I.e., my fault is already committed, so that my only hope is to pray for forgiveness.
9   The thing for which one committed the crime.
10   The hand of the offender offering gold as a bribe.
11   The prize wickedly desired and achieved.

Buys out the law. But 'tis not so above: 60
There is no shuffling,° there the action lies   *evasion, trickery*
In his true nature,[1] and we ourselves compelled,
Even to the teeth and forehead of our faults,[2]
To give in evidence.[3] What then? What rests?[4]
Try what repentance can.° What can it not?   *can do*   65
Yet what can it, when one cannot repent?
O wretched state, O bosom black as death,
O limèd[5] soul, that, struggling to be free,
Art more engaged!° Help, angels! Make assay.[6]   *entangled*
Bow, stubborn knees, and heart with strings of steel,   70
Be soft as sinews of the newborn babe!
All may be well.
[*He kneels.*]

Enter Hamlet.
HAMLET. Now might I do it pat, now 'a is a-praying,[7]
    And now I'll do't.
[*He draws his sword.*]
                        And so 'a goes to heaven,
And so am I revenged. That would be scanned:[8]   75
A villain kills my father, and for that,
I, his sole son, do this same villain send
To heaven.
Why, this is hire and salary, not revenge.
'A took my father grossly, full of bread,[9]   80

---

1 There, in heaven, each deed is seen for what it truly is, in its true form.
2 Face to face with our crimes.
3 To testify against ourselves. (In heaven, an accused can be compelled to do this, not because heaven is tyrannical but because no guiltiness can be evaded at the heavenly bar of justice.)
4 What remains to be said or done?
5 Caught as if with birdlime, a sticky substance smeared on twigs to snare birds.
6 Make some attempt. (Said by the King to himself, or possibly to the angels he hopes can hear him.)
7 Now I might do it opportunely and neatly, now that he is praying.
8 That needs to be looked into, or, could be interpreted as follows.
9 I.e., not spiritually prepared. See Appendix B, p. 272.

With all his crimes broad blown,[1] as flush[2] as May,
And how his audit[3] stands, who knows save° heaven?   *except for*
But in our circumstance and course of thought
'Tis heavy with him.[4] And am I then revenged

85   To take him° in the purging of his soul,   *Claudius*
When he is fit and seasoned for his passage?[5]
No.

[*He sheathes his sword.*]

Up, sword, and know thou a more horrid hent.[6]
When he is drunk asleep, or in his rage,[7]

90   Or in th'incestuous pleasure of his bed,
At gaming, swearing,[8] or about some act
That has no relish° of salvation in't,   *trace, hint*
Then trip him, that his heels may kick at heaven,[9]
And that his soul may be as damned and black

95   As hell, whereto it goes. My mother stays.°   *is waiting*
This physic[10] but prolongs thy sickly days.

                              Exit.

KING. My words fly up, my thoughts remain below.
Words without thoughts never to heaven go.

                              Exit.

---

1   With all of Hamlet Senior's sins in full bloom.
2   Vigorously thriving.
3   Hamlet Senior's spiritual reckoning.
4   But as far as we can tell from our mortal and necessarily limited perspective,
Hamlet Senior's soul is in serious peril. (Hamlet reflects that if his father's soul is
threatened thus because Claudius killed him in a state of spiritual unpreparedness,
to kill Claudius now when he appears to be at prayer and is thus in spiritual readiness for death would be an ironic travesty of vengeful justice.)
5   Prepared spritually for death.
6   I.e., wait for an occasion more horribly threatening to the intended victim.
7   Perhaps "in a fit of sexual passion," though being in an uncontrollable rage
would also put Claudius in danger of hellfire.
8   Gambling, and swearing profusely. ·
9   Kick upwards as the body falls downward, suggesting also a spurning of heavenly reward and ineffectual kicking at the gates of heaven.
10 Medicine; i.e., Hamlet's decision to postpone the killing will act like medicine
in sparing Claudius's life, but not for long.

[3.4 THE QUEEN'S CHAMBER]

Enter Queen [Gertrude] and Polonius.

POLONIUS. 'A will come straight. Look you lay home to him.[1]
   Tell him his pranks have been too broad[2] to bear with,
   And that your grace[3] hath screened and stood between
   Much heat and him. I'll silence me e'en here.
   Pray you, be round with him.°   *be blunt, forthright with him* 5
HAMLET. *(Within)* Mother, mother, mother!
QUEEN. I'll warrant you. Fear me not.[4]
   Withdraw; I hear him coming.

[Polonius conceals himself behind the arras.]

Enter Hamlet.

HAMLET. Now mother, what's the matter?
QUEEN. Hamlet, thou hast thy father[5] much offended.   10
HAMLET. Mother, you have my father[6] much offended.
QUEEN. Come, come, you answer with an idle° tongue.   *a foolish*
HAMLET. Go, go, you question with a wicked tongue.
QUEEN. Why, how now,° Hamlet?   *what's this*
HAMLET.   What's the matter now?
QUEEN. Have you forgot me?[7]
HAMLET.   No, by the rood,[8] not so.   15
   You are the queen, your husband's brother's wife,
   And—would it were not so!—you are my mother.
QUEEN. Nay, then, I'll set those to you that can speak.[9]
HAMLET. Come, come, and sit you down. You shall not budge.
   You go not till I set you up a glass°   *mirror* 20

---

1   He will be here any moment. Be sure to reprove him soundly.
2   Unrestrained, outrageous.
3   (1) Your gracious intervention; (2) Your Grace, the honorific way of addressing the Queen.
4   I assure you on that score. Don't worry about me.
5   Your stepfather, Claudius.
6   The dead King Hamlet.
7   Have you forgotten that I am your mother, to whom you owe respect? (But Hamlet answers in the sense of "How could I forget that you are my mother, in view of what you have done?")
8   By the cross of Christ.
9   I.e., who can talk sense into you.

Where you may see the inmost part of you.

QUEEN. What wilt thou do? Thou wilt not murder me?
Help, help, ho!

POLONIUS. [*Behind the arras*] What ho! Help, help, help!

25   HAMLET. How now, a rat? Dead for a ducat,[1] dead!

[*Hamlet thrusts through the arras with his sword.*]

POLONIUS. [*Behind the arras*] Oh, I am slain!

[*Polonius falls onto the stage floor, dead.*]

QUEEN.   Oh, me, what hast thou done?

HAMLET. Nay, I know not. Is it the King?

QUEEN. Oh, what a rash and bloody deed is this!

HAMLET. A bloody deed—almost as bad, good mother,

30   As kill a king, and marry with his brother.

QUEEN. As kill a king?

HAMLET.   Ay, lady, it was my word.

[*He parts the arras and discovers the dead Polonius.*]

Thou wretched, rash, intruding fool, farewell!
I took thee for thy better.[2] Take thy fortune.
Thou find'st to be too busy° is some danger.   *nosy*

35   [*To the Queen*] Leave wringing of your hands. Peace, sit you down,
And let me wring your heart, for so I shall
If it be made of penetrable stuff,[3]
If damnèd custom° have not brazed[4] it so   *sinful habit*
That it is proof and bulwark against sense.[5]

40   QUEEN. What have I done, that thou dar'st wag thy tongue
In noise so rude against me?

HAMLET.   Such an act
That blurs the grace and blush of modesty,
Calls virtue hypocrite,[6] takes off the rose
From the fair forehead of an innocent love

45   And sets a blister there, makes marriage vows

---

1 I.e., I bet a ducat he's dead; or, a ducat as the price for his life. (A ducat is a gold coin, as at 2.2.348, TLN 1412.)
2 I.e., I mistook you for Claudius, your social and intellectual superior.
3 If your heart still has any sensitivity to feeling and emotion.
4 Brazened, hardened.
5 That it is armored and thus made impenetrable against natural feeling.
6 I.e., slanders virtue itself with an accusation of hypocrisy.

"SETS A BLISTER THERE"
(TLN 2427)

Henry VIII's government threatened, in 1513 and later in 1537, to brand prostitutes and brothel-keepers on the face as a badge of shame. At various times prostitutes might be forbidden to wear aprons (tokens of marital respectability), or they might have their head shaved, or their ears clipped, or their noses slit. These laws seem to have been only fitfully enforced. The idea of imposing tokens of shame is of ancient lineage. Under Roman law, at one time prostitutes were forced to wear the *toga mulieribus*, an acceptably modest gown, signaling the further restriction that women were not allowed to appear in public unaccompanied by a male. Here Hamlet, arraigning his mother of unfaithfulness and immodesty, inveighs against a deed like adultery that "takes off the rose / From the fair forehead of an innocent love / And sets a blister there." Later Laertes, returning in fury to Denmark, exclaims that a failure on his part to avenge the death of his father "proclaims me bastard, / Cries 'Cuckold!' to my father, brands the harlot / Even here between the chaste unsmirchèd brow / Of my true mother" (4.5.118–21, TLN 2860–64).

From *A Harlot's Progress*, William Hogarth, 1731. Pictured here is a courtesan, attended by her turbaned servant, upsetting a coffee table to the consternation of her customer and other alarmed guests.

As false as dicers' oaths—oh, such a deed
As from the body of contraction° plucks   *the marriage contract*
The very soul, and sweet religion makes
A rhapsody of words.[1] Heaven's face doth glow
50   O'er this solidity and compound mass
With tristful visage, as against the doom,
Is thought-sick at the act.[2]

QUEEN.   Ay me, what act,
That roars so loud and thunders in the index?[3]

HAMLET. [*Showing her two likenesses, of his father and of Claudius*]
Look here upon this picture, and on this,
55   The counterfeit presentment° of two brothers.   *painted representation*
See what a grace was seated on this brow:
Hyperion's[4] curls, the front° of Jove himself,   *forehead, brow*
An eye like Mars[5] to threaten and command,
A station° like the herald Mercury[6]   *stance*
60   New lighted on a heaven-kissing hill,[7]
A combination and a form indeed
Where every god did seem to set his seal°   *affix his seal of approval*
To give the world assurance of a man.
This was your husband. Look you now what follows:
65   Here is your husband, like a mildewed ear,°   *ear of grain*
Blasting[8] his wholesome brother. Have you eyes?
Could you on this fair mountain leave° to feed   *leave off, cease*
And batten on this moor?[9] Ha, have you eyes?
You cannot call it love, for at your age
70   The heyday in the blood° is tame, it's humble,   *sexual appetite*

---

1   And turns sweet religion into a mere senseless jumble of words.

2   Heaven's face blushes with shame at this solid earth, compounded as it is of the four elements, with sorrowful face as though the day of doom were at hand, and is sick with thinking of this horrid deed—i.e., Gertrude's second marriage.

3   Table of contents; prologue or preface. (The mere name of Gertrude's crime is in itself a desecration.)

4   The sun-god's; see Appendix A, p. 254.

5   Roman god of war. See Appendix A, pp. 255–56.

6   Winged messenger of the gods. See Appendix A, p. 256.

7   Newly alighted on a hill reaching to the sky.

8   Blighting, infecting.

9   And gorge yourself on this barren, unfertile land (suggesting too a man who is unhandsomely dark of complexion).

And waits upon[1] the judgment, and what judgment
Would step from this to this? Sense,[2] sure, you have,
Else could you not have motion, but sure that sense
Is apoplexed,° for madness would not err,[3]   *paralyzed*
Nor sense to ecstasy was ne'er so thralled   75
But it reserved some quantity of choice
To serve in such a difference.[4] What devil was't
That thus hath cozened you at hoodman-blind?[5]
Eyes without feeling, feeling without sight,
Ears without hands or eyes, smelling sans° all,   *without (French)* 80
Or but a sickly part of one true sense
Could not so mope.[6] O shame, where is thy blush?
Rebellious hell,
If thou canst mutine° in a matron's bones,   *mutiny*
To flaming youth let virtue be as wax   85
And melt in her own fire.[7] Proclaim no shame
When the compulsive ardor gives the charge,
Since frost itself as actively doth burn,
And reason panders will.[8]
QUEEN. Oh, Hamlet speak no more!   90
  Thou turn'st mine eyes into my very soul,
  And there I see such black and grainèd° spots   *ingrained, indelible*

---

1   Is subservient to.
2   Sensation and perception through the five senses.
3   For even madness would not err in this fashion as you have done.
4   Nor could your physical senses ever have been so enslaved to ecstasy (i.e.,
sexual passion) as to have been unable to perceive the difference between Hamlet
Senior and Claudius.
5   Has cheated you at blindman's bluff. (Hamlet imagines a diabolical trick in
which the devil, having covered the eyes of Gertrude with a scarf in the children's
game of blindman's bluff, has steered her in such a way that she gropingly encountered Claudius.)
6   I.e., even a person deprived of the normal use of eyes, touch, hearing, and
smell, or having nothing more than a sickly portion of one of these physical senses,
could err so obtusely and aimlessly.
7   Chastity among the young will melt like wax held over a candle flame. (We
cannot hope for self-restraint in young people when older women set such a bad
example.)
8   Call it no shameful business when the compelling ardor of youth gives the
signal for attack by committing lechery, since even the frost of old age burns with
as active a fire of lust and mature reason perverts its proper function by making
excuses for lust rather than restraining it.

As will not leave their tinct.[1]

HAMLET.   Nay, but to live
In the rank sweat of an enseamèd[2] bed
95   Stewed[3] in corruption, honeying[4] and making love
Over the nasty sty!°   *pigsty*

QUEEN. Oh, speak to me no more!
These words like daggers enter in my ears.
No more, sweet Hamlet.

HAMLET.   A murderer and a villain,
100   A slave that is not twentieth part the tithe[5]
Of your precedent lord,° a vice of kings,[6]   *your previous husband*
A cutpurse[7] of the empire and the rule,°   *kingdom*
That from a shelf the precious diadem° stole   *crown*
And put it in his pocket—
105 QUEEN. No more!

Enter Ghost [in his nightgown].[8]

HAMLET. A king of shreds and patches[9]—
[*Seeing the Ghost*] Save me and hover o'er me with your wings,
You heavenly guards!° What would you, gracious figure?   *angels*

QUEEN. Alas, he's mad!

110 HAMLET. Do you not come your tardy son to chide,
That, lapsed in time and passion,[10] lets go by
Th'important acting of your dread command?
Oh, say!

GHOST. Do not forget. This visitation
115 Is but to whet thy almost blunted purpose.

---

1   Will not lose their dark indelible stain.
2   Saturated with the greasy filth of lust.
3   Steeped (suggesting also "stew," brothel).
4   Indulging in lovey-dovey romantic behavior.
5   Tenth part. (To be a twentieth part of a tenth part would be only 1/200th of something, i.e., virtually none at all.)
6   A nonpareil of evil kings; with an allusion to the character "Vice," a gloating and insidious tempter in late-medieval and sixteenth-century morality plays.
7   Pickpocket.
8   This detail is given in Q1. See Appendix E, pp. 297–302, for some other textual variants unique to Q1.
9   Of ragged patchwork, appropriate for a monarch (Claudius) who is a sham, in Hamlet's view; suitable also for a fool or jester attired in motley.
10 Having let time and passionate commitment (to revenge) slip away.

But look, amazement on thy mother sits.
Oh, step between her and her fighting soul!
Conceit° in weakest bodies strongest works.   *imagination*
Speak to her, Hamlet.
HAMLET.   How is it with you, lady?
QUEEN. Alas, how is't with you,   120
That you do bend your eye on vacancy,
And with th'incorporal° air do hold discourse?   *bodiless*
Forth at your eyes your spirits wildly peep,
And, as the sleeping soldiers in th'alarm,¹
Your bedded° hair, like life in excrements,²   *(previously) lying flat* 125
Start up and stand on end. O gentle° son,   *nobly born; kind*
Upon the heat and flame of thy distemper³
Sprinkle cool patience. Whereon do you look?
HAMLET. On him, on him! Look you how pale he glares!
His form and cause conjoined, preaching to stones,   130
Would make them capable.⁴ [*To the Ghost*] Do not look upon
      me,
Lest with this piteous action you convert
My stern effects. Then what I have to do
Will want true color, tears perchance for blood.⁵
QUEEN. To whom do you speak this?   135
HAMLET. Do you see nothing there?
QUEEN. Nothing at all, yet all that is I see.
HAMLET. Nor did you nothing hear?
QUEEN. No, nothing but ourselves.
HAMLET. Why, look you there, look how it steals away!⁶   140
My father in his habit as he lived.⁷
Look where he goes, even now out at the portal!

                                        Exit Ghost.

---

1 Like sleeping soldiers awakened by the call to arms.
2 As if the hair, an outgrowth of the body, could take on a life of its own.
3 Your disorder, your imbalance of mind.
4 I.e., his ghostly appearance, together with the momentousness of his cause,
would arouse pity even in stones.
5 Do not look at me, lest your pitiful looks divert me from accomplishing what I
have to do, prompting me to weep when I should be shedding blood.
6 The Ghost is presumably starting to leave at this point. "Portal" two lines later
appears to suggest that the Ghost will exit by a stage door, not a trap door in the
stage floor.
7 Dressed as when he was alive.

3.4.125–26:   HAIR STANDING ON END
(TLN 2502–03)

The Queen, astonished at Hamlet's alarming appearance when, so far as she can tell, he is bending his eye "on vacancy" and is holding discourse "with th'incorporal air," notes that his hair is starting up and standing on end. The description matches that of the Ghost at 1.5.16–21 (TLN 700–05), who informs Hamlet that if he were to be told the full horrors of Purgatory, even the "lightest word" would make "each particular hair to stand on end / Like quills upon the fretful porpentine." The famous eighteenth-century actor David Garrick wore a trick wig that enabled him to make his hair stand on end at the appropriate moment.

David Garrick in Hamlet, Act 1, Scene 4, engraving by James McArdell after Benjamin Wilson, 1754.

QUEEN. This is the very coinage° of your brain.   *mere invention*
  This bodiless creation ecstasy
  Is very cunning in.[1]   145
HAMLET. Ecstasy?
  My pulse as yours doth temperately keep time,
  And makes as healthful music. It is not madness
  That I have uttered. Bring me to the test,
  And I the matter will reword,° which madness   *repeat word for word* 150
  Would gambol from.[2] Mother, for love of grace,
  Lay not that flattering unction[3] to your soul
  That not your trespass but my madness speaks.
  It will but skin and film[4] the ulcerous place,
  Whiles rank corruption, mining° all within,   *undermining* 155
  Infects unseen. Confess yourself to heaven,
  Repent what's past, avoid what is to come,
  And do not spread the compost on the weeds
  To make them ranker. Forgive me this my virtue,[5]
  For in the fatness of these pursy times[6]   160
  Virtue itself of vice must pardon beg,
  Yea, curb and woo for leave to do him good.[7]
QUEEN. Oh, Hamlet, thou hast cleft my heart in twain.
HAMLET. Oh, throw away the worser part of it,
  And live the purer with the other half.   165
  Good night. But go not to my uncle's bed;
  Assume° a virtue if you have it not.   *give outward conformity to*
  That monster custom, who all sense doth eat,[8]
  Of habits devil,[9] is angel yet in this,
  That to the use of actions fair and good   170

---

1 Madness (ecstasy) is very skillful in creating this kind of hallucination.
2 Would skip away from.
3 Do not apply an ointment that comforts without healing.
4 Cover with a thin layer of skin.
5 Forgive my urging you to a virtuous course.
6 For in the grossness of this corpulent, swollen, short-winded era. ("Pursy" is
often said of a horse.)
7 Virtue itself must now obsequiously beg for permission to serve vice. (Hamlet's
point is that in these corrupt times virtue must temporize with vice a little if it is to
achieve any reform.)
8 Our proclivity for falling into bad habits, which can so easily consume and
overwhelm the physical senses.
9 Being all too inclined toward evil habits.

He likewise gives a frock or livery
That aptly is put on.[1] Refrain tonight,
And that shall lend a kind of easiness
To the next abstinence; the next more easy:
175 For use almost can change the stamp of nature,[2]
And either [in] the devil, or throw him out[3]
With wondrous potency. Once more good night,
And when you are desirous to be blest,
I'll blessing beg of you.[4] For[5] this same lord,
180 I do repent; but heaven hath pleased it so
To punish me with this, and this with me,[6]
That I must be their scourge and minister.[7]
I will bestow° him, and will answer well[8]   *dispose of*
The death I gave him. So, again, good night.
185 I must be cruel only to be kind.
Thus bad begins, and worse remains behind:[9]
One word more, good lady.

QUEEN.   What shall I do?

HAMLET. Not this, by no means, that I bid you do:
Let the bloat° King tempt you again to bed,   *bloated, puffy*
190 Pinch wanton on your cheek,[10] call you his mouse,[11]
And let him, for a pair of reechy° kisses,   *reeking of filth*

---

1 Custom can instead offer us the garb of outwardly virtuous actions that are
quite easily adopted. (One can incline one's soul, Hamlet says, toward virtue by
consciously behaving in a virtuous way; the outward behavior can then begin to
shape the inner self.)
2 For by rigorously controlling our behavior we can come close to changing our
very inborn selves.
3 I.e., and custom or habit can either admit the devil into our hearts or throw
him out.
4 I.e., and when you are penitently ready to seek God's blessing, I will ask your
blessing as a dutiful son should.
5 As for (turning his attention to the corpse of Polonius).
6 I.e., it is (evidently) heaven's pleasure that I am to be punished for having killed
Polonius, just as he has been fatally punished at my hands for his snooping into
other people's business.
7 I.e., that I must be the heavens' agent of just retribution.
8 Offer a suitable account of, pay for, atone for.
9 I.e., thus we can begin to face difficulties; at least the worst is over.
10 Leave his sensual love pinches on your cheeks.
11 A term of endearment.

Or paddling[1] in your neck[2] with his damned fingers,
Make you to ravel all this matter out° *unravel, disclose all this matter*
That I essentially am not in madness,
But mad in craft.[3] 'Twere good you let him know,[4]   195
For who that's but a queen, fair, sober, wise,
Would from a paddock, from a bat, a gib,
Such dear concernings hide?[5] Who would do so?
No, in despite of sense and secrecy,[6]
Unpeg the basket on the house's top,   200
Let the birds fly, and like the famous ape,
To try conclusions, in the basket creep,
And break your own neck down.[7]

QUEEN. Be thou assured, if words be made of breath
 And breath of life, I have no life to breathe° *to utter* 205
 What thou hast said to me.

HAMLET. I must to England. You know that?

QUEEN. Alack, I had forgot. 'Tis so concluded on.

HAMLET. There's letters sealed, and my two schoolfellows,
 Whom I will trust as I will adders fanged,   210
 They bear the mandate; they must sweep my way[8]
 And marshal me to knavery.[9] Let it work,° *let this matter proceed*
 For 'tis the sport° to have the enginer[10] *it's a fine ironic joke*
 Hoist with his own petard,[11] and 't shall go hard

---

1 Fingering amorously.
2 (Including the breasts.)
3 Only seemingly mad as a cunning device.
4 (Said with a sardonic irony that continues in the following eight lines.)
5 For why would any attractive, temperate, and wise queen wish to hide such important matters from a toad, a bat, a tom-cat? (Said sardonically; of course such a woman would choose not to divulge Hamlet's secret to a repulsive villain.)
6 Despite the secrecy that common sense would seem to require.
7 In this Aesop-like fable, for which no source has been found, an ape releases some birds from a basketlike birdcage on a roof and then, mindlessly wishing to imitate them as an experiment ("To try conclusions"), gets into the cage himself and, attempting to fly, falls to the ground and breaks his neck. Presumably Hamlet is warning the Queen against coming too quickly to conclusions and rashly telling her husband that Hamlet's madness is only pretense. ("Down" here means either "in the fall" or "utterly.")
8 Prepare a path before me.
9 Conduct me to where some treachery lies in wait for me.
10 Deviser of "engines" of war, such as bombs.
11 Blown up by his own explosive device, of a kind used to make a breach in fortifications.

215 But I will delve one yard below their mines,[1]
     And blow them at the moon.[2] Oh 'tis most sweet
     When in one line two crafts directly meet.[3]
     This man shall set me packing.[4]
     I'll lug the guts into the neighbor room.
220 Mother, good night indeed. This counselor
     Is now most still, most secret, and most grave,[5]
     Who was in life a foolish prating knave.°—   *a chattering rascal*
     Come, sir, to draw toward an end with you.[6]—
     Good night, mother.

                              Exit Hamlet, tugging in Polonius.[7]

                        [4.1]

Enter King, with Rosencrantz and Guildenstern.
KING. There's matter[8] in these sighs, these profound heaves.[9]
     You must translate;[10] 'tis fit we understand them.
     Where is your son?
QUEEN. [*To Rosencrantz and Guildenstern*] Bestow this place on us a
     little while.
                  [*Exeunt Rosencrantz and Guildenstern.*]
5   Ah, my good lord, what have I seen tonight!
KING. What, Gertrude? How does Hamlet?
QUEEN. Mad as the sea and wind when both contend

---

1 And it will be bad luck for me if I do not dig my tunnels underneath theirs.
(Tunnels were used to attack enemy fortifications in siege warfare by undermining
them and blowing them up from below.)
2 Blow them moon-high, way up into the air.
3 When two cunning plots are on a collision course, as when mines and counter-
mines confront each other.
4 The death of Polonius will (1) pack me off to England; (2) set me to cooking up
schemes; (3) set me to lugging off the corpse.
5 (Playing on the "grave" where Polonius will now be buried.)
6 (1) Finish up with you; (2) drag you to the place of burial.
7 Q1/Q2/F1 all specify that Hamlet exits here, Q1/F1 adding that he drags the
dead body of Polonius with him. Q1/F1 thus implicitly leave the Queen alone on
stage; in Q2, the simple "Exit" could apply to Hamlet only, also leaving the Queen
alone on stage, but in Q2 the Queen then enters with her husband and the two
courtiers, implying that she has briefly left.
8 Significance, meaning.
9 These great heavings of breast and shoulders as the Queen sobs.
10 I.e., explain why you are weeping.

Which is the mightier. In his lawless fit,
Behind the arras hearing something stir,
Whips out his rapier, cries, "A rat, a rat!"   10
And in this brainish apprehension¹ kills
The unseen good old man.
KING.   Oh, heavy° deed!   *grievous*
It had been so with us had we been there.²
His liberty is full of threats to all—
To you yourself, to us, to everyone.   15
Alas, how shall this bloody deed be answered?³
It will be laid to us,⁴ whose providence°   *foresight*
Should have kept short,⁵ restrained, and out of haunt⁶
This mad young man. But so much was our love,
We would not understand what was most fit,   20
But like the owner° of a foul disease,   *sufferer*
To keep it from divulging,⁷ let° it feed   *allowed*
Even on the pith° of life. Where is he gone?   *essential part*
QUEEN. To draw apart the body he hath killed,
O'er whom his very madness, like some ore   25
Among a mineral of metals base,
Shows itself pure:⁸ 'a weeps for what is done.
KING. Oh, Gertrude, come away!
The sun no sooner shall the mountains touch
But we will ship him hence, and this vile deed   30
We must with all our majesty and skill
Both countenance and excuse.⁹—Ho, Guildenstern!

Enter Rosencrantz and Guildenstern.
Friends both, go join you with some further aid.¹⁰

---

1   In this brainsick misapprehension.
2   If I had been there instead of Polonius.
3   Explained, responded to, accounted for.
4   Laid at our (my) doorstep, blamed on me.
5   Kept on a short leash.
6   Secluded, away from public gatherings.
7   From being made publicly known.
8   The Queen argues that Hamlet's weeping over Polonius's dead body shows his madness to be like a vein of pure gold amidst a mine of baser metals, i.e., revealing his finer nature even though he has madly done this deed.
9   Put the best face on and justify as well as we can.
10 Take with you some others to help.

Hamlet in madness hath Polonius slain,
35   And from his mother's closet hath he dragged him.
Go seek him out, speak fair,[1] and bring the body
Into the chapel. I pray you haste in this.

>   *Exit Gentlemen [Rosencrantz and Guildenstern].*

Come, Gertrude, we'll call up our wisest friends
To let them know both what we mean to do
40   And what's untimely done. [So envious slander,]
Whose whisper o'er the world's diameter,
As level as the cannon to his blank,
Transports his poisoned shot, may miss our name
And hit the woundless air.[2] Oh, come away!
45   My soul is full of discord and dismay.

>   *Exeunt.*

[4.2]

Enter Hamlet.

HAMLET. Safely stowed.

ROSENCRANTZ AND GUILDENSTERN. (*Within*)[3] Hamlet! Lord
    Hamlet!

HAMLET. But soft, what noise? Who calls on Hamlet? Oh, here they
5   come.

Enter Rosencrantz and Guildenstern.

ROSENCRANTZ. What have you done, my lord, with the dead
    body?

HAMLET. Compounded° it with dust, whereto 'tis kin.[4]   *mixed*

ROSENCRANTZ. Tell us where 'tis, that we may take it thence
10   And bear it to the chapel.

HAMLET. Do not believe it.

---

1   Speak gently and courteously to him.
2   In that way, envious slander, spreading far and wide its poisonous whisper as
if shot from a cannon at point-blank range, may be deflected from me as its target
and expend itself harmlessly on the invulnerable air. (The phrase "So envious
slander" does not appear in the early texts.)
3   Off stage.
4   See Appendix B, p. 272.

ROSENCRANTZ. Believe what?

HAMLET. That I can keep your counsel and not mine own.[1] Besides,
to be demanded of[2] a sponge, what replication[3] should be made
by the son of a king?   15

ROSENCRANTZ. Take you me for a sponge, my lord?

HAMLET. Ay, sir, that soaks up the King's countenance,[4] his rewards,
his authorities.[5] But such officers do the King best service in the
end: he keeps them, like an ape an apple in the corner of his jaw,
first mouthed to be last swallowed.[6] When he needs what you   20
have gleaned, it is but squeezing you, and, sponge, you shall be
dry again.[7]

ROSENCRANTZ. I understand you not, my lord.

HAMLET. I am glad of it. A knavish speech sleeps in a foolish ear.[8]

ROSENCRANTZ. My lord, you must tell us where the body is, and go   25
with us to the King.

HAMLET. The body is with the King, but the King is not with the
body.[9] The King is a thing—

GUILDENSTERN. A thing, my lord?

HAMLET. Of nothing.[10] Bring me to him. Hide fox, and all after![11]   30

Exeunt.

---

1 I.e., don't expect me to do as you bid me and not follow my own counsel.
2 Interrogated by.
3 Reply.
4 Favor.
5 The benefits that he authorizes.
6 I.e., Rosencrantz and Guildenstern are kept in reserve by the King, always
there but to be used only when it serves the King's purposes, not theirs.
7 I.e., the King will squeeze you dry, ceasing to bestow benefits on you.
8 A crafty insult is not understood as such by the fool to whom the insult is
directed.
9 A riddle, perhaps suggesting that although Claudius's body is necessarily a part
of him, the essence of true kingship is not to be found there. Claudius can order
the body of Polonius to be brought to him, but that also will not make him any
more a true king than he really is.
10 See Appendix B, p. 272.
11 This cry from the children's game of fox-and-hounds, similar to hide-and-seek,
suggests that Hamlet runs away from Rosencrantz and Guildenstern.

[4.3]

Enter King, and two or three.

KING. I have sent to seek him and to find the body.
How dangerous is it that this man goes loose!
Yet must not we put the strong law on him;
He's loved of the distracted multitude,[1]

5 Who like not in their judgment but their eyes,[2]
And where 'tis so, th'offender's scourge is weighed,
But ne'er the offense.[3] To bear all smooth and even,[4]
This sudden sending him away must seem
Deliberate pause.[5] Diseases desperate grown

10 By desperate appliance are relieved,[6]
Or not at all.

Enter Rosencrantz.

KING.   How now, what hath befall'n?[7]
ROSENCRANTZ. Where the dead body is bestowed, my lord,
We cannot get from him.
KING.   But where is he?
ROSENCRANTZ. Without,[8] my lord, guarded, to know your
        pleasure.

15 KING. Bring him before us.
ROSENCRANTZ. [*Calling*] Ho, Guildenstern! Bring in my lord.

Enter Hamlet and Guildenstern [with Guards].

KING. Now Hamlet, where's Polonius?
HAMLET. At supper.
KING. At supper? Where?

---

1 By the irrationally unstable commoners.
2 Who choose not rationally but by appearances.
3 And in such cases people are likely to censure the severity of the punishment
without sufficiently considering the gravity of the offense.
4 In order to manage the business without arousing suspicion.
5 Must seeem the result of careful planning.
6 Diseases that are grown desperate can be cured only by the applying of desperate remedies.
7 Now, what has happened?
8 Outside (the door).

HAMLET. Not where he eats, but where 'a is eaten. A certain 20
convocation of politic worms are e'en[1] at him. Your worm is your
only emperor for diet.[2] We fat all creatures else to fat us, and we
fat ourselves for maggots. Your fat king and your lean beggar is
but variable service;[3] two dishes but to one table. That's the end.

KING. Alas, alas! 25

HAMLET. A man may fish with the worm that hath eat[4] of a king,
and eat of the fish that hath fed of that worm.

KING. What dost thou mean by this?

HAMLET. Nothing but to show you how a king may go a progress[5]
through the guts of a beggar. 30

KING. Where is Polonius?

HAMLET. In heaven. Send thither to see. If your messenger find him
not there, seek him i'th' other place yourself. But if indeed you
find him not within this month, you shall nose[6] him as you go up
the stairs into the lobby. 35

KING. [*To some attendants*] Go seek him there.

HAMLET. 'A will stay till you come.

[*Exeunt attendants.*]

KING. Hamlet, this deed of thine, for thine especial safety—
Which we do tender,[7] as we dearly° grieve   *intensely*
For that which thou hast done—must send thee hence 40
With fiery quickness. Therefore prepare thyself.
The bark° is ready, and the wind at help,   *ship*
Th'associates tend,[8] and everything is bent°   *is in readiness*
For England.

HAMLET. For England! 45

KING. Ay, Hamlet.

HAMLET. Good.

---

1   Even now.
2   I.e., an ordinary worm feeds more grandly than even an emperor, since worms
will feed on the decaying bodies of all creatures, high or low.
3   Are simply various dishes or courses served at table. (Worms feed on kings and
beggars alike.)
4   Has eaten.
5   Royal state journey.
6   Smell.
7   Value, hold dear.
8   The companions are waiting.

KING. So is it if thou knew'st our purposes.

HAMLET. I see a cherub[1] that sees them. But come, for England!
50   Farewell, dear mother.

KING. Thy loving father, Hamlet.

HAMLET. My mother. Father and mother is man and wife, man and
    wife is one flesh,[2] and so, my mother. Come, for England!

                                            Exit.

KING. Follow him at foot.[3] Tempt[4] him with speed aboard.
55   Delay it not. I'll have him hence tonight.
    Away! For everything is sealed and done
    That else leans on th'affair.[5] Pray you, make haste.

                       [Exeunt all but the King.]

    And England,[6] if my love thou hold'st at aught,
    As my great power thereof may give thee sense,[7]

---

1   Cherubim, in the second order of angels, were possessors of a special wisdom
and knowledge that would enable them, in Hamlet's view, to perceive the full
extent of Claudius's treachery.
2   See Appendix B, p. 272.
3   Close at his heels.
4   Entice, persuade.
5   Everything else that relates to this business is taken care of.
6   The King of England.
7   As indeed my great power should persuade you of the importance of valuing
my high regard for you.

4.3.21–22:   **EDICT OF WORMS**
                     (TLN 2686–87)

When Hamlet alludes to a "convocation of politic worms" and speaks of
such worms as "your only emperor for diet," some scholars see an allusion to the Imperial Diet (i.e., Assembly) of Worms, a celebrated convocation of the Holy Roman Empire assembled in the Heylshof Garden,
Worms, Germany, on 28 January 1521, to inquire into and to condemn
as heretical many of the 95 theses that Martin Luther had proposed
in 1517, generally seen as the first salvo of the Protestant Reformation.
The Emperor Charles V presided. In the previous year, Pope Leo X had
issued a Papal Bull identifying some 41 errors in Luther's pronounce-
ments. See also extended note on p. 76.

Since yet thy cicatrice looks raw and red   60
After the Danish sword,[1] and thy free awe[2]
Pays homage to us, thou mayst not coldly set
Our sovereign process, which imports at full
By letters congruing to that effect
The present death of Hamlet.[3] Do it, England,   65
For like the hectic[4] in my blood he rages,
And thou must cure me. Till I know 'tis done,
Howe'er my haps, my joys were ne'er begun.[5]

                                             Exit.

[4.4 THE DANISH COAST]

Enter Fortinbras [and a Captain] with his army over the stage.[6]

FORTINBRAS. Go, Captain, from me greet the Danish King.
    Tell him that by his license° Fortinbras   *permission*
    Craves the conveyance of a promised march[7]
    Over his kingdom. You know the rendezvous.
    If that his majesty would aught with us,[8]   5
    We shall express our duty in his eye;[9]
    And let him know so.
CAPTAIN. I will do't, my lord.
FORTINBRAS. [*To his soldiers*] Go softly on.[10]

                          [*Exeunt all but the Captain.*]

---

1   Since the scar still looks fresh that you suffered in having been subjugated to Danish rule.
2   Your unconstrained show of respect and obedience.
3   You cannot simply ignore Denmark's command, which orders fully in writing that Hamlet be put immediately to death.
4   Fluctuating but persistent fever.
5   Whatever else fortune holds in store for me, I cannot begin to be happy until I know that Hamlet is dead.
6   With his army, marching across the stage (and then exiting at line 9).
7   Requests unhindered and escorted passage, in fulfillment of a promise made.
8   If the Danish King wishes to confer with me for any reason.
9   I will pay my respects in person.
10 Go quietly on, without creating a disturbance.

Enter Hamlet, Rosencrantz, [Guildenstern,] etc.

10 HAMLET. [*To the Captain*] Good sir, whose powers[1] are these?

CAPTAIN. They are of Norway, sir.

HAMLET. How purposed, sir, I pray you?

CAPTAIN. Against some part of Poland.

HAMLET. Who commands them, sir?

15 CAPTAIN. The nephew to old Norway, Fortinbras.

HAMLET. Goes it against the main of Poland,[2] sir,
    Or for some frontier?

CAPTAIN. Truly to speak, and with no addition,°   *exaggeration*
    We go to gain a little patch of ground

20   That hath in it no profit but the name.[3]
    To pay five ducats, five, I would not farm it,[4]
    Nor will it yield to Norway or the Pole[5]
    A ranker° rate, should it be sold in fee.[6]   *higher*

HAMLET. Why then the Polack never will defend it.

25 CAPTAIN. Yes, it is already garrisoned.

HAMLET. Two thousand souls and twenty thousand ducats
    Will not debate the question of this straw.[7]
    This is th'impostume[8] of much wealth and peace,
    That inward breaks,[9] and shows no cause without°   *externally*

30   Why the man dies. I humbly thank you, sir.

CAPTAIN. God b'wi' you, sir.

                                   [*Exit.*]

ROSENCRANTZ.   Will't please you go, my lord?

HAMLET. I'll be with you straight.° Go a little before.   *right away*

                               [*Exeunt all but Hamlet.*]

    How all occasions do inform against° me,   *accuse, denounce*
    And spur my dull revenge! What is a man

---

1   Soldiers, armed forces.

2   Does this army march against the whole of Poland.

3   I.e., other than the reputation to be gained by conquering it.

4   I.e., I would not take a lease on it as tenant farmer even for a mere five ducats a year.

5   To either the King of Norway or of Poland.

6   Sold outright as a freehold, in "fee simple."

7   I.e., appear to be insufficient stakes in a quarrel about this trifling matter.

8   The abscess, cancerous growth.

9   Festers within.

If his chief good and market° of his time   *profit, advantage* 35
Be but to sleep and feed? A beast, no more.
Sure he that made us with such large discourse,[1]
Looking before and after,[2] gave us not
That capability and godlike reason
To fust° in us unused. Now, whether it be   *grow moldy* 40
Bestial oblivion,[3] or some craven° scruple   *cowardly*
Of thinking too precisely on th'event[4]—
A thought which, quartered, hath but one part wisdom
And ever three parts coward—I do not know
Why yet I live to say this thing's to do,[5]   45
Sith° I have cause, and will, and strength, and means   *since*
To do't. Examples gross° as earth exhort me.   *as obvious*
Witness this army of such mass and charge,°   *of such size and cost*
Led by a delicate and tender° prince,   *refined and youthful*
Whose spirit with divine ambition puffed°   *inspired* 50
Makes mouths at the invisible event,[6]
Exposing what is mortal and unsure
To all that fortune, death, and danger dare,°   *can threaten him with*
Even for an eggshell.[7] Rightly to be great
Is not to stir without great argument,   55
But greatly to find quarrel in a straw
When honor's at the stake.[8] How stand I, then,
That have a father killed, a mother stained,
Excitements of my reason and my blood,[9]
And let° all sleep, while to my shame I see   *and yet I let* 60

---

1 With such wide-ranging capacity for reasoning.
2 Enabling us to recall past events and anticipate the future.
3 Forgetfulness and heedlessness of the sort one sees in animals.
4 Caused by thinking too scrupulously about what might happen as a consequence of one's actions.
5 This thing is not yet accomplished, still to be done.
6 Presents a scornful face to unforeseeable outcomes.
7 Even for a thing proverbially of no value.
8 True greatness is not to be measured solely in terms of being moved to action
by a great cause; rather, it is to respond stirringly even to an apparently trivial
cause when honor is at stake. (Hamlet sees the irrationality of such a devotion to
honor even as he admires it in Fortinbras.)
9 Enough cause to awaken a keen response in me that is both reasonable and
passionate.

The imminent death of twenty thousand men
That for a fantasy and trick of fame[1]
Go to their graves like beds, fight for a plot
Whereon the numbers cannot try the cause,[2]
65 Which is not tomb enough and continent°   *receptacle, container*
To hide the slain? Oh, from this time forth,
My thoughts be bloody, or be nothing worth!

                   Exit.

[4.5 THE CASTLE]

Enter Queen and Horatio.
QUEEN. I will not speak with her.
HORATIO.   She is importunate,
 Indeed, distract.° Her mood will needs be pitied. *distraught*
QUEEN. What would she have?
HORATIO. She speaks much of her father, says she hears
5 There's tricks[3] i'th' world, and hems,[4] and beats her heart,[5]
Spurns enviously at straws,[6] speaks things in doubt° *obscurely*
That carry but half sense. Her speech is nothing,
Yet the unshapèd use[7] of it doth move
The hearers to collection;[8] they yawn[9] at it,
10 And botch° the words up fit to[10] their own thoughts, *patch*
Which,[11] as her winks and nods and gestures yield[12] them,
Indeed would make one think there might be thought,

---

1 That for the illusory and trifling business of striving to gain a reputation for bravery.
2 A plot of ground containing insufficient room even for the bodies of the soldiers who are fighting over it.
3 Deceptions.
4 Clears her throat with a "hem" sound.
5 Breast.
6 Kicks bitterly (i.e., takes offense and reacts suspiciously) at trifles.
7 Incoherent manner.
8 To inference, guessing at some sort of meaning.
9 Gape in wonderment; gasp.
10 In such a way as to match.
11 Which words.
12 Deliver, represent.

Though nothing sure, yet much unhappily.[1]
QUEEN. 'Twere good she were spoken with, for she may strew
    Dangerous conjectures in ill-breeding[2] minds.   15
    Let her come in.
                      [Horatio withdraws to admit Ophelia.]
    [*Aside*] To my sick soul, as sin's true nature is,[3]
    Each toy° seems prologue to some great amiss.°   *trifle / calamity*
    So full of artless jealousy is guilt,
    It spills itself in fearing to be spilt.[4]   20

Enter Ophelia distracted, playing on a lute, and her hair down, singing.
OPHELIA. Where is the beauteous majesty of Denmark?
QUEEN. How now,° Ophelia?   *what's this*
OPHELIA. (*She sings*)
    "How should I your true love know
      From another one?
    By his cockle hat[5] and staff,   25
      And his sandal shoon."°   *shoes (an archaic plural)*
QUEEN. Alas, sweet lady, what imports° this song?   *signifies*
OPHELIA. Say you? Nay, pray you, mark.°   *listen, pay attention*
    (*Song*) "He is dead and gone, lady,
      He is dead and gone.   30
    At his head a grass-green turf,
      At his heels a stone."°   *gravestone*
    Oho!°   *(evidently a sigh)*
QUEEN. Nay, but Ophelia—
OPHELIA. Pray you, mark. (*Song*)   35
    "White his shroud as the mountain snow—"

Enter King.

---

1   That there might be, buried in her wild speech, an idea that, however incoher-
ently expressed, could have distressing implications, even if one can't be sure.
2   Suspicious, prone to expect the worst.
3   As is the case in sin's true nature.
4   Guilt is so burdened with a self-incriminating fear of detection that it betrays
itself by the very fear of being detected.
5   Hat with cockleshell (a mollusk scallop-like shell) stuck in it as a sign (along
with a walking staff and sandals) that the wearer has been a pilgrim to the shrine of
Saint James of Compostela in Spain (often associated with forlorn lovers).

QUEEN. Alas, look here, my lord.

OPHELIA. [*Song*]

    "Larded° with sweet flowers,   *strewn, bedecked*

    Which bewept to the grave did not go

40   With true-love showers."°   *i.e., tears*

KING. How do you, pretty lady?

OPHELIA. Well God'ield you.[1] They say the owl was a baker's daughter.[2] Lord, we know what we are, but know not what we may be. God be at your table!

45 KING. Conceit° upon her father.   *fantasy, brooding*

OPHELIA. Pray you, let's have no words of this, but when they ask you what it means, say you this: (*Song*)

    "Tomorrow is Saint Valentine's Day,[3]

    All in the morning betime,°   *early*

50 And I a maid at your window

    To be your Valentine.

Then up he rose, and donned his clothes

    And dupped° the chamber door,   *unlatched*

Let in the maid, that out a maid

55   Never departed more."[4]

KING. Pretty Ophelia—

OPHELIA. Indeed, la? Without an oath I'll make an end on't.°   *of it*

[*Song*]

    "By Gis and by Saint Charity,[5]

    Alack, and fie for shame!

60 Young men will do't if they come to't;

    By Cock,[6] they are to blame.

Quoth she, 'Before you tumbled me,

    You promised me to wed.'

He answers,

---

1   God yield (i.e., reward) you.

2   In a folk tale, Christ in disguise begs hospitality at a baker's shop. When the baker's daughter stingily allows him no more than a small loaf, she is turned into an owl.

3   A feast day (14 February) in honor of Saint Valentine; traditionally a day on which the first person one meets is destined to be one's lovemate.

4   Who, when she departed, was no longer a virgin.

5   By Jesus and in the name of Christian love and fellow feeling (a mild oath).

6   A euphemism for "By God"; with verbal play on the slang term for "penis."

'So would I ha' done, by yonder sun,   65
   An° thou hadst not come to my bed.'"   *if*
KING. How long hath she been thus?
OPHELIA. I hope all will be well. We must be patient. But I cannot
   choose but weep to think they would lay him i'th' cold ground.
   My brother shall know of it. And so I thank you for your good   70
   counsel. Come, my coach! Good night, ladies, good night, sweet
   ladies, good night, good night.

                                            Exit.

KING. [*To Horatio*] Follow her close. Give her good watch, I pray
   you.

                                   [*Exit Horatio.*]
Oh, this is the poison of deep grief! It springs
All from her father's death, and now behold!   75
Oh, Gertrude, Gertrude,
 When sorrows come, they come not single spies
But in battalions.[1] First, her father slain;
Next, your son gone, and he most violent author
Of his own just remove;[2] the people muddied,°   *stirred up, confused* 80
Thick[3] and unwholesome in their thoughts and whispers
For good Polonius' death, and we have done but greenly[4]
In hugger-mugger[5] to inter him; poor Ophelia
Divided from herself and her fair judgment,
Without the which we are pictures or mere beasts;   85
Last, and as much containing° as all these,   *and as serious*
Her brother is in secret come from France,
Feeds on this wonder,[6] keeps himself in clouds,[7]
And wants not buzzers[8] to infect his ear
With pestilent speeches of his father's death,   90

---

1   When sorrows come, they come not one at a time but in swarms, or (militarily)
battalions. ("Spies" are scouts sent in advance of the main army.)
2   Of his own justly deserved removal (to England).
3   Bewildered, muddled.
4   We have acted foolishly, naively.
5   Secret haste. See also Appendix A, "Plutarch," p. 260.
6   Feeds his feeling of resentment about this whole shocking turn of events.
7   Behaves suspiciously and in ways that are hard to interpret or predict, arousing
uncertainty and suspicion.
8   Is not lacking in gossipers and scandal mongers.

>Wherein necessity, of matter beggared,
>Will nothing stick our person to arraign
>In ear and ear.[1] O my dear Gertrude, this,
>Like to a murd'ring piece,[2] in many places
95 >Gives me superfluous death.°   *kills me over and over*
>*A noise within.*

>*Enter a Messenger.*
>QUEEN. Alack, what noise is this?
>KING. Where is my Switzers?[3] Let them guard the door.
>What is the matter?
>MESSENGER.   Save yourself, my lord!
>The ocean, overpeering of his list,[4]
100 >Eats not the flats[5] with more impiteous° haste   *unpitying, merciless*
>Than young Laertes, in a riotous head,[6]
>O'erbears your officers. The rabble call him lord,
>And, as the world were now but to begin,
>Antiquity forgot, custom not known,
105 >The ratifiers and props of every word,[7]
>They cry, "Choose we! Laertes shall be king!"
>Caps,[8] hands, and tongues applaud it to the clouds:
>"Laertes shall be king, Laertes king!"
>QUEEN. How cheerfully on the false trail they cry![9]
>*A noise within.*
110 >Oh, this is counter,[10] you false Danish dogs!
>KING. The doors are broke.

---

1   In which business, since the gossips are unprovided with accurate information and yet long for some plausible explanation, they will not hesitate to whisper insinuations about me, their king.

2   Like a cannon loaded with shrapnel.

3   Where are my Swiss mercenary guards?

4   Overflowing (literally, rising above and looking over) its shore or boundary.

5   Low-lying lands near shore.

6   Insurrectionary advance, like a tidal wave.

7   And, as if the world were to begin all over again, utterly neglecting all ancient traditional customs that should confirm and underprop everything that we say and promise.

8   Caps thrown into the air in celebration of Laertes.

9   Bay loudly (said of hunting dogs).

10 You are following a contrary or false scent (a metaphor from hunting).

Enter Laertes with others.

LAERTES. Where is this king?—Sirs,[1] stand you all without.°   *outside*

ALL. No, let's come in.

LAERTES. I pray you, give me leave.[2]

ALL. We will, we will.   115

LAERTES. I thank you. Keep° the door.   *guard*

[*Exeunt followers.*]
                                O thou vile king,
    Give me my father!

QUEEN.   Calmly, good Laertes.

LAERTES. That drop of blood that's calm proclaims me bastard,
    Cries "Cuckold!" to my father, brands the harlot
    Even here between the chaste unsmirchèd brow   120
    Of my true mother.[3]

KING.   What is the cause, Laertes,
    That thy rebellion looks so giant-like?—
    Let him go, Gertrude. Do not fear our person.[4]
    There's such divinity doth hedge[5] a king
    That treason can but peep to what it would,[6]   125
    Acts little of his will.[7]—Tell me, Laertes,
    Why thou art thus incensed?—Let him go, Gertrude.—
    Speak, man.

LAERTES.   Where is my father?

KING.   Dead.

QUEEN. But not by him.

KING.   Let him demand his fill.

LAERTES. How came he dead? I'll not be juggled with.[8]   130
    To hell, allegiance! Vows, to the blackest devil!

---

1 ("Sirs" is a standard form of address to commoners.)
2 I.e., leave matters to me, let me converse with the King alone.
3 I.e., brands me on the forehead with the stigma and punishment allotted to
prostitutes, shaming me thus with the (invisible) horns of cuckoldry despite my
being the true son of my chaste mother.
4 Do not fear for my personal safety.
5 That protects, surrounds defensively.
6 That treason can only peep furtively, as through a barrier, at what it wishes to
accomplish.
7 While performing little of what it intends.
8 Deceived, played with.

Conscience and grace, to the profoundest pit!
I dare damnation. To this point I stand,°   *I am resolved in this*
That both the worlds I give to negligence,[1]
135   Let come what comes, only I'll be revenged
Most throughly° for my father.   *thoroughly*
KING. Who shall stay° you?   *prevent, hinder*
LAERTES. My will, not all the world's.[2]
And for° my means, I'll husband[3] them so well   *as for*
They shall go far with little.
140   KING.   Good Laertes,
If you desire to know the certainty
Of your dear father's death, is't writ in your revenge
That, swoopstake, you will draw both friend and foe,[4]
Winner and loser?
145   LAERTES. None but his enemies.
KING. Will you know them, then?
LAERTES. To his good friends thus wide I'll ope my arms,
And, like the kind life-rend'ring pelican,
Repast them with my blood.
KING.   Why, now you speak
150   Like a good child and a true gentleman.
That I am guiltless of your father's death,
And am most sensibly in grief° for it,   *feelingly grief-stricken*
It shall as level° to your judgment 'pear°   *straightforward, plain / appear*
As day does to your eye.
A noise within.
155   VOICES. (*Within*) Let her come in!
LAERTES. How now, what noise is that?

Enter Ophelia [as before].
O heat, dry up my brains! Tears seven times salt
Burn out the sense and virtue° of mine eye!   *function, power*

---

1   That I fear nothing either in this world or in the life to come.
2   I will cease when my will is accomplished, not for anyone else's.
3   Manage prudently and economically.
4   I.e., is it set down in and required by your need for revenge that you will sweep
up friend and foe indiscriminately, like a gambler in a sweepstake, winning all the
stakes on the gambling table?

4.5.148: "THE KIND LIFE-REND'RING PELICAN"
(TLN 2896)

The female pelican was credited, in medieval and Renaissance bestiaries, with great capacity in caring for her young, to the point of plucking blood from her own breast to feed her young when other sustenance was unavailable. For this reason the bird became a symbol of the great sacrifice that Christ made in his Passion of dying for humankind. Queen Elizabeth I made this a symbol of her self-devotion to her country. Here, Laertes alludes to this myth by way of explaining to the King how he will treat Polonius's friends differently from his enemies.

St. Johann (Rot an der Rot), Johann Michael Biehle, 1740. "Rot an der Rot," "red on red," points to the pelican's breast where she is feeding her young.

By heaven, thy madness shall be paid by weight[1]
160   Till our scale turns the beam.[2] O rose of May,
Dear maid, kind sister, sweet Ophelia!
O heavens, is't possible a young maid's wits
Should be as mortal as an old man's life?
Nature is fine in love, and where 'tis fine
165   It sends some precious instance of itself
After the thing it loves.[3]

OPHELIA. (*Song*)
"They bore him bare-faced on the bier,[4]
    Hey non nonny, nonny, hey nonny,
And on his grave rained many a tear."

170   Fare you well, my dove.

LAERTES. Hadst thou thy wits, and didst persuade[5] revenge,
It could not move thus.

OPHELIA. You must sing "a-down, a-down," an[6] you call him
"a-down-a." Oh, how the wheel[7] becomes it! It is the false
175   steward that stole his master's daughter.[8]

LAERTES. This nothing's more than matter.[9]

OPHELIA. There's rosemary; that's for remembrance. Pray you, love,
remember. And there is pansies; that's for thoughts.

LAERTES. A document[10] in madness, thoughts and remembrance
180   fitted.

OPHELIA. There's fennel for you, and columbines. There's rue
for you, and here's some for me; we may call it herb of grace

---

1   Will be avenged with equal gravity.
2   Until our cause of justice outweighs, as in a balance scales, the wrongful deed
of the offender.
3   Human nature's sensitivity in matters of love is such that it sends some precious part of itself after a lost object of that love. (In this case, Ophelia's sanity has
deserted her under the burden of grief for her dead father.)
4   In an open coffin on the litter.
5   Argue for, urge.
6   If.
7   Perhaps Ophelia imagines a spinning wheel, where women might sit and work
as they sang; or Fortune's wheel.
8   The story is unknown, but false stewards do sometimes steal their masters'
daughters in romance tales. Perhaps Ophelia is madly fantasizing about her
father's uneasy fear that Hamlet might in effect steal her away by seducing her.
9   Ophelia's ravings are more eloquent than ordinary sane utterance.
10 An object lesson.

o' Sundays. You may wear your rue with a difference. There's a
daisy. I would give you some violets, but they withered all when
my father died. They say 'a made a good end. [*She sings.*]   185
"For bonny sweet Robin is all my joy."

LAERTES. Thought and afflictions,[1] passion,° hell itself   *suffering*
She turns to favor° and to prettiness.   *grace, beauty*

OPHELIA. (*Song*)
"And will 'a not come again?
And will 'a not come again?   190
   No, no, he is dead,
   Go to thy deathbed,
He never will come again.

His beard was as white as snow,
All flaxen was his poll.°   *His head of hair was as white as flax*   195
   He is gone, he is gone,
   And we cast away moan.°   *We loudly but unavailingly proclaim our grief*
God 'a' mercy on his soul!"
And of all Christian souls, I pray God. God b'wi' you!
                        Exeunt Ophelia [and the Queen, following her].

LAERTES. Do you see this, O God?   200

KING. Laertes, I must commune with your grief,
   Or you deny me right.[2] Go but apart,[3]
   Make choice of whom your° wisest friends you will,   *of whichever of*
   And they shall hear and judge 'twixt you and me.
   If by direct or by collateral hand°   *or by indirect agency* 205
   They find us touched,[4] we will our kingdom give,
   Our crown, our life, and all that we call ours
   To you in satisfaction;° but if not,   *as recompense*
   Be you content to lend your patience to us,
   And we shall jointly labor with your soul   210
   To give it due content.

LAERTES.   Let this be so.
   His means of death, his obscure burial—

---

1   Melancholy, sad thoughts.
2   I insist on my right to communicate with you and take part in your grief.
3   Withdraw with me to some other place where we can talk privately.
4   They conclude that I am implicated.

No trophy, sword, nor hatchment[1] o'er his bones,
No noble rite, nor formal ostentation°— *ceremony*
215 Cry to be heard as 'twere from heaven to earth,
That I must call't in question.[2]
KING. So you shall,
And where th'offense is, let the great ax fall.
I pray you go with me.

Exeunt.

[4.6]

Enter Horatio, with an Attendant [i.e., Servingman].
HORATIO. What[3] are they that would speak with me?
SERVINGMAN. Sailors, sir. They say they have letters for you.
HORATIO. Let them come in. [*Exit Servingman.*]
I do not know from what part of the world I should be greeted,
5 if not from Lord Hamlet.

Enter Sailors.
SAILOR. God bless you, sir.
HORATIO. Let him bless thee too.
SAILOR. 'A shall, sir, an't[4] please him. There's a letter for you, sir. It
comes from th'ambassador[5] that was bound for England, if your
10 name be Horatio, as I am let to know[6] it is. [*He gives a letter.*]
HORATIO. (*Reads the letter.*) "Horatio, when thou shalt have over-
looked[7] this, give these fellows some means[8] to the King;
they have letters for him. Ere we were two days old at sea,[9] a
pirate[10] of very warlike appointment[11] gave us chase. Finding
15 ourselves too slow of sail, we put on a compelled valor, and in

---

1 No memorial display, sword betokening knightly prowess, or tablet displaying
the coat of arms of the deceased.
2 So that I must demand an explanation for that.
3 What sort of men; who.
4 If it.
5 I.e., from Hamlet.
6 Led to believe.
7 Looked over, read.
8 Means of access.
9 Before we had been at sea for two days.
10 Pirate ship.
11 Equipment.

the grapple[1] I boarded them. On the instant they got clear of our
ship, so I alone became their prisoner. They have dealt with me
like thieves of mercy but they knew what they did:[2] I am to do a
good turn for them. Let the King have the letters I have sent, and
repair thou to me[3] with as much haste as thou wouldest fly death.   20
I have words to speak in thine ear will make thee dumb, yet are
they much too light for the bore[4] of the matter. These good fellows will bring thee where I am. Rosencrantz and Guildenstern
hold their course for England. Of them I have much to tell thee.
Farewell.   25

He that thou knowest thine,
Hamlet.”

Come, I will give you way for these your letters,[5]
And do't the speedier that you may direct me
To him from whom you brought them.   30

Exeunt.

[4.7 A PRIVATE ROOM IN THE CASTLE]

Enter King and Laertes.

KING. Now must your conscience my acquittance seal,[6]
   And you must put me in your heart for friend,
   Sith° you have heard, and with a knowing ear,   *since*
   That he which hath your noble father slain
   Pursued my life.

LAERTES.   It well appears. But tell me   5
   Why you proceeded not against these feats°   *acts*
   So crimeful and so capital° in nature,   *punishable by death*
   As by your safety,[7] greatness, wisdom, all things else,
   You mainly° were stirred up.   *greatly*

KING. Oh for two special reasons,   10

---

1   And during the action in which the pirate ship bound itself to the side of our
vessel by means of grappling irons to facilitate close combat.
2   I.e., they have dealt mercifully with me, but they knew I could be useful to
them.
3   Come to me.
4   Caliber, size, importance.
5   I will provide means of access for you to deliver your letters.
6   Your conscience must confirm my release from any guilt in Polonius's death.
7   Your need to be protected against attack.

Which may to you perhaps seem much unsinewed,[1]
And yet to me they're strong. The Queen his mother
Lives almost by his looks, and for myself—
My virtue or my plague, be it either which[2]—
15   She's so conjunctive[3] to my life and soul
That, as the star moves not but in his[4] sphere,
I could not but by her. The other motive
Why to a public count[5] I might not go
Is the great love the general gender° bear him,   common people
20   Who, dipping all his faults in their affection,[6]
Would, like the spring that turneth wood to stone,[7]
Convert his gyves[8] to graces, so that my arrows,
Too slightly timbered for so loud a wind,[9]
Would have reverted to my bow again,
25   And not where I had aimed them.
LAERTES. And so have I a noble father lost,
A sister driven into desp'rate terms,°   condition, circumstances
Whose worth, if praises may go back again,[10]
Stood challenger on mount of all the age
30   For her perfections.[11] But my revenge will come.
KING. Break not your sleeps for that. You must not think
That we are made of stuff so flat and dull

---

1   Weak, lacking sinew.
2   Whichever it may be.
3   She is so closely united. (A metaphor from astronomy: two or more celestial
bodies meeting or passing in the same degree of the zodiac are said to be in
conjunction.)
4   Its. (The Ptolemaic astronomical concept here is of the stars and planets
revolving around the earth in concentric spheres or transparent globes.)
5   Accounting, indictment.
6   I.e., who, testing all his faults by the forgiving standard of their affection for
him.
7   Like a spring water with such a heavy concentration of lime that it can in effect
petrify a piece of wood and thus make it more perfect and unflawed.
8   Fetters; here signifying "crimes," "faults."
9   Provided with too slight a shaft of wood to be able to cope with so mighty a
gust of popular opinion.
10   If praising her can sufficiently recall what she once was.
11   Would stand like a supreme challenger daring the world to match her perfections.

That we can let our beard be shook with danger[1]
And think it pastime. You shortly shall hear more.
I loved your father, and we love ourself,   35
And that, I hope, will teach you to imagine—

Enter a Messenger with letters.
   How now? What news?
MESSENGER.   Letters, my lord, from Hamlet.
   This to your majesty, this to the Queen.
[*He gives letters.*]
KING. From Hamlet! Who brought them?
MESSENGER. Sailors, my lord, they say. I saw them not.   40
   They were given me by Claudio.[2] He received them.
KING. Laertes, you shall hear them. [*To the Messenger*] Leave us.
                                 Exit Messenger.
[*He reads.*] "High and mighty, you shall know I am set naked[3]
on your kingdom. Tomorrow shall I beg leave to see your kingly
eyes, when I shall first, asking your pardon thereunto,[4] recount   45
the occasion of my sudden and more strange return.
                                     Hamlet."

What should this mean? Are all the rest come back?
Or is it some abuse, and no such thing?[5]
LAERTES. Know you the hand?
KING.   'Tis Hamlet's character.[6] "Naked!"   50
   And in a postscript here he says "alone."
   Can you advise me?
LAERTES. I am lost in it, my lord. But let him come.
   It warms the very sickness in my heart
   That I shall live and tell him to his teeth   55
   "Thus diddest thou."[7]

---

1   That I would allow anyone to threaten and insult me with shaking or plucking
my beard.
2   Presumably another servingman or messenger, who does not appear in the
play.
3   Unarmed; without possessions or followers.
4   I.e., asking your pardon for having returned without permission.
5   Or is it some deception, and not what it appears to be?
6   Handwriting.
7   I.e., I am repaying you for what you did to my father.

KING.   If it be so, Laertes—
   As how should it be so, how otherwise?[1]—
   Will you be ruled by me?
LAERTES.   Ay, my lord,
   If so° you'll not o'errule me to a peace.   *so long as*
60 KING. To thine own peace. If he be now returned
   As checking at his voyage,[2] and that he means
   No more to undertake it, I will work him
   To an exploit, now ripe in my device,°   *devising*
   Under the which he shall not choose but fall;[3]
65 And for his death no wind of blame shall breathe,
   But even his mother shall uncharge the practice[4]
   And call it accident.
LAERTES.   My lord, I will be ruled,
   The rather if you could devise it so
   That I might be the organ.°   *agent, instrument*
KING.   It falls right.
70 You have been talked of since your travel much,
   And that in Hamlet's hearing, for a quality
   Wherein they say you shine. Your sum of parts[5]
   Did not together pluck such envy from him
   As did that one, and that, in my regard,
75 Of the unworthiest siege.°   *least worthy in rank of importance*
LAERTES. What part is that, my lord?
KING. A very ribbon in the cap of youth,
   Yet needful too, for youth no less becomes
   The light and careless livery that it wears
80 Than settled age his sables and his weeds
   Importing health and graveness.[6] Two months since

---

1 I.e., how could it be true that Hamlet has returned, and yet how could it be
otherwise than true since we have this letter from him?
2 As one who has been diverted from his journey (like a falcon turning away
from its intended quarry to fly at a chance bird).
3 From which he cannot possibly escape.
4 Declare the matter to be blameless.
5 All your admirable qualities.
6 Youth and stylishly informal dress suit each other admirably, just as rich
fur-lined robes and other sober garments are well suited to the concern for good
health and the grave dignity of men in advancing years.

Here was a gentleman of Normandy.
I have seen myself, and served against, the French,
And they can well on horseback,° but this gallant   *are skillful riders*
Had witchcraft in't;[1] he grew into his seat,   85
And to such wondrous doing brought his horse
As had he been incorpsed and demi-natured
With the brave beast.[2] So far he passed my thought[3]
That I in forgery of shapes and tricks[4]
Come short of what he did.

LAERTES.   A Norman[5] was't?   90

KING. A Norman.

LAERTES. Upon my life, Lamord.

KING.   The very same.

LAERTES. I know him well. He is the brooch° indeed   *ornament*
And gem of all the nation.

KING. He made confession of you,[6]   95
And gave you such a masterly report
For art and exercise in your defense,[7]
And for your rapier most especially,
That he cried out 'twould be a sight indeed
If one could match you. Th'escrimers° of their nation,   *fencers*   100
He swore, had neither motion, guard, nor eye[8]
If you opposed them. Sir, this report of his
Did Hamlet so envenom with his envy[9]
That he could nothing do but wish and beg
Your sudden coming o'er to play with him.[10]   105
Now, out of this—

LAERTES.   What out of this,[11] my lord?

---

1   But this dashing young man had an almost magical skill in horsemanship.
2   As if he had become one body with the horse (like the fabled centaur, with the torso and legs of a horse and the head and arms of a man). See Appendix A, p. 249.
3   He surpassed my expectation so greatly.
4   In my imagining what devices and feats might be possible (in horsemanship).
5   Someone from Normandy.
6   He testified to and conceded your superior ability.
7   With respect to your skill and practice in the art of self-defense.
8   Would seem to lack movement, defensive strategy, or visual acuity.
9   Did so embitter Hamlet with poisonous envy.
10   That you would quickly come from France and fence with him.
11   Why are you saying "out of this"?

KING. Laertes, was your father dear to you?
Or are you like the painting of a sorrow,
A face without a heart?
LAERTES.   Why ask you this?
110 KING. Not that I think you did not love your father,
But that I know love is begun by time,[1]
And that I see, in passages of proof,[2]
Time qualifies[3] the spark and fire of it.
There lives within the very flame of love
115 A kind of wick or snuff[4] that will abate it,
And nothing is at a like goodness still,[5]
For goodness, growing to a pleurisy,[6]
Dies in his own too much.[7] That° we would do   *that which*
We should do when we would, for this "would" changes
120 And hath abatements° and delays as many   *diminutions*
As there are tongues, are hands, are accidents,[8]
And then this "should" is like a spendthrift's sigh,[9]
That hurts by easing.[10] But to the quick of th'ulcer:[11]
Hamlet comes back. What would you undertake
125 To show yourself your father's son in deed
More than in words?
LAERTES.   To cut his throat i'th' church.
KING. No place, indeed, should murder sanctuarize.[12]
Revenge should have no bounds. But, good Laertes,

---

1 Love comes into being under certain circumstances (and is subject to change).
2 When other circumstances test that love.
3 Weakens, moderates.
4 The charred end of the candlewick that needs occasional trimming to improve the light and reduce smoke. (Love is like a candle in that it consumes itself in its own ardor.)
5 Nothing remains always at a constant level of goodness.
6 Excess, plethora (literally, an inflammation of the chest).
7 Of its own excess.
8 As there are tongues to dissuade, hands to prevent, and chance events to intervene.
9 Is like the regretful sigh of one who has squandered his wealth.
10 That causes pain even while it affords relief.
11 I.e., heart of the disease.
12 Shield from punishment, by offering the shelter of the church.

Will you do this:[1] keep close[2] within your chamber.
Hamlet returned shall know you are come home.   130
We'll put on those shall[3] praise your excellence
And set a double varnish on the fame[4]
The Frenchman gave you, bring you in fine[5] together,
And wager on your heads. He being remiss,°   *carelessly unwary*
Most generous,° and free from all contriving,   *noble-minded*   135
Will not peruse the foils,° so that with ease,   *fencing weapons*
Or with a little shuffling, you may choose
A sword unbated,[6] and in a pass of practice[7]
Requite him for your father.

LAERTES.   I will do't,
And for that purpose I'll anoint my sword.   140
I bought an unction[8] of a mountebank°   *quack, charlatan*
So mortal that, but dip a knife in it,
Where it draws blood no cataplasm[9] so rare,[10]
Collected from all simples that have virtue[11]
Under the moon,[12] can save the thing from death   145
That is but scratched withal.° I'll touch my point   *with it, by it*
With this contagion, that if I gall him slightly,[13]
It may be death.

KING.   Let's further think of this,
Weigh what convenience both of time and means
May fit us to our shape.[14] If this should fail,   150
And that our drift look through our bad performance,[15]

---

1 If you will do this.
2 Remain out of sight.
3 I will arrange for some people to.
4 And enhance the lustrous reputation.
5 Finally, in conclusion.
6 Not blunted by a button at its tip (as was customary when dueling for sport).
7 In a treacherous thrust instead of a conventional fencing move.
8 Ointment.
9 Medicinal plaster or poultice.
10 Excellent, distinctive; uncommon, seldom found.
11 Composed of herbs with potent healing properties.
12 I.e., anywhere on earth.
13 Graze, wound him even slightly.
14 To the roles we propose to act.
15 And if our intentions should be betrayed by inept performance.

'Twere better not essayed.° Therefore this project   *attempted*
Should have a back or second, that might hold
If this should blast in proof.[1] Soft,[2] let me see.
155 We'll make a solemn wager on your cunnings[3]—
I ha't![4]
When in your motion you are hot and dry—
As[5] make your bouts more violent to that end—
And that he calls for drink, I'll have prepared him
160 A chalice for the nonce,[6] whereon but sipping,
If he by chance escape your venomed stuck,°   *sword thrust*
Our purpose may hold there.

Enter Queen.
                              How [now], sweet queen?
QUEEN. One woe doth tread upon another's heel,
So fast they follow. Your sister's drowned, Laertes.
165 LAERTES. Drowned! Oh, where?
QUEEN. There is a willow grows aslant[7] a brook
That shows his hoar leaves[8] in the glassy stream.
Therewith fantastic garlands did she make
Of crowflowers,[9] nettles, daisies, and long purples,[10]
170 That liberal[11] shepherds give a grosser name,[12]
But our cold° maids do dead men's fingers call them.   *chaste*
There on the pendent° boughs her crownet weeds[13]   *overhanging*
Clamb'ring to hang, an envious sliver° broke,   *malicious branch*

---

1 If this plot should come to grief (literally, blow up in our faces) when put to the test.
2 Gently, wait a minute.
3 Your respective skills.
4 I have it, I have a plan.
5 I.e., and you should.
6 A drinking cup just for this occasion.
7 Obliquely across.
8 Its gray-white leaves reflected.
9 Wild buttercups, bluebells, or ragged robins.
10 Early purple wild orchids.
11 Free-speaking, hedonistic.
12 A more indecent name (such as "dogstones" or "cullions," in reference to the testicle-shaped tubers of some of these flowers).
13 Coronet-like garland of wild flowers.

When down her weedy trophies¹ and herself
Fell in the weeping brook. Her clothes spread wide,   175
And mermaid-like awhile they bore her up,
Which time² she chanted snatches of old lauds,°   *hymns*
As one incapable of³ her own distress,
Or like a creature native and endued
Unto that element.⁴ But long it could not be   180
Till that° her garments, heavy with their drink,   *until*
Pulled the poor wretch⁵ from her melodious lay°   *song*
To muddy death.

LAERTES.   Alas, then she is drowned.

QUEEN. Drowned, drowned.

LAERTES. Too much of water hast thou, poor Ophelia,   185
And therefore I forbid my tears. But yet
It is our trick; nature her custom holds,⁶
Let shame say what it will. [*He weeps.*] When these are gone,
The woman will be out.⁷ Adieu, my lord.
I have a speech of fire that fain° would blaze,   *willingly, eagerly*   190
But that this folly douts⁸ it.

                                                    Exit.

KING.   Let's follow, Gertrude.
How much I had to do to calm his rage!
Now fear I this will give it start again;
Therefore let's follow.

                                            Exeunt.

---

1   Her garland of wild flowers.
2   During which time.
3   Lacking the ability to comprehend or do anything about.
4   Naturally adapted to a watery existence.
5   (Here, as often, a term of endearment and pity.)
6   Weeping is the natural and characteristic way for us humans to express grief;
nature holds to her customary course.
7   When my tears are all shed, this womanly weakness in me will have run its
course.
8   My weeping douses, extinguishes.

[5.1 A CHURCHYARD]

Enter two Clowns° [*with tools for digging*].   *rustics*

CLOWN. Is she to be buried in Christian burial,[1] that willfully seeks
her own salvation?[2]

OTHER. I tell thee she is, and therefore make her grave straight.[3]
The crowner hath sat on her, and finds it Christian burial.[4]

5   CLOWN. How can that be, unless she drowned herself in her own
defense?[5]

OTHER. Why, 'tis found so.[6]

CLOWN. It must be *se offendendo*,[7] it cannot be else, for here lies the
point: if I drown myself wittingly, it argues an act, and an act

10   hath three branches: it is to act, to do, and to perform. Argal,[8]
she drowned herself wittingly.

OTHER. Nay, but hear you, Goodman Delver.[9]

CLOWN. Give me leave. Here lies the water; good. Here stands the
man; good. If the man go to this water and drown himself, it is,

15   will he, nill he,[10] he goes. Mark you that. But if the water come
to him and drown him, he drowns not himself. Argal, he that is
not guilty of his own death shortens not his own life.

OTHER. But is this law?

CLOWN. Ay, marry, is't, crowner's quest[11] law.

---

1   Burial in consecrated ground—something that the Church would deny to any
who had committed mortal sin, such as suicide.
2   Seemingly a blunder for "damnation," though possibly suggesting that Ophelia
was seeking a shortcut to heaven.
3   Right away. (And with wordplay on "not crooked" and on strait, "narrow.")
4   The coroner, the official charged with conducting an inquest into cases of
accidental or violent death, has done so in this case, and has judged the deceased
worthy of burial in sanctified ground.
5   (Though self-defense could be a legitimate defense against a charge of murder,
it is a ludicrous thought for suicide to be committed in self-defense.)
6   Determined to be thus in the coroner's verdict.
7   Presumably an attempt at *se defendendo*, killing in self-defense.
8   Ergo, therefore.
9   Master Digger; worthy digger.
10   Willy-nilly, whether he is willing or not.
11   Coroner's inquest.

OTHER. Will you ha' the truth on't?[1] If this had not been a gentle- 20
woman, she should have been buried out o' Christian burial.[2]

CLOWN. Why, there thou say'st,[3] and the more pity that great folk
should have countenance[4] in this world to drown or hang themselves more than their even-Christian.[5] Come, my spade. There is
no ancient[6] gentlemen but gardeners, ditchers, and gravemakers. 25
They hold up[7] Adam's profession.

OTHER. Was he a gentleman?

CLOWN. 'A was the first that ever bore arms.[8]

OTHER. Why, he had none.

CLOWN. What, art a heathen? How dost thou understand the 30
Scripture? The Scripture says Adam digged.[9] Could he dig without arms? I'll put another question to thee. If thou answerest me
not to the purpose, confess thyself[10]—

OTHER. Go to.[11]

CLOWN. What is he that builds stronger than either the mason,[12] 35
the shipwright, or the carpenter?

OTHER. The gallows-maker, for that frame[13] outlives a thousand
tenants.

CLOWN. I like thy wit well, in good faith, the gallows does well. But
how does it well? It does well[14] to those that do ill. Now, thou 40

---

1 Of it.
2 Outside of, not in, the graveyard reserved for those who have died good
Christians.
3 I.e., you certainly spoke the truth that time.
4 Privilege, authority.
5 Fellow Christians.
6 Venerable, going back to ancient times.
7 Uphold, practice.
8 (1) Was entitled to display the coat of arms of a gentleman; (2) had arms on his
body; (3) wielded a spade.
9 See Appendix B, pp. 272–73.
10 I.e., prepare yourself spiritually for death. (Suggesting too the proverbial
phrase, "Confess [thyself] and be hanged," Dent C587. The dash suggests that the
speaker is here interrupted by his comrade's impatient interruption, "Go to.")
11 An expression of impatience.
12 Stonemason.
13 Since that frame, the gallows (used for hanging criminals).
14 (1) It provides a good answer; (2) the gallows serves well as an instrument of
execution.

dost ill to say the gallows is built stronger than the church. Argal, the gallows may do well to thee.[1] To't again, come.

OTHER. "Who builds stronger than a mason, a shipwright, or a carpenter?"

45 CLOWN. Ay, tell me that, and unyoke.[2]

OTHER. Marry, now I can tell.

CLOWN. To't.

OTHER. Mass, I cannot tell.

Enter Hamlet and Horatio afar off.

CLOWN. Cudgel thy brains no more about it, for your dull ass[3] will
50 not mend[4] his pace with beating; and when you are asked this question next, say "a grave-maker." The houses that he makes lasts till doomsday. Go get thee to Johan.[5] Fetch me a stoup[6] of liquor.

[*Exit Second Clown.*]

[*The First Clown digs.*]

(*Sings*) "In youth when I did love, did love,
55   Methought it was very sweet
To contract—oh—the time for—a—my behove,[7]
Oh, methought there—a—was nothing—a—meet."[8]

HAMLET. Has this fellow no feeling of his business, that 'a sings at grave-making?

60 HORATIO. Custom hath made it in him a property of easiness.[9]

HAMLET. 'Tis e'en so.[10] The hand of little employment hath the daintier sense.[11]

CLOWN. (*Clown sings*) "But age with his stealing steps

---

1   May serve your turn when it comes time for you to be hanged.
2   I.e., unharness your wit, like a tired team of plow animals; put an end to your mental efforts.
3   Any ordinary plodding ass. (Not implying ownership by the gravedigger's assistant; the idea is general. Varying the proverbial phrase, "A dull ass must have a sharp spur," Dent A 348.1.)
4   Improve.
5   The name, apparently, of a nearby tavern-keeper.
6   Flagon, tankard.
7   To shorten the time for my own benefit. (Perhaps he means "to pass the time." The dashes here may represent the Clown's grunting as he digs.)
8   Suitable, more appropriate.
9   A thing he can do easily, without distress.
10 Exactly.
11 One who seldom does such things is apt to be more squeamish.

Hath clawed me in his clutch,
And hath shipped me intil the land,[1]   65
    As if I had never been such."[2] [*The Clown throws up a skull.*]

HAMLET. That skull had a tongue in it and could sing once. How
the knave jowls[3] it to the ground, as if 'twere Cain's jawbone,[4]
that did the first murder! This might be the pate of a politician,[5]
which this ass now o'er-offices,[6] one that would circumvent God,   70
might it not?

HORATIO. It might, my lord.

HAMLET. Or of a courtier, which could say, "Good morrow, sweet
lord, how dost thou, good lord?" This might be my Lord Such-a-
one, that praised my Lord Such-a-one's horse when 'a meant to   75
beg it,[7] might it not?

HORATIO. Ay, my lord.

HAMLET. Why, e'en so. And now my Lady Worm's,[8] chapless,[9] and
knocked about the mazard[10] with a sexton's spade. Here's fine
revolution,[11] an[12] we had the trick to see't. Did these bones cost 80
no more the breeding but to play at loggets with 'em?[13] Mine ache
to think on't.

CLOWN. (*Sings*) "A pickax and a spade, a spade,
    For and[14] a shrouding sheet;
Oh, a pit of clay for to be made   85
    For such a guest is meet." [*He throws up another skull.*]

---

1   I.e., sent me on my way toward death.
2   As if I had never lived.
3   Dashes, hurls.
4   See Appendix B, p. 273.
5   The skull of a scheming manipulator intent on gaining political advantage.
6   Puts in his place, lords it over him (since the gravedigger now has the upper
hand).
7   I.e., who praised that lord's horse with the intent of suggesting that the horse
be presented to the praiser as a gift.
8   I.e., a skull belonging to Lady Worm; or perhaps (as Thompson and Taylor suggest) the skull of a lady who is now food for worms.
9   Lacking the lower jaw.
10 Literally a drinking vessel, here applied to the head.
11 Reversal of destiny, by the turning of Fortune's wheel.
12 If.
13 Was so little care taken in bringing up the owner of these bones that we can
now play a game like skittles or horse-shoes with the bones, throwing them in
sport at a stake to see who comes closest?
14 And also.

HAMLET. There's another. Why might not that be the skull of a
lawyer? Where be his quiddities now, his quillets,[1] his cases, his
tenures,[2] and his tricks? Why does he suffer this rude[3] knave now
90   to knock him about the sconce[4] with a dirty shovel, and will not
tell him of his action of battery?[5] H'm! This fellow might be in's
time a great buyer of land, with his statutes, his recognizances,
his fines, his double vouchers, his recoveries.[6] Is this the fine[7]
of his fines, and the recovery of his recoveries, to have his fine
95   pate full of fine dirt?[8] Will his vouchers vouch him no more of
his purchases, and double ones too, than the length and breadth
of a pair of indentures?[9] The very conveyances of his lands[10] will
hardly lie in this box,[11] and must th'inheritor[12] himself have no
more, ha?
100   HORATIO. Not a jot more, my lord.

HAMLET. Is not parchment made of sheepskins?

HORATIO. Ay, my lord, and of calves' skins too.

HAMLET. They are sheep and calves which seek out assurance in
that.[13] I will speak to this fellow.—Whose grave's this, sirrah?
105   CLOWN. Mine, sir. [Sings]
"Oh, a pit of clay for to be made
For such a guest is meet."

HAMLET. I think it be thine indeed, for thou liest in't.

---

1   His subtleties and legal niceties.
2   Property titles.
3   Foolish, ignorant.
4   Head.
5   Legal action charging physical assault.
6   His securities acknowledging obligation of a debt, his bonds undertaken to
repay debts, his procedures for converting entailed estates into "fee simple" or
freehold, his vouchers signed by two signatories guaranteeing the validity of titles
to land, (and) his suits to obtain possession of land.
7   End.
8   To have the skull of his once elegant head filled with minutely sifted dirt? (With
multiple puns on "fine" and "fines.")
9   Will his vouchers, no matter how carefully duplicated, guarantee him no more
land than is needed to bury him in, being no bigger than the deed of conveyance?
10 Legal documents pertaining to the purchases of his lands.
11 (1) In this coffin; (2) in this deed box.
12 The purchaser, owner.
13 Any persons who place their trust in such legal documents are simpletons and
fools.

CLOWN. You lie out on't, sir, and therefore 'tis not yours. For my
part, I do not lie in't, and yet it is mine. 110

HAMLET. Thou dost lie in't, to be in't and say 'tis thine. 'Tis for the
dead, not for the quick;[1] therefore thou liest.

CLOWN. 'Tis a quick[2] lie, sir; 'twill away again from me to you.

HAMLET. What man dost thou dig it for?

CLOWN. For no man, sir. 115

HAMLET. What woman, then?

CLOWN. For none, neither.

HAMLET. Who is to be buried in't?

CLOWN. One that was a woman, sir, but, rest her soul, she's dead.

HAMLET. [To Horatio] How absolute[3] the knave is! We must speak 120
by the card,[4] or equivocation[5] will undo us. By the Lord, Horatio,
these three years I have taken note of it, the age is grown so picked
that the toe of the peasant comes so near the heel of the courtier
he galls his kibe.[6]—How long hast thou been grave-maker?

CLOWN. Of all the days i'th' year, I came to't that day that our last 125
King Hamlet overcame Fortinbras.

HAMLET. How long is that since?

CLOWN. Cannot you tell that? Every fool can tell that. It was the
very day that young Hamlet was born—he that is mad and sent
into England. 130

HAMLET. Ay, marry, why was he sent into England?

CLOWN. Why, because 'a was mad. 'A shall recover his wits there, or
if 'a do not, 'tis no great matter there.

HAMLET. Why?

CLOWN. 'Twill not be seen in him there. There the men are as mad 135
as he.

HAMLET. How came he mad?

CLOWN. Very strangely, they say.

HAMLET. How strangely?

---

1 The living.
2 Nimble (punning on "quick" in the previous speech).
3 Precise.
4 I.e., precisely.
5 Quibbling.
6 The age is grown so contentiously hair-splitting that the peasant nearly treads
on the heels of the courtier, chafing his sore heel.

140 CLOWN. Faith, e'en with losing his wits.

HAMLET. Upon what ground?[1]

CLOWN. Why, here in Denmark. I have been sexton[2] here, man and boy, thirty years.

HAMLET. How long will a man lie i'th' earth ere he rot?

145 CLOWN. I'faith, if 'a be not rotten before 'a die—as we have many pocky corses[3] nowadays that will scarce hold the laying in[4]—'a will last you[5] some eight year, or nine year. A tanner will last you nine year.

HAMLET. Why he more than another?

150 CLOWN. Why, sir, his hide is so tanned with his trade that 'a will keep out water a great while; and your water is a sore[6] decayer of your whoreson[7] dead body. [*He picks up a skull.*] Here's a skull now: this skull hath lain you i'th' earth three-and-twenty years.

HAMLET. Whose was it?

155 CLOWN. A whoreson mad fellow's it was. Whose do you think it was?

HAMLET. Nay, I know not.

CLOWN. A pestilence on him for a mad rogue! 'A poured a flagon of Rhenish[8] on my head once. This same skull, sir, was Yorick's skull, the King's jester.

160 HAMLET. This?

CLOWN. E'en that.

HAMLET. Let me see. [*He takes the skull.*] Alas, poor Yorick! I knew him, Horatio, a fellow of infinite jest, of most excellent fancy. He hath borne me on his back a thousand times, and now how 165 abhorred in my imagination it is! My gorge rises[9] at it. Here hung those lips that I have kissed I know not how oft.—Where be your gibes[10] now? Your gambols,[11] your songs, your flashes of

---

1 Cause, reason. (But the Gravedigger answers in the sense of "land," "country.")
2 A minor official who tends to church property, ringing bells, digging graves, etc.
3 Diseased, rotten corpses; literally, riddled with the pox or syphilis.
4 Hold together long enough to be buried.
5 He (or "it") will last. (The "you" is colloquial here and in lines 151–52: "your water," "your whoreson dead body.")
6 Keen, veritable.
7 Son-of-a-bitch. (A colloquial expression of contempt.)
8 Rhenish wine.
9 I feel nauseated.
10 Taunts.
11 Skipping or leaping about in play and in playful wit.

merriment that were wont to set the table on a roar? Not one[1]
now to mock your own grinning? Quite chopfall'n?[2] Now get
you to my lady's chamber and tell her, let her paint an inch thick, 170
to this favor[3] she must come. Make her laugh at that. Prithee,
Horatio, tell me one thing.

HORATIO. What's that, my lord?

HAMLET. Dost thou think Alexander[4] looked o'this fashion i'th'
earth?   175

HORATIO. E'en so.

HAMLET. And smelt so? Pah! [*He throws the skull down.*]

HORATIO. E'en so, my lord.

HAMLET. To what base uses we may return, Horatio! Why may
not imagination trace the noble dust of Alexander till 'a find it   180
stopping a bunghole?[5]

HORATIO. 'Twere to consider too curiously[6] to consider so.

HAMLET. No, faith, not a jot. But to follow him thither with mod-
esty enough, and likelihood[7] to lead it, as thus: Alexander died,
Alexander was buried, Alexander returneth into dust,[8] the dust   185
is earth, of earth we make loam,[9] and why of that loam whereto
he was converted might they not stop a beer-barrel?
Imperial Caesar,[10] dead and turned to clay,
Might stop a hole to keep the wind away.
Oh, that that earth[11] which kept the world in awe   190
Should patch a wall t'expel the winter's flaw![12]

---

1 (1) No one; or, (2) not one of your gibes or gambols.
2 (1) Lacking the lower jaw; (2) downcast, dejected.
3 Aspect, appearance.
4 Alexander the Great, the Macedonian king who conquered much of the known
world in the fourth century BCE. See Appendix A, p. 248.
5 Hole for filling or emptying a cask or barrel.
6 Consider too minutely, over-subtly.
7 With moderation and plausibility.
8 See Appendix B, p. 273.
9 A mixture of moistened sandy clay and straw used to make bricks, plaster, or
(in this case) bungs for beer barrels.
10 The term can apply to Julius Caesar, or to the Roman emperors starting with
Augustus Caesar who adopted the title for themselves, or more generally to
Alexander or any powerful emperor.
11 I.e., Caesar's body.
12 Winter's squalls and destructive force (with "flaw" as a spelling variant of "flow"
chosen to rhyme with "awe" in the previous line).

Enter King, Queen, Laertes, and a coffin [containing the corpse of Ophelia,
in funeral procession, with the "Doctor" or Priest], with Lords attendant.
But soft, but soft; aside! Here comes the King,
The Queen, the courtiers. Who is that they follow?
And with such maimèd rites?[1] This doth betoken
195   The corpse they follow did with desp'rate hand
Fordo it° own life. 'Twas of some estate.[2]   destroy its
Couch we[3] awhile and mark.
[*Hamlet and Horatio conceal themselves. Ophelia's body is taken to the*
grave.]
LAERTES. What ceremony else?
HAMLET. [*Aside to Horatio*] That is Laertes, a very noble youth. Mark.
200   LAERTES. What ceremony else?
PRIEST. Her obsequies° have been as far enlarged   funeral rites
As we have warrantise. Her death was doubtful,[4]
And, but that great command o'ersways the order,[5]
She should in ground unsanctified have lodged
205   Till the last trumpet. For° charitable prayers,   in place of
Shards, flints, and pebbles should be thrown on her;
Yet here she is allowed her virgin crants,[6]
Her maiden strewments,[7] and the bringing home
Of bell and burial.[8]
LAERTES. Must there no more be done?
210   PRIEST.   No more be done.
We should profane the service of the dead
To sing sage requiem and such rest[9] to her
As to peace-parted souls.[10]

---

1   Truncated ceremonies.
2   Of considerable social rank.
3   Let's conceal ourselves, lie low.
4   I.e., suspected of being a suicide.
5   Were it not that royal command overrules the customary practice (as prescribed too by our monastic order) of denying sacred burial to suicides.
6   Garlands betokening maidenhood.
7   Flowers strewn on a coffin.
8   Laying the body to rest, to the tolling of the church bell and the recitation of
the burial ceremony.
9   A solemn mass for the dead and other rituals beseeching heaven to grant rest
to those who have died at peace with God.
10 As to the souls of those who have died at peace with God.

LAERTES.   Lay her i'th' earth,
And from her fair and unpolluted flesh
May violets spring! I tell thee, churlish priest,   215
A minist'ring angel shall my sister be
When thou liest howling.°   *i.e., in hell*
HAMLET. [*To Horatio*]   What, the fair Ophelia!
QUEEN. [*Scattering flowers*] Sweets to the sweet! Farewell.
I hoped thou shouldst have been my Hamlet's wife.
I thought thy bride-bed to have decked, sweet maid,   220
And not t'have strewed thy grave.
LAERTES.   Oh, treble woe
Fall ten times treble on that cursèd head
Whose wicked deed thy most ingenious sense
Deprived thee of!¹—Hold off the earth awhile,
Till I have caught her once more in mine arms.   225
[*He*] *leaps in the grave.*
Now pile your dust upon the quick and dead,²
Till of this flat° a mountain you have made   *level place*
T'o'ertop old Pelion, or the skyish head
Of blue Olympus.³
HAMLET. [*Coming forward*] What is he whose grief
Bears such an emphasis,⁴ whose phrase of sorrow   230
Conjures the wand'ring stars,⁵ and makes them stand⁶
Like wonder-wounded° hearers? This is I,   *struck with amazement*
Hamlet the Dane.⁷
LAERTES. [*Grappling with Hamlet*] The devil take thy soul!
HAMLET. Thou pray'st not well.   235
I prithee take thy fingers from my throat,

---

1 Deprived you of your fine, quick intelligence.
2 The living and the dead. See Appendix B, p. 273.
3 I.e., to tower above Greece's highest mountains, including Mount Pelion and
Mount Olympus, the reputed home of the Olympian gods. In Greek mythological
legends, the rebellious Giants attempted to scale Mount Olympus by piling still
another mountain, Ossa (mentioned in line 261, below), on top of Pelion. See
Appendix A, p. 259.
4 Is conveyed so forcefully.
5 Whose sorrowful speech invokes the planets to come to his aid.
6 Remain stationary in their heavenly paths.
7 A customary form of title for the King of Denmark, as at 1.1.17, 1.2.44, etc.

For, though I am not splenative and rash,°   *hot-tempered*
Yet have I something in me dangerous,
Which let thy wiseness fear. Away thy hand!

240 KING. Pluck them asunder.

QUEEN. Hamlet, Hamlet!

ALL. Gentlemen!

HORATIO. Good my lord, be quiet.

[*Hamlet and Laertes are parted.*]

HAMLET. Why, I will fight with him upon this theme

245   Until my eyelids will no longer wag.[1]

QUEEN. Oh, my son, what theme?

HAMLET. I loved Ophelia. Forty thousand brothers
    Could not with all their quantity of love
    Make up my sum.—What wilt thou do for her?

250 KING. Oh, he is mad, Laertes.

QUEEN. For love of God, forbear him.°   *let Hamlet alone*

HAMLET. 'Swounds, show me what thou'lt do.
    Woo't weep? Woo't fight? Woo't fast? Woo't tear thyself?
    Woo't drink up eisil?° Eat a crocodile?   *will you drink vinegar*

255   I'll do't. Dost thou come here to whine?
    To outface me with leaping in her grave?
    Be buried quick° with her, and so will I.   *alive*
    And if thou prate of mountains, let them throw
    Millions of acres on us, till our ground,

260   Singeing his pate against the burning zone,
    Make Ossa like a wart.[2] Nay, an thou'lt mouth,°   *if you want to rant*
    I'll rant as well as thou.

QUEEN.   This is mere° madness,   *utter*
    And thus awhile the fit will work on him;
    Anon, as patient as the female dove

265   When that her golden couplets are disclosed,[3]
    His silence will sit drooping.

HAMLET. [*To Laertes*]   Hear you, sir,

---

1   Move, flutter (as a sign that the person is still living).

2   Until the vast acres of land that have been thrown on top of us, scorching the very top of this huge mound by its nearness to the burning sun, make Mount Ossa seem comparatively as small as a wart. See Appendix A, p. 259.

3   When her baby pigeons clad in golden-colored down are hatched.

What is the reason that you use me thus?
I loved you ever. But it is no matter.
Let Hercules himself do what he may,
The cat will mew, and dog will have his day.[1]   270

Exit Hamlet.

KING. I pray you, good Horatio, wait upon° him.   *attend*

And Horatio [exits too].

[*Aside to Laertes*] Strengthen your patience in[2] our last night's
     speech;
We'll put the matter to the present push.°—   *immediate test*
Good Gertrude, set some watch over your son.—
This grave shall have a living monument.[3]   275
An hour of quiet shortly shall we see;
Till then, in patience our proceeding be.

Exeunt.

[5.2 THE CASTLE]

Enter Hamlet and Horatio.

HAMLET. So much for this, sir. Now let me see, the other.[4]
     You do remember all the circumstance?
HORATIO. Remember it, my lord![5]
HAMLET. Sir, in my heart there was a kind of fighting
     That would not let me sleep. Methought[6] I lay   5
     Worse than the mutines in the bilboes.[7] Rashly,[8]
     And praised be rashness for it: let us know,°   *acknowledge*

---

1 I.e., despite all that Hercules himself (or Laertes) could do, my day will come.
On Hercules, see Appendix A, pp. 253–54.
2 I.e., by recalling.
3 I.e., a lasting memorial—and perhaps with the suggestion, for Laertes's ears
only, that this memorial will be accomplished by the death of the now-living
Hamlet.
4 Hamlet and Horatio enter in mid-conversation. Hamlet's "this" may refer to
what he has told Horatio about his abortive voyage to England, "the other" to
what Hamlet is about to add to that account.
5 I.e., how could I ever forget such a thing?
6 It seemed to me that.
7 Mutineers in shackles.
8 On impulse. (The adverb looks forward to lines 12 ff.)

Our indiscretion[1] sometime serves us well

When our deep[2] plots do pall,[3] and that should learn° us   *teach*

10   There's a divinity that shapes our ends,

Rough-hew° them how we will.   *shape roughly*

HORATIO.   That is most certain.

HAMLET. Up from my cabin,

My sea-gown scarfed[4] about me, in the dark

Groped I to find out them,[5] had my desire,

15   Fingered° their packet, and in fine[6] withdrew   *pilfered, lifted*

To mine own room again, making so bold,

My fears forgetting manners, to unseal

Their grand commission; where I found, Horatio—

Oh, royal knavery!—an exact command,

20   Larded° with many several° sorts of reasons   *garnished / various*

Importing[7] Denmark's health, and England's too,

With, ho! such bugs and goblins in my life,[8]

That on the supervise, no leisure bated,[9]

No, not to stay the grinding[10] of the ax,

My head should be struck off.

25 HORATIO.   Is't possible?

HAMLET. [*Showing a document*] Here's the commission. Read it at
     more leisure.

But wilt thou hear me how I did proceed?

HORATIO. I beseech you.

HAMLET. Being thus benetted round with villainies—

30   Ere I could make a prologue to my brains,

---

1   An action that is not premeditated. (Hamlet does not mean an action that is indiscreet or reckless.)

2   Secret, obscure.

3   Lose strength, falter, fade away.

4   My seaman's coat loosely wrapped, as with a scarf.

5   Find out Rosencrantz and Guildenstern, uncover their villainy.

6   Finally, in conclusion.

7   Concerning, relating to.

8   I.e., with all sorts of imagined fanciful terrors if I were allowed to remain alive. ("Bugs" are bugbears, hobgoblins.)

9   That on the reading of this commission, no delay being permitted.

10   Not to await the sharpening.

They had begun the play[1]—I sat me down,
Devised a new commission, wrote it fair.[2]
I once did hold° it, as our statists° do,   *regard / statesmen*
A baseness[3] to write fair, and labored much
How to forget that learning, but, sir, now   35
It did me yeoman's service.[4] Wilt thou know
Th'effect of what I wrote?

HORATIO.   Ay, good my lord.

HAMLET. An earnest conjuration° from the King,   *entreaty*
As England was his faithful tributary,[5]
As love between them like the palm[6] should flourish,   40
As peace should still° her wheaten garland[7] wear   *always*
And stand a comma[8] 'tween their amities,
And many suchlike "as"es of great charge,[9]
That on the view and knowing° of these contents,   *understanding*
Without debatement further more or less,[10]   45
He should the bearers put to sudden death,
Not shriving time[11] allowed.

HORATIO.   How was this sealed?

HAMLET. Why, even in that was heaven ordinant.°   *directing, ordaining*
I had my father's signet° in my purse,   *small seal*
Which was the model° of that Danish seal;   *duplicate, likeness* 50

---

1   Before I could consciously formulate a scheme for proceeding further, my brain had started working on a plan all by itself.
2   In the formal handwriting used in official documents.
3   As something beneath my dignity.
4   I.e., it stood me in good stead, by providing me with secretarial handwriting skills.
5   Whereas England was obligated to pay tribute to Denmark.
6   The palm tree, symbol of amity. Cf. Psalm 92:12: "The righteous shall flourish like the palm tree."
7   A symbol of peace and fruitful plenty.
8   I.e., and stand as a link uniting two entities that, though separate, are closely integrated.
9   And many similarly weighty clauses, each introduced (as in formal legal documents or proclamations) by "As" or "Whereas." (With wordplay on "'as'es" and "asses.")
10 Without any further discussion. (Hamlet continues to speak mockingly in legal jargon.)
11 With no time for confession and absolution.

Folded the writ up in the form of th'other,[1]
Subscribed[2] it, gave't th'impression,[3] placed it safely,
The changeling[4] never known. Now the next day
Was our sea fight, and what to this was sequent°   *what followed this*
55   Thou know'st already.
HORATIO. So Guildenstern and Rosencrantz go to't.
HAMLET. Why, man, they did make love to this employment.
They are not near my conscience. Their defeat
Does by their own insinuation grow.[5]
60   'Tis dangerous when the baser nature comes
Between the pass and fell incensèd points
Of mighty opposites.[6]
HORATIO.   Why, what a King is this!
HAMLET. Does it not, think thee, stand me now upon[7]—
He that hath killed my King and whored my mother,
65   Popped in between th'election and my hopes,[8]
Thrown out his angle[9] for my proper life,°   *my very life*
And with such coz'nage°—is't not perfect conscience   *duplicity*
To quit him with this arm?[10] And is't not to be damned
To let this canker of our nature come
70   In further evil?[11]
HORATIO. It must be shortly known to him from England
What is the issue° of the business there.   *the outcome*
HAMLET. It will be short.
The interim's mine, and a man's life's no more

---

1 I folded the written document just as the original had been folded.
2 Signed (forging the King's name).
3 Sealed it by stamping the official seal into the wax.
4 I.e., the substituted document. (Literally, an elfish child substituted by fairies for a human child they steal.)
5 Their destruction follows as a consequence of their own intrusive intervention, ingratiating themselves with the King by doing his dirty business.
6 I.e., it's dangerous when persons of lower social station and capability come between the deadly and enraged weapon-thrusts of two such mighty opponents as the King and Hamlet.
7 Is it not incumbent on me now.
8 I.e., between me and my hopeful expectation of being "elected" to the Danish throne after the death of my father.
9 Fishing hook and line.
10 To repay him with my strong right arm.
11 To allow this ulcerous sore that afflicts human nature to commit further evil?

Than to say one.¹ But I am very sorry, good Horatio,   75
That to Laertes I forgot myself,
For by the image of my cause I see
The portraiture of his. I'll court his favors.²
But sure the bravery° of his grief did put me   *extravagance*
Into a tow'ring passion.

HORATIO.   Peace, who comes here?   80

Enter young Osric, a courtier.

OSRIC. Your lordship is right welcome back to Denmark.

HAMLET. I humbly thank you, sir. [*Aside to Horatio*] Dost know this
water-fly?³

HORATIO. [*Aside to Hamlet*] No, my good lord.

HAMLET. [*Aside to Horatio*] Thy state is the more gracious,⁴ for 'tis a   85
vice to know him. He hath much land, and fertile. Let a beast be
lord of beasts, and his crib shall stand at the King's mess.⁵ 'Tis a
chuff,⁶ but, as I say, spacious in the possession of dirt.⁷

OSRIC. Sweet lord, if your lordship were at leisure,⁸ I should impart
a thing to you from his majesty.   90

HAMLET. I will receive it, sir, with all diligence of spirit. Put your
bonnet⁹ to his¹⁰ right use. 'Tis for the head.

OSRIC. I thank your lordship, it is very hot.

HAMLET. No, believe me, 'tis very cold. The wind is northerly.

OSRIC. It is indifferent¹¹ cold, my lord, indeed.   95

---

1   A man's life lasts no longer than it takes to count to one.
2   Try to ingratiate myself with Laertes.
3   I.e., a giddy, superficial person.
4   Blessed.
5   Provided a man, no matter how beastlike, is rich in livestock and possessions
(as Osric appears to be), he may eat at the King's meal-table. (A crib is a manger or
trough for feeding livestock.)
6   (1) Boor, churl; (2) chatterer, jackdaw.
7   He's a large landowner.
8   I.e., if you have the time, if I'm not interrupting. ("Your lordship" is a polite
form of address, as at line 81.)
9   Hat.
10   Its.
11   Somewhat, rather.

HAMLET. But yet methinks it is very sultry and hot for my complexion.[1]

OSRIC. Exceedingly, my lord, it is very sultry, as 'twere—I cannot tell how. But, my lord, his majesty bade me signify to you that 'a has laid a great wager on your head. Sir, this is the matter—

HAMLET. [*Reminding Osric once more about his hat*] I beseech you, remember.

OSRIC. Nay, good my lord, for my ease, in good faith.[2] Sir, here is newly come to court Laertes—believe me, an absolute[3] gentlemen, full of most excellent differences,[4] of very soft society[5] and great showing.[6] Indeed, to speak feelingly[7] of him, he is the card or calendar of gentry,[8] for you shall find in him the continent of what part a gentleman would see.[9]

HAMLET. Sir, his definement suffers no perdition in you, though I know to divide him inventorially would dazzle th'arithmetic of memory, and yet but yaw neither, in respect of his quick sail.[10] But in the verity of extolment, I take him to be a soul of great article, and his infusion of such dearth and rareness as, to make true diction of him, his semblable is his mirror, and who else would trace him, his umbrage, nothing more.[11]

OSRIC. Your lordship speaks most infallibly of him.

---

1 For a person of my constitution.
2 A polite declining of Hamlet's adjuration to Osric that he put on his hat.
3 Perfect, complete.
4 Superior and distinctive qualities.
5 Agreeable manners.
6 Distinguished appearance.
7 With just perception, appreciatively.
8 He is the model or paradigm (literally, the map or directory) of good breeding.
9 You'll find him to be one who contains in himself all the attributes a gentleman might wish for.
10 Your characterizing of Laertes's qualities in no way diminishes his excellence, though I know that to enumerate all his graces would stupify one's powers of reckoning, and even so could do no more than veer unsteadily off-course (yaw) in a vain attempt to track the brilliance of his accomplishments. (Hamlet is satirizing Osric's overly fancy mode of speech.)
11 But to speak truthful praise of him, I take him to be a person of remarkable substance, one whose essence is of such rarity and excellence that, to speak truly of him, no one can be compared with him other than his own likeness; anyone else attempting to emulate him can only hope to attain the shadow of his substance, not the real thing. (Hamlet is parodying Osric's pomposity.)

HAMLET. The concernancy,[1] sir? Why do we wrap the gentleman in
our more rawer breath?[2]

OSRIC. Sir?

HORATIO. [*To Hamlet*] Is't not possible to understand in another   120
tongue?[3] You will do't, sir, really.[4]

HAMLET. [*To Osric*] What imports the nomination[5] of this gentleman?

OSRIC. Of Laertes?

HORATIO. [*To Hamlet*] His purse is empty already; all's golden words   125
are spent.

HAMLET. [*To Osric*] Of him, sir.

OSRIC. I know you are not ignorant—

HAMLET. I would you did, sir. Yet in faith if you did, it would not
much approve me.[6] Well, sir?   130

OSRIC. Sir, you are not ignorant of what excellence Laertes is—

HAMLET. I dare not confess that, lest I should compare with him in
excellence. But to know a man well were to know himself.[7]

OSRIC. I mean, sir, for his weapon. But in the imputation laid on
him by them, in his meed he's unfellowed.[8] You are not ignorant   135
of what excellence Laertes is at his weapon.

HAMLET. What's his weapon?

---

1 What is the import, the relevance, of this?

2 I.e., why do we undertake to describe Laertes in our inelegant speech, more
inelegant indeed than can hope to succeed in praising him worthily enough?

3 I.e., (speaking aside to Hamlet) are we really to understand that Osric cannot
understand when someone speaks to him in the stilted language that he himself
uses? Or (if speaking to Osric), are you simply unable to understand and communicate in any other tongue than the overblown rhetoric you have used?

4 I.e., (to Hamlet) you will truly have your joke at Osric's expense; or (if to Osric),
you can speak plainly if you just try hard enough.

5 Naming, mention.

6 I.e., I wish you would admit me to be knowledgeable ("not ignorant") in these
matters, though, even if you did allow that, it would not be much of a commenda-
tion, coming from you.

7 I.e., I dare not claim to know that Laertes is an excellent young man lest I
seem to imply a comparable excellence in myself (since common wisdom holds
that it takes excellence to recognize excellence in others). Certainly, to know
another person well, one must know oneself.

8 I.e., I mean his excellence with his rapier, not his general excellence. But in the
reputation he enjoys among knowledgeable people for use of his weapon, in that
merit he is unrivaled.

OSRIC. Rapier and dagger.

HAMLET. That's two of his weapons—but well.[1]

140 OSRIC. The King, sir, hath wagered with him six Barbary horses,[2] against the which he has impawned,[3] as I take it, six French rapiers and poniards,[4] with their assigns,[5] as girdle,[6] hangers, or so.[7] Three of the carriages,[8] in faith, are very dear to fancy, very responsive to the hilts, most delicate carriages, and of very
145 liberal conceit.[9]

HAMLET. What call you the carriages?

HORATIO. [To Hamlet] I knew you must be edified by the margin ere you had done.[10]

OSRIC. The carriages, sir, are the hangers.

150 HAMLET. The phrase would be more germane to the matter if we could carry cannon by our sides; I would it might be "hangers" till then. But on. Six Barbary horses against six French swords, their assigns, and three liberal-conceited[11] carriages: that's the French bet against the Danish. Why is this "impawned," as you call it?

155 OSRIC. The King, sir, hath laid, sir, that in a dozen passes between yourself and him, he shall not exceed you three hits. He hath laid on't twelve for nine,[12] and it would come to immediate trial, if your lordship would vouchsafe the answer.[13]

---

1 But never mind that.
2 Arabian horses, originally from the Barbary region of northern Africa, especially (today) Morocco, Algeria, and Tunisia.
3 Laertes has staked, wagered.
4 Daggers.
5 Accessories.
6 Sword belt.
7 Strap on the girdle or sword belt from which the sword hung, and so on.
8 Another term for "hangers," straps (as Osric explains in line 149, below).
9 Are very appealing to the "fancy" or imagination, decoratively matched as they are with the hilts or the cases for the swords, finely wrought in workmanship, and elaborately designed.
10 I knew you'd need to have the matter explained to you more clearly, as if by an explanatory note (often printed in the margins of books), before you're finished asking about "carriages." (Said sotto voce to Hamlet.)
11 Elaborately designed. (Hamlet mockingly throws back at Osric the grandiose term the courtier has used at line 145 above.)
12 Seemingly, though the phrasing is difficult and may be corrupt, the King has "laid" or wagered that, in a dozen "passes" or bouts of fencing, the total number of hits scored by Laertes will not exceed Hamlet's total by three.
13 If you would be so good as to accept the challenge.

HAMLET. How if I answer no?[1]

OSRIC. I mean, my lord, the opposition of your person in trial. 160

HAMLET. Sir, I will walk here in the hall. If it please his majesty, it
is the breathing time of day[2] with me. Let[3] the foils be brought,
the gentleman willing, and the King hold his purpose, I will win
for him an I can; if not, I will gain nothing but my shame and
the odd hits. 165

OSRIC. Shall I re-deliver you e'en so?[4]

HAMLET. To this effect, sir, after what flourish your nature will.

OSRIC. I commend my duty[5] to your lordship.

HAMLET. Yours, yours.

[*Exit Osric.*]

'A does well to commend it himself; there are no tongues else 170
for's turn.[6]

HORATIO. This lapwing[7] runs away with the shell on his head.

HAMLET. 'A did comply with his dug[8] before 'a sucked it. Thus
has he, and many more of the same bevy that I know the drossy
age dotes on, only got the tune of the time and outward habit 175
of encounter, a kind of yeasty collection, which carries them
through and through the most fanned and winnowed opinions;
and do but blow them to their trial, the bubbles are out.[9]

---

1   By replying in pretended ignorance as though he has been asked for a simple
"yes" or "no" answer, Hamlet mischievously refuses to acknowledge that the
polite formula in which the challenge has been delivered to him requires that he
acquiesce.

2   Time for exercise.

3   I.e., if.

4   Shall I report your answer in this way?

5   I dedicate my service (a conventionally polite phrase of departure).

6   I.e., he needs to commend his own virtues; no one else will do it for him.

7   Plover, a wading bird known to flap its wings and scurry about in a wily fashion
calculated to draw intruders away from the nest. According to legend, when newly
hatched the lapwing was thought to run around with the egg-shell still on its head.

8   He bowed ceremoniously to his mother's or nurse's nipple.

9   Thus has he—and many more of the same sort that our frivolous age dotes
on—acquired the trendy manner of speech of the time and formulaic conversation
with courtiers of their own kind: a kind of frothy repertoire of current phrases
which enables such gallants to pass themselves off as persons of the most select
and well-sifted views; and yet do but test these creatures by merely blowing on
them, and their bubbles burst. ("Fanned and winnowed" means sifted and sepa-
rated out, like grain in the process of threshing.)

Enter a Lord.

LORD. My lord, his majesty commended him[1] to you by young Osric,
180   who brings back to him that you attend him in the hall. He sends
to know if your pleasure hold to play[2] with Laertes, or that you
will take longer time?[3]

HAMLET. I am constant to my purposes; they follow the King's
pleasure. If his fitness speaks, mine is ready;[4] now or whensoever,
185   provided I be so able as now.

LORD. The King and Queen and all are coming down.

HAMLET. In happy time.[5]

LORD. The Queen desires you to use some gentle entertainment to
Laertes before you fall to play.[6]

190 HAMLET. She well instructs me.

                                                          [Exit Lord.]

HORATIO. You will lose this wager, my lord.

HAMLET. I do not think so. Since he went into France, I have been
in continual practice; I shall win at the odds.[7] But thou wouldst
not think how ill all's here about my heart, but it is no matter.

195 HORATIO. Nay, good my lord—

HAMLET. It is but foolery, but it is such a kind of gaingiving[8] as
would perhaps trouble a woman.

HORATIO. If your mind dislike anything, obey it. I will forestall their
repair[9] hither and say you are not fit.

200 HAMLET. Not a whit, we defy augury.[10] There's a special providence[11]
in the fall of a sparrow.[12] If it be now, 'tis not to come; if it be
not to come, it will be now; if it be not now, yet it will come. The

---

1   Has sent his commendations, his greetings.
2   Fence.
3   Or if you would prefer to put this off.
4   If this suits his convenience, it suits me as well.
5   I.e., they come at an opportune time.
6   To greet Laertes courteously before you begin fencing.
7   The odds are in my favor.
8   Misgiving.
9   Their coming.
10 I.e., not at all, I defy superstition, or hunches. (Literally, divination from auspices or omens, such as the flight of birds.)
11 Providential direction overseeing even the smallest details of human history.
12 See Appendix B, p. 274.

readiness is all. Since no man has aught of what he leaves, what
is't to leave betimes?[1] Let be.[2]

Trumpets, drums, and officers with cushions. Enter King, Queen, and
Lords [including Laertes and Osric, and all the state], with other
Attendants with foils and gauntlets, a table, and flagons of wine on it.

KING. Come, Hamlet, come, and take this hand from me.

[*The King puts Laertes's hand into Hamlet's.*]

HAMLET. [*To Laertes*] Give me your pardon, sir. I've done you   205
    wrong,
But pardon't as you are a gentleman.
This presence° knows,   *royal assembly*
And you must needs have heard, how I am punished
With a sore distraction.[3] What I have done
That might your nature, honor, and exception[4]   210
Roughly awake, I hear proclaim was madness.
Was't Hamlet wronged Laertes? Never Hamlet.
If Hamlet from himself be ta'en away,
And when he's not himself does wrong Laertes,
Then Hamlet does it not; Hamlet denies it.   215
Who does it, then? His madness. If't be so,
Hamlet is of the faction° that is wronged;   *party*
His madness is poor Hamlet's enemy.
Sir, in this audience
Let my disclaiming from a purposed evil[5]   220
Free me so far in your most generous thoughts
That I have shot my arrow o'er the house
And hurt my brother.[6]

LAERTES.   I am satisfied in nature,[7]

---

1   Being in readiness is the crucially important thing, since no one can truly
be said to possess the worldly goods and physicality that must be left behind at
the moment of death. Why then should it matter if one must leave those things
"betimes," i.e., earlier rather than later?

2   Enough; say no more. Leave things as they are.

3   Afflicted by a serious mental disturbance.

4   Disapproval, dissatisfaction.

5   Let my denial of having had any evil intention.

6   I.e, I have hurt my comrade, my fellow gentleman. The notion that Hamlet is
thinking here of Laertes as brother-in-law because of Hamlet's love for Ophelia
seems unlikely; he has not alluded to her in this scene.

7   I.e., as to my personal feelings.

Whose motive[1] in this case should stir me most
225 To my revenge. But in my terms of honor
I stand aloof, and will° no reconcilement,   *desire, will allow*
Till by some elder masters of known honor
I have a voice and precedent of peace
To keep my name ungored.[2] But till that time
230 I do receive your offered love like love,
And will not wrong it.
HAMLET.   I do embrace it freely,
And will this brother's wager frankly play.—
Give us the foils. Come on.
LAERTES.   Come, one for me.
HAMLET. I'll be your foil,[3] Laertes. In mine ignorance[4]
235 Your skill shall like a star i'th' darkest night
Stick fiery off° indeed.   *stand out brilliantly*
LAERTES. You mock me, sir.
HAMLET. No, by this hand.
KING. Give them the foils, young Osric.
[*Foils are handed to Hamlet and Laertes.*]
                                        Cousin Hamlet,
You know the wager.
240 HAMLET.   Very well, my lord.
Your grace has laid the odds o'th' weaker side.[5]
KING. I do not fear it; I have seen you both.
But since he is bettered, we have therefore odds.[6]
LAERTES. This is too heavy. Let me see another.
[*He exchanges his foil for another.*]
245 HAMLET. This likes° me well. These foils have all a length?[7]   *pleases*

---

1   The promptings of which.
2   Until persons of high social standing, acting in accord with social precedent, determine that I can make a peaceful reconcialition without injuring my
reputation.
3   Hamlet puns on the term "foil." Literally, a foil is a thin metal background
used to set off and enhance the brilliance of a jewel. Hamlet modestly suggests
that he will make Laertes look skillful by comparison.
4   I.e., given my comparative inexperience as a fencer.
5   You have bet on the weaker side.
6   I.e., but since Laertes is the favored contestant, we have settled on odds.
7   Are these rapiers of equal length?

OSRIC. Ay, my good lord.

[*They*] *prepare to play.*

KING. Set me the stoups° of wine upon that table.   *flagons*
 If Hamlet give the first or second hit,
 Or quit in answer of the third exchange,¹
 Let all the battlements their ordnance fire.²   250
 The King shall drink to Hamlet's better breath,³
 And in the cup an union⁴ shall he throw
 Richer than that which four successive kings
 In Denmark's crown have worn. Give me the cups,
 And let the kettle to the trumpet speak,⁵   255
 The trumpet to the cannoneer without,⁶
 The cannons to the heavens, the heaven to earth,
 "Now the King drinks to Hamlet." Come, begin.

*Trumpets the while.*⁷
 And you, the judges, bear a wary eye.

HAMLET. Come on, sir.   260

LAERTES. Come, my lord.

They play. [*Hamlet scores a hit.*]

HAMLET. One.

LAERTES. No.

HAMLET. [*To Osric*] Judgment.

OSRIC. A hit, a very palpable hit.   265

LAERTES. Well, again.

KING. Stay.° Give me drink. Hamlet, this pearl is thine. *stop*

[*He drinks, and throws a pearl in Hamlet's cup.*]
 Here's to thy health.—Give him the cup.

Trumpets sound, and shot goes off.

---

1 Or counters Laertes's winning the first and second bout by winning on the third exchange.
2 Let the soldiers stationed on the battlements or parapets fire their cannon.
3 Better health and performance.
4 I.e., a pearl, which the King may intend to be dissolved in the wine. (The King calls it a pearl at line 267 below.) An onyx (the Q2 reading, corrected in F1) is literally a precious stone, a translucent chalcedony (a kind of quartz) in parallel layers of different colors.
5 And let the kettledrum answer the trumpeters.
6 Whereupon the trumpeters are to signal to soldiers outside to fire their cannon.
7 The trumpeters sound their trumpets (and the cannons are fired) while the King drinks.

HAMLET. I'll play this bout first. Set it by awhile.
270   Come. [*They fence.*] Another hit. What say you?
LAERTES. A touch, a touch, I do confess.
KING. [*To the Queen*] Our son shall win.

5.2.248–89:   FINAL SCENE: DUEL
                         (TLN 3727–80)

Dueling among gentlemen was governed by a system of punctilious
etiquette in the Renaissance, and indeed earlier as well. Dueling as a
sport would of course be treated as a matter of exercise and competitive recreation; but in the case of an insult to a person's honor, dueling could become deadly. An insult had to be answered by a challenge,
usually to a duel, and a challenge had to be accepted. Touchstone, in
As You Like It, satirizes seven stages of quarreling, from the Retort
Courteous and the Quip Modest to the Lie Circumstantial and the
Lie Direct (5.4.66–102). Earlier in *Hamlet*, Polonius presumes that
his son Laertes, in Paris, knows how to conduct himself in matters
of "drinking, fencing, swearing, / Quarreling, drabbing" (2.1.26–27,
TLN 917–18)—all allowable and even admirable in young men of spirit
so long as those behaviors are not carried to excess. In soliloquy, Hamlet
berates himself for cowardice by imagining how he would respond to
a challenge: "Am I a coward? / Who calls me villain? Breaks my pate
across? / Plucks off my beard and blows it in my face? / Tweaks me by
th' nose? Gives me the lie i'th' throat / As deep as to the lungs? Who
does me this, / Ha?" (2.2.539–44, TLN 1611–16). Claudius, at 4.7.33
(TLN 3041), assures Laertes that he will not let his "beard be shook with
danger." Hamlet cringes at the very thought of mildly accepting such
insults, all of them deeply personal affronts that no gentleman could
endure without challenging the offender to a duel. The matter comes up
here again in Act 5 when Osric conveys to Hamlet what appears to be
a challenge to a gentlemanly duel from Laertes. Hamlet—and indeed
almost everyone present at the duel—believes this to be some harmless
entertainment, but we know that Claudius and Laertes intend it to be
a fight to the death.

QUEEN.   He's fat[1] and scant of breath.—
Here, Hamlet, take my napkin,° rub thy brows.   *handkerchief*
[*The Queen takes a cup of wine to offer a toast to Hamlet.*]
The Queen carouses° to thy fortune, Hamlet.   *drinks a toast*

---

1   Not physically fit, out of training.

Fencing School at Leiden University, engraving by Willem Swanenburgh, drawing by
Johannes Woudanus, 1610.

Duels might be fought with rapier and dagger, such as those mentioned
by Osric at 5.2.138 (TLN 3614), or the foils employed at 5.2.233–45 (TLN
3708–25). Foils were light fencing swords, usually with a cup-shaped
guard to protect the hand and a flexible blade tapered to a point that
could be blunted with a button; a foil lacking such a blunted point was
said to be "Unbated" (5.2.303, TLN 3798). The word "foil" could also refer
to a thin metal background used to set off and enhance the brilliance of
a jewel or similar valuable object. When Hamlet says to Laertes, "I'll be
your foil, Laertes" (5.2.234, TLN 3710), he punningly and self-deprecat-
ingly suggests that he will show Laertes to advantage by proving to be
less skillful in fencing.

More detail on duels is available in the online edition at
internetshakespeare.uvic.ca.

275 HAMLET. Good madam.

KING. Gertrude, do not drink.

QUEEN. I will, my lord, I pray you pardon me.

[*She drinks.*]

KING. [*Aside*] It is the poisoned cup. It is too late.

HAMLET. I dare not drink yet, madam; by and by.

280 QUEEN. Come, let me wipe thy face.

LAERTES. [*Aside to the King*] My lord, I'll hit him now.

KING. [*Aside to Laertes*]   I do not think't.

LAERTES. [*Aside*] And yet 'tis almost 'gainst my conscience.

HAMLET. Come for the third, Laertes, you do but dally.

I pray you, pass° with your best violence;   *thrust*

285 I am afeard you make a wanton of me.¹

LAERTES. Say you so? Come on.

[*They*] *play.*

OSRIC. Nothing neither way.

LAERTES. Have at you now!

[*Laertes wounds Hamlet with his unbated rapier.*] *In scuffling they*
change rapiers. [*Hamlet wounds Laertes.*]

KING.   Part them! They are incensed.

HAMLET. Nay, come again.

[*Laertes falls down. The Queen falls down.*]

OSRIC.   Look to the Queen there, ho!

290 HORATIO. They bleed on both sides. [*To Hamlet*] How is it, my
      lord?

OSRIC. How is't, Laertes?

LAERTES. Why, as a woodcock to mine own springe,² Osric;

I am justly killed with mine own treachery.

HAMLET. How does the Queen?

KING.   She swoons to see them bleed.

295 QUEEN. No, no, the drink, the drink, O my dear Hamlet,

The drink, the drink! I am poisoned.

[*She dies.*]

HAMLET. Oh, villainy! Ho! Let the door be locked.

Treachery! Seek it out.

[*Exit Osric.*]

---

1   I fear you are trifling with me, treating me as if I were a spoiled child.
2   I am like that proverbially stupid bird, the woodcock, caught in my own trap.

LAERTES. It is here, Hamlet. Hamlet, thou art slain.
    No med'cine in the world can do thee good;   300
    In thee there is not half an hour of life.
    The treacherous instrument is in thy hand,
    Unbated¹ and envenomed. The foul practice°   *plot, stratagem*
    Hath turned itself on me. Lo, here I lie
    Never to rise again. Thy mother's poisoned.   305
    I can no more. The King, the King's to blame.
HAMLET. The point envenomed too? Then, venom, to thy work.
[*He*] *hurts the King.*
ALL. Treason, treason!
KING. Oh, yet defend me, friends, I am but hurt.
HAMLET. [*Forcing the King to drink*] Here, thou incestuous,   310
        murd'rous, damnèd Dane,
    Drink off this potion. Is thy union² here?
    Follow my mother.
[*The*] *King dies.*
LAERTES.   He is justly served.
    It is a poison tempered° by himself.   *mixed*
    Exchange forgiveness with me, noble Hamlet.
    Mine and my father's death come not upon thee,   315
    Nor thine on me!
[*He*] *dies.*
HAMLET. Heaven make thee free of it! I follow thee.
    I am dead, Horatio. Wretched Queen, adieu.
    You that look pale and tremble at this chance,°   *mischance*
    That are but mutes³ or audience to this act,   320
    Had I but time, as this fell sergeant⁴ Death
    Is strict in his arrest, oh, I could tell you—
    But let it be. Horatio, I am dead,
    Thou liv'st. Report me and my cause aright
    To the unsatisfied.
HORATIO.   Never believe it.   325
    I am more an antique Roman⁵ than a Dane.

---

1   Not blunted with a button.
2   (1) The pearl, as at line 252 above; (2) your marriage.
3   Silent lookers-on; actors with nonspeaking roles.
4   Since this remorseless arresting officer.
5   I.e., I am one who embraces death, if necessary by suicide, before dishonor.

Here's yet some liquor left.
[He attempts to drink from the poisoned cup, but is prevented by Hamlet.]
HAMLET.   As thou'rt a man,
Give me the cup! Let go! By heaven I'll ha't.
Oh, God, Horatio, what a wounded name,
330 Things standing thus unknown, shall live behind me!
If thou didst ever hold me in thy heart,
Absent thee from felicity awhile,
And in this harsh world draw thy breath in pain
To tell my story.
March afar off, and shout within.
                              What warlike noise is this?

Enter Osric.

335 OSRIC. Young Fortinbras, with conquest come from Poland,
To th'ambassadors of England gives this warlike volley.[1]
HAMLET. Oh, I die, Horatio.
The potent poison quite o'ercrows[2] my spirit.
I cannot live to hear the news from England,
340 But I do prophesy th'election lights
On Fortinbras. He has my dying voice.[3]
So tell him, with th'occurrents more and less
Which have solicited.[4] The rest is silence.
Oh, oh, oh, oh!
[He] dies.
345 HORATIO. Now cracks a noble heart. Good night, sweet prince,
And flights of angels sing thee to thy rest!
[March within.]
Why does the drum come hither?

Enter Fortinbras and the English Ambassadors, with Drum, Colors, and Attendants.

---

1 This simultaneous firing of weapons in a military salute.
2 Proclaims triumph over (like the winner of a cockfight).
3 Vote (in "th'election" referred to in the previous line).
4 The events of greater or lesser importance that have urged me on (in what I have done or attempted, and in my wish to support the succession of Fortinbras to the throne).

FORTINBRAS. Where is this sight?

HORATIO.   What is it ye would see?
  If aught of woe or wonder, cease your search.

FORTINBRAS. This quarry cries on havoc.¹ O proud Death,   350
  What feast is toward in thine eternal cell,²
  That thou so many princes at a shot
  So bloodily hast struck?

AMBASSADOR.   The sight is dismal,
  And our affairs from England come too late.
  The ears are senseless that should give us hearing,   355
  To tell him his° commandment is fulfilled,   *Claudius's*
  That Rosencrantz and Guildenstern are dead.
  Where should we have our thanks?

HORATIO.   · Not from his mouth,
  Had it th'ability of life to thank you;
  He never gave commandment for their death.   360
  But since so jump upon this bloody question³
  You from the Polack wars and you from England
  Are here arrived, give order that these bodies
  High on a stage° be placèd to the view,   *platform*
  And let me speak to th'yet unknowing world   365
  How these things came about. So shall you hear
  Of carnal, bloody, and unnatural acts,
  Of accidental judgments,⁴ casual° slaughters,   *chance*
  Of deaths put on by cunning and forced cause,⁵
  And, in this upshot, purposes mistook   370
  Fall'n on th'inventors' heads. All this can I
  Truly deliver.°   *report*

FORTINBRAS.   Let us haste to hear it,
  And call the noblest to the audience.
  For me, with sorrow I embrace my fortune.

---

1 This heap of corpses (literally, slaughtered game) loudly proclaims a general
slaughter.
2 O thou insolent and mighty Death, what feasting on the slain is being prepared
in your everlasting dwelling place.
3 So hard on the heels of this bloody business.
4 Acts brought about by accident (such as the death of Polonius).
5 Of deaths gratuitously instigated by cunning stratagems and contrivances.

375   I have some rights of memory[1] in this kingdom,
       Which now to claim my vantage doth invite me.[2]
   HORATIO. Of that I shall have also cause to speak,
       And from his mouth whose voice will draw on more.[3]
       But let this same be presently° performed,   *immediately*
380   Even while men's minds are wild, lest more mischance
       On plots° and errors happen.   *on top of plots*
   FORTINBRAS.   Let four captains
       Bear Hamlet like a soldier to the stage,
       For he was likely, had he been put on,[4]
       To have proved most royal; and for his passage,[5]
385   The soldiers' music[6] and the rites of war
       Speak[7] loudly for him.
       Take up the body. Such a sight as this
       Becomes the field,[8] but here shows much amiss.
       Go bid the soldiers shoot.
           Exeunt marching, after the which a peal of ordnance are shot off.

FINIS

---

1   Claims that must not be forgotten.
2   Which my favorable position and opportunity now invite me to claim.
3   And speaking on behalf of Hamlet, whose vote will influence still others.
4   Invested in royal office (and thereby given the opportunity to prove what sort of ruler he would be).
5   To mark his passing from this world to the next.
6   I.e., muffled drumbeat.
7   (Let the beating drums) speak.
8   Is appropriate to a battlefield.

APPENDIX A: REFERENCES TO
CLASSICAL HISTORY AND MYTHOLOGY

AENEAS'S TALE TO DIDO. Hamlet's recital of a speech to the players, which is then continued by the First Player, is a blank-verse tragic composition adapted by Shakespeare from Virgil's *Aeneid*, a Latin epic poem written c. 29–19 BCE. Designed to grace the Roman literary world in the era of Caesar Augustus, to whom Virgil dedicated the poem, the *Aeneid* clearly took as its model Homer's *Iliad* and *Odyssey*. Virgil tells what purports to be a continuation of Homer's account of the Trojan War, with the Greeks gaining access to Troy by the ruse of the Trojan Horse, their sacking of that city, and Aeneas's escape from the ruins with his father, Anchises, his wife, Creusa, and his son, Ascanius; then Aeneas's journey to Queen Dido's Carthage (where he relates to her the story of Troy's fall), and then to Italy, where eventually his triumph over the Latins enables him to found the city of Rome. Renaissance English historians regarded this foundational myth as the back-story of their own civilization, since, according to a medieval continuation of that myth, Aeneas's great-grandson Brut or Brutus made an epic journey similar to his great-grandfather's that resulted in the founding of Troynovant (New Troy), or London.

The passage, beginning at 2.2.423 (TLN 1492), retells the Virgilian story of the sack of Troy, focusing on Pyrrhus' savage slaughter of the old and unarmed Priam, King of Troy, and then the grieving of Queen Hecuba. Pyrrhus, also known as Neoptolemus, is the son of the heroic Greek warrior Achilles, usually regarded as the central figure of Homer's *Iliad*. The slaughter of Priam is the price that the furious Pyrrhus demands as vengeance for the death of his own father. Homer does not portray the death of Achilles, but other sources report that he was killed near the end of the Trojan War by Paris, a son of Priam and husband of Helen. Paris managed to shoot Achilles with an arrow in his heel, the one vulnerable spot on his body since (according to the first-century Roman historian Statius in his *Achilleid*) Achilles' mother Thetis had endeavored to bestow immortality on her son by dipping him as an infant into the river Styx; in doing so, she left vulnerable that one part of the body by which she was holding her son, the heel (hence the terms Achilles heel and Achilles tendon).

Christopher Marlowe and Thomas Nashe wrote *Dido Queen of Carthage* (c. 1585), a dramatization of the love affair of Aeneas and Dido and his reluctant decision to leave in obedience to the gods, who have decreed that he is to found Rome. See also, "Virgil, *Aeneid*," pp. 265–66.

ALEXANDER. The Emperor Alexander III, Alexander the Great, 356–323 BCE, was famed for his conquest of the known world all the way east to India. When Hamlet playfully imagines in conversing with Horatio that the dust of Alexander's corpse might be made into the loam used to stop a bunghole in a beer barrel, he is calling upon a commonplace view of Alexander's worldly achievement as ultimately mocked by his death and burial (5.1.180–87, TLN 3391–99).

Image 1: *Apollo Belvedere*, c. 120–140 CE. Photograph by Jean-Pol Grandmont.

APOLLO. The god of the sun, and of medicine, music, archery, and prophecy, known to the Romans as Phoebus Apollo. His "cart" or chariot is emblematic of the sun as a heavenly body, going around the earth daily and thus, at 3.2.139 (TLN 2024), a way of marking the passage of a year.

BRUTUS, LUCIUS JUNIUS. The founder of the Roman republic. His name, "Brutus," was synonymous with "stupid"; according to legend, he feigned madness in order to evade the plotting of his enemies, the Tarquins, whom he eventually overthrew. Polonius and Hamlet exchange words about the assassination of Julius Caesar by Lucius Junius Brutus's descendant, Marcus Brutus, at 3.2.92–95 (TLN 1957–61). See below, "Caesar, Gaius Julius," p. 249, and *Henry V*, 2.4.37–38, where the Constable of France compares King Henry's "vanities forespent" to "the outside of the Roman Brutus, / Covering discretion with a coat of folly."

BRUTUS, MARCUS JUNIUS. This patrician descendant of Lucius Junius Brutus was a leader of the Republican cause and one of the conspirators who assassinated Julius Caesar in 44 BCE. Polonius and Hamlet refer to the assassination at 3.2.90–95 (TLN 1953–61), in the action leading up to the performance of "The Murder of Gonzago" before the King, Queen, and court.

CAESAR, GAIUS JULIUS. The assassination of Gaius Julius Caesar on 15 March 44 BCE is the subject of Shakespeare's *Julius Caesar* (1599). Horatio cites this famous episode in the first scene of *Hamlet* as an instance when ominous prognostications preceded and foretold disaster (1.1.118, TLN 124.7). Later, when Polonius describes how he acted the part of Julius Caesar once in a play "i'th' university," and was accounted "a good actor" in the part, having been killed by Brutus "i'th' Capitol," Hamlet replies with a biting wit that "It was a brute part

Image 2: *Bust of Gaius Julius Caesar,* c. 100 CE.

of him to kill so capital a calf there" (3.2.90–95, TLN 1953–61). The word "brute" plays on "brutus," Latin for "stupid," referring to a legendary story in the life of Lucius Junius Brutus (p. 248).

CENTAUR. When Claudius, in conversation with Laertes, undertakes to praise the horsemanship of a Frenchman named Lamord, he describes how the rider "brought his horse / As had been incorpsed and demi-natured / With the brave beast" (4.6.86–88, TLN 3083–85). The image Claudius raises is that of the centaur, a fabled creature shaped with the legs and body of a horse and a man's body in place of the horse's head and neck. The centaurs dwelt near Mount Pelion (mentioned at 5.1.228, TLN 3447).

CYCLOPS. These giants, supposedly the sons of Coelus (or Uranus, the most ancient of the gods) and his own mother Terra (Earth), had only

Image 3: *Bust of Polyphemus*, Johann Heinrich Wilhelm Tischbein, c. 1790.

one eye positioned in the middle of the forehead; hence the name "Cyclopes," literally "round-eyed." The ancient Greek poet Hesiod says they were three in number; other accounts speak of more of them, governed by Polyphemus as their king in Sicily. This location places them near Mount Etna; hence the tradition that they were workers in the smithy of Vulcan. In *Hamlet*, at 3.2.75–76 (TLN 1934–35), Hamlet speaks of faulty imagining of evil things as "foul / As Vulcan's stithy." (See "Vulcan," pp. 266–67.) The account of the fall of Troy in 2.2 compares Pyrrhus's vengeful rage to the remorseless blows with which "the Cyclops' hammers fall / On Mars his armor forged for proof eterne" (2.2.461–62, TLN 1529–30). This reference shows no awareness of the well-known story in Book 9 of Homer's *Odyssey* about Odysseus' encounter with the man-eating Cyclops named Polyphemus and Odysseus' narrow escape by means of his wit.

DAMON AND PYTHIAS. Hamlet evidently quotes, at 3.2.263 (TLN 2153), some unknown ballad about the fabled friendship of Damon and Pythias. When Damon, condemned to death by the tyrant Dionysius, obtains leave to settle his affairs before dying, his friend Pythias takes his place as surety for Damon's return. Damon returns barely in time, inspiring Dionysius to spare them both in recognition of their noble fidelity to each other. Sources for this often-told tale include Aristoxenus (fourth century BCE), Cicero (*De officiis*, first century BCE), Diodorus Siculus and Valerius Maximus (both first century CE), and Castiglione (*The Courtier*, translated into English by Sir Thomas Hoby, 1561). Hamlet implicitly acknowledges his deep friendship with Horatio as like that of Damon and Pythias.

DIANA AND THE MOON. The moon is associated with Diana, the Roman goddess, equivalent to the Greek moon-goddess Artemis, a

Image 4: *Diana of Versailles*, first century CE.

virgin huntress of wildlife, also goddess of childbirth and chaste affections; sometimes conflated with Phoebe, a Titan associated with the moon and with Phoebus Apollo. Elizabethans associated these goddesses with their Queen Elizabeth, who readily adopted the myth.

The Moon is called "the moist star" at 1.1.122 (TLN 124.11) because of its association with the ocean tides in "Neptune's empire," the sea. A lunar eclipse is here seen as a harbinger of ominous events, such as the assassination of Julius Caesar. Laertes warns his sister at 1.3.36–37 (TLN 499–500) that "The chariest maid is prodigal enough / If she unmask her beauty to the moon." On the moon as a monthly measure of time, see below, "Neptune" (3.2.140, TLN 2025). "Under the moon" (4.7.145, TLN 3136) expresses the idea of all that is sublunary, beneath the moon, hence all living things on earth.

ENCELADUS. One of the Giants who rebelled against the Olympian gods and was imprisoned under Mount Etna in Sicily. See "Giants," p. 252.

ETNA, MOUNT. A volcanic mountain in Sicily, where Enceladus, one of the Giants, was imprisoned. See "Giants," p. 252.

FORTUNA OR FORTUNE. See extended note, p. 90.

GIANTS. When Claudius speaks of Laertes's threatened rebellion as "giant-like" (4.5.122, TLN 2866), he may be referring to the unsuccessful rebellion of the Giants, sons of Ge or Gaia (Earth), against Zeus and the Olympian gods. When the Giants were overthrown, Enceladus, one of their number, was buried under Mount Etna in Sicily. This rebellion is sometimes confused or conflated with that of the Titans against Uranus or Coelus; possibly Shakespeare has both in mind here. The Titans were also gigantic and were the offspring of Uranus and Ge, mother of the Giants, so both the Giants and the Titans were imagined to have sprung from the earth (Ge).

The wars of both the Giants and the Titans against the gods are cited often in Greek mythology and are sometimes conflated. When Laertes hyperbolically begs that the dust of Ophelia's grave be heaped upon him "Till of this flat a mountain you have made / T'o'ertop old Pelion, or the skyish head / Of blue Olympus" (5.1.227–29, TLN 3446–48), he evidently has in mind the attempts of the Giants to scale Mount Olympus by piling still another mountain, Ossa, on top of Mount Pelion. Hamlet matches Laertes allusion for allusion when he vaunts, "And if thou prate of mountains, let them throw / Millions of acres on us, till our ground, / Singeing his pate against the burning zone, / Make Ossa like a wart" (5.1.258–61, TLN 3477–80).

Image 5: *Triple-formed representation of Hecate*, Musei Vatacani, Vatican City.

HECATE. Goddess of witchcraft, associated with Diana and the moon, Hecate presided over magic and enchantments. Lucianus, the murderer in "The Murder of Gonzago," invokes her baleful curse "thrice blasted, thrice infected" (3.2.240, TLN 2128) in the poisonous concoction he pours into the sleeping ears of his royal victim.

HECUBA. The queen and then the grieving widow of King Priam of Troy. See "Virgil, *Aeneid*," pp. 265–66. The recitation about the fall of Troy in 2.2 is based on the *Aeneid*. It focuses at 2.2.473 ff. (TLN 1541 ff.) on the pitiable spectacle of the inconsolable

Hecuba, running up and down as Troy burns, bereft of crown and regal attire. Perhaps Hamlet has chosen this passage because Queen Gertrude's mourning for her dead husband has been, in Hamlet's view, deplorably brief.

HERCULES. "Hercules" is the Latin form of the Greek Heracles. He is the most famous hero of Greek mythology, noted especially for his fulfillment of the twelve "Labors" imposed on him by Eurystheus, King of Argos and Mycenae and grandson of Pelops. Eurystheus was jealous of Hercules because Zeus had decreed that one of them would be subservient to the other. The first of Hercules' labors was the slaying of the Nemean lion, an otherwise invulnerable monster; Hamlet alludes to this when he cries out to the soldiers who are attempting to restrain him from following his father's Ghost on the battlements: "My fate cries

Image 6: *Herakles and the Nemean Lion*. Attic white-ground black-figured oinochoe, c. 520–500 BCE.

out, / And makes each petty artery in this body / As hardy as the Nemean lion's nerve" (1.4.83–85, TLN 668–70). Earlier, Hamlet speaks of his hated uncle Claudius as "no more like my father / Than I to Hercules" (1.2.152–53, TLN 336–37).

In a discussion about the rivalry between adult actors and juvenile companies (see extended note, pp. 124–25), Hamlet asks "Do the boys carry it away?," to which Rosencrantz replies, "Ay, that they do, my lord, Hercules and his load too" (2.2.344–45, TLN 1407–08). The reference is seemingly to Hercules' bearing the world on his shoulders, a veritable "Herculean" labor even though not one of the twelve famous labors imposed on him by Eurystheus. According to one legend, it was Atlas who bore the world on his shoulders as a punishment meted out by Zeus. When Hercules sought Atlas's help to fetch the apples of the Hesperides, Atlas agreed on the condition that Hercules take his place as upholder of the world, but Hercules then tricked Atlas into taking on the load briefly while Hercules found a pad for his shoulders, whereupon Hercules left Atlas with his burden. The familiar image of Hercules holding up the world may have been used as the sign of the Globe Theatre, though the evidence for this rests chiefly on this passage from *Hamlet* (2.2.244–45).

Hamlet invokes the name of Hercules at Ophelia's gravesite, when he and Laertes have quarreled violently. Hamlet asks Laertes, "What is the reasons that you use me thus? / I loved you ever. But it is no matter. / Let Hercules himself do what he may, / The cat will mew, and dog will have his day" (5.1.267–70, TLN 3488–91).

HYMEN. Also called Hymenaeus, the Greek god of marriage. He is personified at 3.2.143 (TLN 2028) by the Player King as the god presiding over the Player King's marriage to his queen.

HYPERION. Hyperion (Greek for "the High One") was one of the twelve Titans, offspring of Ge or Gaia (Earth) and Uranus (the sky, the heavens). In partnership with his sister, the Titaness Theia, Hyperion fathered Helios (the Sun), Selene (the Moon), and Eos (the Dawn). The sun-god Hyperion is often invoked by poets as an embodiment of the Sun itself, as in Shakespeare's *Henry V*, 4.1.273, when King Henry, on the night before the battle of Agincourt, reflects on the lot of the happy peasant who sleeps peacefully after his day's labor and then, at dawn the next day, "Doth rise and help Hyperion to his horse."

Led by Cronus, the Titans overthrew Uranus and ruled during the mythological Golden Age until they were in turn displaced by Zeus and the Olympian gods. The ancient Greek poet Hesiod's *Theogony* depicts Cronus, the youngest of the Titans, as envious of Uranus's power as ruler of the universe. The Romantic poet John Keats (1795–1821) wrote two versions of a fragment of a poem on Hyperion, in which this last of the Titans is dethroned by Apollo. To Hamlet at 1.2.140 (TLN 324), Hyperion is, like Hamlet's own dead father, an icon of regal splendor and gracious majesty, to be contrasted with the satyr-like Claudius. Similarly, when Hamlet confronts his mother with two contrasting images, one of the dead King Hamlet and the other of Claudius, he imagines his father's graceful brow to be adorned with "Hyperion's curls" and "the front of Jove himself" (3.4.57, TLN 2440).

HYRCANIAN BEAST. I.e., tiger. Hyrcania, a province of the Median Empire, bordered on the southern and southeastern shore of the Caspian Sea, in modern-day Iran and Turkmenistan. The name "Hyrcania" suggests "Wolf-land." The entire region, though fertile and beautiful, was fabled to be inhabited by wild and dangerous beasts. In 2.2, Hamlet begins his Virgilian recital of the fall of Troy by comparing "The rugged Pyrrhus" to "th'Hyrcanian beast" (2.2.423, TLN 1492–93), only to pause and start again with a different image.

JOVE. Another name for Jupiter (Roman) or Zeus (Greek), the most powerful of the Olympian gods. He overthrew his father Saturn for conspiring against him. Hamlet compares his own father to Jove, Hyperion, Mars, and Mercury in stark contrast to Claudius, who is "like a mildewed ear" and a "moor" (3.4.65–68, TLN 2448–51). Earlier, at 3.2.265–66 (TLN 2154–56), Hamlet alludes to the realm of "Jove himself" as dismantled by "A very, very—pajock."

LETHE. The river of forgetfulness and oblivion, one of five rivers in Hades. The others are Acheron, the river of pain; Styx, the river of hatred; Phlegethon, the river of fire; and Cocytus, the river of wailing. The Ghost mentions "Lethe wharf" at 1.5.34 (TLN 720).

MARCUS AURELIUS. Roman Emperor and Stoic philosopher (121–180 CE). See below, "Stoicism," p. 243.

MARS. God of War, Roman equivalent of Ares. A pen-and-ink sketch by the late-seventeenth-century artist Raymond de la Fage (p. 256) (see Image 7) shows "Venus watching Vulcan and Cyclops forge armor for Mars." In it, Mars is accompanied by his workmen, the Cyclopes, as they hammer with a vengeful fury like that alluded to by the First Player when he exclaims, "And never did the Cyclops' hammers fall / On Mars his armor forged for proof eterne / With less remorse than Pyrrhus' bleeding sword" (2.2.462–64, TLN 1529–31). This episode reflects the well-earned reputation of Vulcan (or his Greek equivalent

Hephaestus) as armorer for the gods. For the story of Vulcan's jealous response to Venus's affair with Mars, see "Vulcan" below, pp. 266–67.

At 3.4.56–66 (TLN 2439–49), Hamlet compares his own father to Jove, Hyperion, Mars, and Mercury; see also "Jove," p. 255.

Image 7: *Venus watching Vulcan and Cyclops forge armor for Mars*, Raymond de la Fage, late seventeenth century.

MERCURY. The messenger of Jupiter on Mount Olympus, known as Hermes to the Greeks. He was often portrayed with winged heels, enabling him to move with extraordinary rapidity. At 3.4.56–66 (TLN 2439–49), Hamlet compares his own father to Jove, Hyperion, Mars, and Mercury as contrasted with Claudius. Hamlet's father is here endowed with a "station" or stance like that of "the herald Mercury / New-lighted on a heaven-kissing hill."

NEMEAN LION. See "Hercules," pp. 253–54, the first of whose twelve labors was to quell the Nemean lion. This monster, born of the hundred-headed Typhon, terrorized the inhabitants of Nemea, in Argolis in the Peloponnesus peninsula of Greece. According to one legend the lion was thought to be protected by a fur that was impervious to attack, but Hercules (Heracles) had the sagacity to use the beast's own claws to destroy the monster and then skin it, thereby fashioning for himself a cloak with extraordinary protective properties. In *Hamlet*, when Horatio and the guard attempt to prevent Hamlet from following his father's ghost on the battlements, he throws off their restraint,

Image 8: *Hercules and the Nemean Lion*, Peter Paul Rubens, originally painted c. 1615.

exclaiming, "My fate cries out / And makes each petty artery in this body / As hardy as the Nemean lion's nerve" (1.4.83–85, TLN 668–70).

NEPTUNE. The Roman god of the sea, with attributes of the Greek equivalent Poseidon. See also "Diana and the Moon," pp. 250–51. At 3.2.139–41 (TLN 2024–26), the Player King reckons the amount of time that he and his queen have been happily married as "thirty dozen moons," during which span of time the sun ("Phoebus' cart") has gone around "Neptune's salt wash and Tellus' orbèd ground" (the earth) some thirty times (thirty years). Twelve complete cycles of the moon are here seen as equivalent to a calendar year. Horatio refers to "Neptune's empire" at 1.1.123 (TLN 124.12).

NERO. This Roman emperor from 54–68 CE was infamous for many things: for taking on a female identity and marrying one of his eunuchs, for bringing about the deaths of Seneca, Lucan, Petronius, and his wife Octavia Poppaea, and much more. He caused Rome to be set on fire in various places, and sang of the destruction of Troy while his own city burned. He built sumptuous palaces and indulged in every imaginable sort of debauchery. He was fascinated with theater, and was himself an actor. Most relevant to Hamlet's citing of him at 3.2.363–66 (TLN 2264–67) is Nero's having ordered the assassination of his own mother. As Hamlet goes to confront his mother with her

Image 9: *Niobe and her children killed by Apollo and Artemis*, Aniçet Charles Gabriel Lemonnier, 1772.

guilty behavior, he vows to be cruel with her but not "unnatural"; he will not let "The soul of Nero enter this firm bosom." He will "speak daggers to her, but use none."

NIOBE. Daughter of Tantalus, King of Sipylus in Lydia. Her brothers' families were cursed over successive generations, culminating in the tragic story of Agamemnon's family dramatized by Aeschylus in his *Oresteia* trilogy. Niobe became the wife and Queen of King Amphion of Thebes. Hubris prompted her to boast that in her 12 or 14 children (or 20, in Hesiod's account) she was more fortunate than Leto (Latona in

Roman myth), mother of Apollo and Artemis. In some accounts, Apollo avenged this insult by causing her to lose all her children; in some others, Artemis joined in punishing Niobe. Shakespeare is likely to have encountered the story in Ovid's *Metamorphoses*, Book 6, where Niobe is turned into a marble slab atop Mount Sipylus, incessantly dropping tears. In Homer's *Iliad*, Book XXIV, the children of Niobe are left lying in their own blood for nine days when Zeus turns into stone all the people of Thebes who attempt to bury them. The gods finally bury the children on the tenth day. Shakespeare's chief interest is the image of Niobe as "all tears" (1.2.149, TLN 333). The weeping rock on Mount Sipylus in western Turkey, not far from the Aegean Sea, still flows today, having been associated since ancient times with the legend of Niobe. She weeps in stone statuary at the tomb of Harry Houdini in New York City.

OLYMPUS. A mountain in Macedonia and Thessaly, so high that it was thought to touch the very heavens and thus well suited for the court of Jupiter and the Olympian gods. Laertes speaks of "the skyish head / Of blue Olympus" (5.1.228–29, TLN 3447–48). See "Ossa" and "Pelion," below.

OSSA. A mountain in Thessaly, at one point the residence of the Centaurs. The Giants, in their war against the gods, attempted to scale Mount Olympus by piling Ossa on top of Mount Pelion, an incident alluded to by Hamlet. When Laertes, having jumped into Ophelia's grave, begs to be covered with dust until a mountain is formed that will overtop Pelion and Olympus (5.1.226–29, TLN 3445–48), Hamlet replies in kind: "And if thou prate of mountains, let them throw / Millions of acres on us, till our ground, / Singeing his pate against the burning zone, / Make Ossa like a wart" (5.1.258–61, TLN 3477–80).

PELION. A wooded mountain near the coast of Thessaly. According to Greek mythology, some Giants, notably Otus and Ephialtes, attempted to pile Ossa and Pelion on Mount Olympus in their failed rebellion against the Olympian gods. Laertes seemingly refers to this rebellion of the Giants when he leaps into Ophelia's grave and exclaims, "Now pile your dust upon the quick and dead, / Till of this flat a mountain you have made / T'o'ertop old Pelion, or the skyish head / Of blue Olympus" (5.1.226–29, TLN 3445–48; see also 258–61, TLN 3477–80).

PLAUTUS. Titus Maccus (or Maccius) Plautus (c. 254–184 BCE) was widely regarded in the Renaissance as the supreme exemplar of Roman comedy. Along with the younger Terence (c. 190–159 BCE), Plautus excelled as the Roman successor to Athenian comic writers, from the so-called Old Comedy of Aristophanes (late fifth century BCE) and Middle Comedy to the New Comedy of Menander (c. 324–291 BCE). Renaissance England knew little about Aristophanes, but Latin drama was much more widely read and studied, and the comedies of Plautus, often expurgated, were well known and imitated. His focus on the lives of ordinary Romans typically featured charismatic young people outwitting their elders. Character types included gullible or libertine fathers, knavish servants who assisted their masters in their plotting, greedy parasite slaves and pimps, courtesans, and braggart soldiers (most notably in his play *Miles Gloriosus*). Shakespeare's *The Comedy of Errors* is modeled on Plautus's *Menaechmi* or *Twins*, and Falstaff owes much to the tradition of *Miles Gloriosus*. The love plot of Shakespeare's *The Taming of the Shrew* is based on Ludivico Ariosto's *I Suppositi* (1509), which in turn belongs to the comic tradition of Plautus's *Captivi* and Terence's *Eunuchus*. In *Hamlet*, Polonius fatuously preens himself on his knowledge of ancient drama by opining that "Seneca cannot be too heavy nor Plautus too light" (2.2.379–80, TLN 1448–49). See also "Seneca," pp. 262–63.

PLUTARCH. Claudius's worry that he has done "but greenly" to bury Polonius "In hugger-mugger" (4.5.83–84, TLN 2820–21)—that is, in secret haste—may recall Thomas North's description, in his translation of Plutarch's *Life of Julius Caesar*, of the hasty burial "in hugger mugger" of Julius Caesar without ceremonial honors.

POLYXENA. See "Pyrrhus," p. 261.

PRIAM. Book 2 of Virgil's *Aeneid* tells of the death of Priam, King of Troy. The speech of the First Player about the fall of Troy and the slaughter of Priam (2.2.423 ff., TLN 1491 ff.) bears an interesting resemblance to Marlowe and Nashe's *Dido Queen of Carthage* (late 1580s), to whom Hamlet refers at 2.2.420 (TLN 1489–90). That play in turn is derived from Virgil's *Aeneid*, Books 1, 2, and 4. See also "Virgil, *Aeneid*," pp. 265–66.

Image 10: *Neoptolemus and Andromache*, Pierre-Narcisse Guérin, 1810.

PYRRHUS. "Pyrrhus," meaning "yellow-haired," is a familiar name for Neoptolemus, the son of Achilles. After his father's death (at the hands of Paris, according to some post-Homeric accounts), Neoptolemus was summoned to Troy, since the seer Calchas had decreed that Troy could not be taken without the assistance of Achilles' son. "Neoptolemus," meaning "New Soldier," was given to him as a name because he had come so late to the field of battle. He was the first warrior to enter the wooden horse and was infamous for his barbaric cruelty, not only in the slaying of the old and defenseless Priam but in other atrocities as well. He furiously sacrificed Astyanax, the son of Hector and Andromache, and Polyxena, the daughter of Priam and Hecuba. He was awarded Hector's widow, Andromache, as his prize among the captives. In *Hamlet*, the violence of his vengeful acts (2.2.423 ff., TLN 1492 ff.) invites comparison with the vengeful duties imposed on Laertes, Fortinbras, and Hamlet. See also "Virgil, *Aeneid*," pp. 265–66.

SATYR. In Greek mythology, a follower of Pan and Dionysus, gods respectively of shepherds and of wine and ritual frenzy. Satyrs were imagined to have goat-like bodies, with goat tail, legs, phallus, hooves, horns, and ears, combined with human torsos, faces, and curly hair and

Image 11: *Nymphs and Satyr*, William-Adolphe Bouguereau, 1873.

beards. Often they wore wreaths of vine or ivy leaves on their balding heads, and they played on flutelike pipes. They were associated with fertility, sensual pleasure, wine, song, and the music of cymbals, castanets, and bagpipes. In the cult of Dionysus, the males were satyrs and the females were maenads or bacchants. Hamlet invokes satyrs at 1.2.140 (TLN 324) as resembling Claudius in their promiscuous lechery and hence the very opposite of Hyperion and of Hamlet's father.

SENECA. Lucius Annaeus Seneca the Younger (c. 4 BCE–65 CE) was widely regarded in the Renaissance as the supreme writer of classical tragedy. (The works of the Greek tragedians Aeschylus, Sophocles, and Euripides, to which the Roman Seneca was indebted, were lesser known.) This second son of the rhetorician Seneca the Elder became a major Stoic philosopher who served as counselor for the emperor Nero, helping to keep the emperor under some control for a time but then withdrawing from court when Nero's conduct became unmanageable. Seneca was ultimately ordered by Nero to take his own life because of alleged participation in a conspiracy against the emperor. He died with notable calm, in the stoic vein of Socrates. Although his nine tragedies were much emulated in the Renaissance as models of Aristotelean correctness of tragic form, they did not, on the whole, offer workable models for a public and popular dramatist such as Shakespeare. Dealing with the tragic accounts of such figures as Agamemnon, Thyestes, Oedipus, Hercules, Phaedra, and Medea—which had fascinated dramatists in the great days of Athens's fifth century BCE—Seneca's tragedies feature long moral disquisitions in a declamatory style more suited to philosophical inquiry than to the give-and-take of dramatic action. Indeed, his plays may not have been intended for live dramatic presentation on stage. Nonetheless, their influence was considerable, especially on classically correct tragedy in Italy, France, and England during the Renaissance. Stock characters of Senecan drama, including the nurse, the ghost, and the remorseless villain, are an important part of theater's dramatic ancestry, on the popular stage as well as in more rigorously classical plays such as Ben Jonson's *Sejanus* (1603) and *Catiline* (1611). Thomas Kyd's *The Spanish Tragedy* (c. 1582) owes much to Senecan drama, and Shakespeare's *Hamlet* is fully aware of this theatrical ancestry. In *Hamlet*, Polonius fatuously preens himself on his knowledge of ancient drama by opining that "Seneca cannot be too heavy nor Plautus too light" (2.2.379–80, TLN 1448–49). See also "Plautus," p. 260.

STOICISM. Although *Hamlet* never mentions Stoicism by name, the ideas of that ancient philosophy emerge strongly in Hamlet's admiring account of Horatio as one who, "in suff'ring all," suffers nothing; he is a man "that Fortune's buffets and rewards / Hast ta'en with equal thanks." Hamlet enlarges this portrait to include all those "Whose blood and judgment are so well commingled / That they are not a pipe for Fortune's finger / To sound what stop she please." Such a person "is not passion's slave" (3.2.58–64, TLN 1915–23). Hamlet's warm praise aptly summarizes some of the tenets of Stoicism, originally a school of Hellenistic philosophy founded in Athens by Zeno in the third century BCE and then practiced by such Roman philosophers as Seneca, Epictetus, and the Roman emperor Marcus Aurelius. It taught wise persons how to avoid the destructive dangers of uncontrolled emotions and flawed judgment. To learn a true indifference to the blandishments of Fortune is to find a way to be immune to the vicissitudes of life. If one refuses to crave the rewards of Fortune, one cannot be hurt by misfortune. For "Fortune," see extended note on p. 90.

STYX. The river of hatred, one of the five rivers of Hades. See "Lethe," p. 255.

TELLUS. The Roman goddess of the earth, an ancient Titan, mother of Hyperion and Saturn, among others. She was associated with agricultural growth and decay. She personifies the earth itself when the

Player King, in the performance of "The Murder of Gonzago," marks the passage of thirty years by the number of times that "Phoebus' cart" has gone round "Neptune's salt wash and Tellus' orbèd ground" (3.2.139–40, TLN 2024–25).

THETIS. A sea nymph, one of the fifty Nereids. Mother of Achilles, she held him by the ankle as an infant and dipped him in the River Styx. Though not mentioned directly in *Hamlet*, she is pertinent to the story of Achilles and his son Pyrrhus. See p. 261.

TITANS. The Titans were the gigantic primeval offspring of Caelus (or Uranus in Greek mythology) and Caelus's mother Terra (or Ge or Gaia), a marriage of heaven and earth. According to Hesiod, their number included Oceanus, Hyperion, Cronus, Themis, Mnemosysne, Phoebe, and Tethys. Cronus, who corresponds to the Roman Saturn, led a rebellion against Uranus (who had confined his children to Tartarus) and castrated him. Cronus presided over a Golden Age. Warned in turn that one of his children would overthrow him, Cronus swallowed them as they were born, but Zeus, the youngest, was saved by the wiles of his mother, Rhea. Olympus formed itself into a home for the gods after the defeat of the Titans, when Cronus (or Saturn) was replaced on the throne by his son Zeus (or Jupiter).

Claudius, when he speaks of the incipient rebellion of Laertes as "so giant-like" (4.5.122, TLN 2866), may be referring to the Titans or the Giants, or both; see "Giants," p. 252. Hyperion, whom Hamlet compares to his own father (1.2.140, TLN 324), was one of the Titans. See also "Tellus," pp. 263–64.

THE TROJAN HORSE. The memorable episode about the Trojan Horse and the fall of Troy is post-Homeric. It figures prominently in Virgil's *Aeneid*, on which the First Player's recitation in 2.2 about the fall of Troy is based. See "Virgil, *Aeneid*," pp. 265–66. This recital describes Pyrrhus as lying "couchèd in the ominous horse" (2.2.427, TLN 1496), assuming that hearers would readily understand the reference.

URANUS. This ancient deity was overthrown by his son Cronus (Saturn) in the rebellion of the Titans that is sometimes conflated with the unsuccessful one of the Giants. See "Giants," p. 252, and "Titans," above.

Image 12: *Zeus defeating the Titans*, detail from the altar-frieze at Pergamon.
Photograph by Miguel Hermoso Cuesta.

VENUS. Goddess of beauty, wife of Vulcan. Not mentioned directly in *Hamlet*, but pertinent to the story of Vulcan at 3.2.76 (TLN 1935). See also 2.2.462–63 (TLN 1529–30) and "Vulcan," pp. 266–67.

VIRGIL, *AENEID*. Publius Vergilius Maro, known universally as Virgil (70–19 BCE), became the great poet of the early Roman empire under Augustus. He completed his *Eclogues* in 37 BCE and the *Georgics* in 30 BCE, whereupon he devoted the remaining 11 years of his life to the *Aeneid*. Consciously modeled on Homer's *Iliad* and *Odyssey*, the *Aeneid* tells the story of the founding of Rome and celebrates its religious heritage. It was extraordinarily important to Renaissance England as a foundational epic that embraced the history of England as well as that of Rome. Aeneas's journeyings took him to the Carthage of Queen Dido, where he told her the story of the fall of Troy, and thence eventually to the founding of Rome. A subsequent legend, first told by the British historian Nennius in the ninth century and then by Geoffrey of Monmouth in his *Historia Regum Britanniae* or *History of the Kings of Britain* (twelfth century), proposed that Aeneas's great-grandson (or grandson), Brut (or Brutus), responding to a divine vision of the land where he was destined to found a new nation, set sail across the Mediterranean and through the Straits of Gibraltar until he finally arrived at a place on the banks of what was to be known as the River Thames, where he founded Troia Nova, or New Troy. The name of this settlement was in time corrupted to Trinovantum and eventually became known as London. Brut's three sons—Locrinus, Albanactus, and Kamber—divided the kingdom after Brut's death into the regions of England, Scotland, and Wales. In this way, Nennius and Geoffrey provided England with a dignified and glorious foundational ancestry based on the *Aeneid*, a work read and studied by virtually all those in England who acquired Latin during the Middle Ages and Renaissance. Versions of the story after Geoffrey's included the *Roman de Brut* (c. 1155), a verse chronicle in Anglo-Saxon by the Norman poet Wace, a subsequent chronicle in early Middle English by the English priest Layamon that is generally known as *Layamon's Brut* (c. 1190–1215), and at least two Welsh medieval chronicles. *The Chronicles of England*, printed in 1480 by William Caxton, was one of the earliest books in English to be produced by the new method of printing. An immensely popular work in its time, it comprehensively gave an account of supposed British history from Brut and Locrinus on downward through a succession of legendary rulers, including Mempricius, Bladud, Leir or Lear, Gorboduc and his sons Ferrex and Porrex, and many more, proceeding to the recorded British history of the Norman conquest of 1066 and all that. This legendary account of British history remained part of the record throughout the sixteenth century. It was told again in Raphael Holinshed's *Chronicles of England, Scotland, and Ireland*, first printed in 1577. Shakespeare used Holinshed's text extensively in its second edition of 1587.

For *Hamlet*'s particular indebtednesses to the *Aeneid* in 2.2.423 ff. (TLN 1489 ff.), see "Priam," p. 260, "Pyrrhus," p. 261, "Trojan Horse," p. 264, and "Hecuba," pp. 252–53.

VULCAN. Vulcan's stithy (characterized as "foul" at 3.2.75, TLN 1934) is the smithy or place of stiths (anvils), where Vulcan and his menials fashioned armor and weapons. Vulcan, the Roman counterpart of the Greek deity Hephaestus, was the god of fire and volcanoes, often portrayed as crippled and with a blacksmith's hammer in hand. The worship of Vulcan began very early in Roman history. As the husband of Venus (Aphrodite), this god was sometimes portrayed as a cuckold betrayed by his voluptuous wife with Mars (Ares). The scene in Book 8 of Homer's *Odyssey* is highly satirical: the jealous husband fashions in his forge a net with which to entrap his wife and her lover *in flagrante delicto* and then hoists the two aloft for all the gods to laugh at. In *Hamlet*, Hamlet's dark brooding on Claudius's seduction of his dead brother's wife calls to mind Vulcan's plot to ensnare his wife and her lover; see "Cyclops," pp. 249–50, and "Virgil, *Aeneid*," pp. 265–66.

APPENDIX B: REFERENCES TO THE BIBLE

[The plentiful references to the Bible in *Hamlet* are appropriate to Hamlet's having studied at Wittenberg, a university associated in Shakespeare's day with the beginnings of the Protestant Reformation. Hamlet shows himself an avid student of Christian teachings. Shakespeare relied primarily on the Geneva Bible, the most widely read and influential Bible of his time. It generally took the place of the so-called Great Bible of 1539, the first authorized edition of the Bible in English. The New Testament Geneva Bible was published in 1557, the complete Bible in 1560. John Calvin of Geneva, greatly admired by English Protestants, supplied many of the copious interpretive notes. The numbering of chapters and verses, introduced by the Geneva Bible, became standard. The King James Version of the Bible was completed in 1611, too late for most of Shakespeare's work.]

1.1.124: "SICK ALMOST TO DOOMSDAY" (TLN 124.10–13)

Horatio's description of the frightening omens seen shortly before the assassination of Julius Caesar, with "stars with trains of fire and dews of blood, / Disasters in the sun; and the moist star, / Upon whose influence Neptune's empire stands, / Was sick almost to doomsday with eclipse," recalls Revelation 6:12 and Matthew 24:29: "Immediately after the tribulation of those days shall the sun be darkened, and the moon shall not give her light, and the stars shall fall from heaven, and the powers of the heavens shall be shaken." See also note below at 2.2.235 (TLN 1282–84), p. 270, and extended note on p. 120.

1.2.70–71: "DO NOT FOREVER WITH THY VAILÈD LIDS / SEEK FOR THY NOBLE FATHER IN THE DUST" (TLN 250–51)

This admonition from Gertrude to her son is one among several recollections in the play of Genesis 3:19: "for dust thou art, and unto dust shalt thou return." See also p. 270 regarding Hamlet's characterization of humankind as a "quintessence of dust" (2.2.297–98, TLN 1355), and his meditation on how "Alexander returneth into dust" (5.1.185,

TLN 3396–97), p. 273. When Hamlet is asked what he has done with the dead body of Polonius, he replies: "Compounded it with dust, whereto 'tis kin" (4.2.8, TLN 2636). See also Ecclesiastes 3:20: "All go unto one place; all are of the dust, and all turn to dust again," and 12:7: "Then shall the dust return to the earth as it was."

1.2.105: "FROM THE FIRST CORPSE TILL HE THAT DIED TODAY" (TLN 287)

Claudius is recalling the first murder on earth of Abel by his brother Cain, Genesis 4:1–16.

1.2.156–57: "OH, MOST WICKED SPEED, TO POST / WITH SUCH DEXTERITY TO INCESTUOUS SHEETS!" (TLN 340–41)

Hamlet's brooding over his mother's second marriage recalls Leviticus 18:16: "Thou shalt not uncover the nakedness of thy brother's wife," and 20:21: "And if a man shall take his brother's wife, it is an unclean thing." See also Appendix D1, pp. 293–94.

2.2.235: "THEN IS DOOMSDAY NEAR" (TLN 1284)

For information on Hamlet's invoking the concept of apocalypse, as vividly portrayed in The Book of Revelation, see extended note on p. 120.

2.2.297–98: "QUINTESSENCE OF DUST" (TLN 1355)

See entry above at 1.2.70–71 (TLN 250–51), pp. 269–70, and extended note on p. 297.

2.2.382: "O JEPHTHAH, JUDGE OF ISRAEL, WHAT A TREASURE HADST THOU?" (TLN 1451)

The patriarch Jephthah vowed that he would sacrifice the first living thing he saw coming forth from his own house if God granted him victory over the Ammonites in battle (Judges 11:30–40). The first living thing he saw on his return from battle turned out to be his daughter and only child. Though racked with sorrow, he fulfilled his vow.

3.1.126–27: "WE ARE ARRANT KNAVES, ALL; BELIEVE NONE OF US" (TLN 1784)

On the concept of Original Sin, see extended note on p. 145.

3.1.142: "YOU ... NICKNAME GOD'S CREATURES" (TLN 1800–01)

Here Hamlet seems to be recalling the story of God's creating the world and then bidding Adam name all living creatures, Genesis 1:10–25 and 2:19–20.

3.2.12: "IT OUT-HERODS HEROD" (TLN 1861–62)

When Hamlet inveighs against exaggerated acting, he has in mind the story of Herod's ordering the massacre of the innocents, as told in Matthew 2:16–18, an event that in the medieval cycle plays was plentifully accompanied with Herod's blustering rage. See extended note on p. 151.

3.3.37–38: "IT HATH THE PRIMAL ELDEST CURSE UPON'T, / A BROTHER'S MURDER" (TLN 2313–14)

Claudius, attempting unsuccessfully to pray, points to Cain's murder of his brother Abel, the first such crime on earth (Genesis 4:1–16.). See also below, 5.1.68, p. 273, where Hamlet compares a skull to "Cain's jawbone, that did the first murder," and above, 1.2.105, p. 270, on "the first corpse" in human history.

3.3.43–46: "WHAT IF THIS CURSÈD HAND / WERE THICKER THAN ITSELF WITH BROTHER'S BLOOD, / IS THERE NOT RAIN ENOUGH IN THE SWEET HEAVENS / TO WASH IT WHITE AS SNOW?" (TLN 2319–22)

Claudius's desperate question, asked when he is preparing to pray, recalls Isaiah 1:15–18: "I will not hear: your hands are full of blood. / Wash ye, make ye clean; put away the evil of your doings from before mine eyes ... though they [your sins] be red like scarlet, they shall be as wool."

3.3.80: "'A TOOK MY FATHER GROSSLY, FULL OF BREAD" (TLN 2356)

Here Hamlet uses the language of Ezekiel 16:49: "Behold, this was the iniquity of thy sister Sodom, pride, fullness of bread, and abundance of idleness."

4.2.8: "COMPOUNDED IT WITH DUST, WHERETO 'TIS KIN" (TLN 2636)

See above, 1.2.70–71, pp. 269–70.

4.2.28–30: "THE KING IS A THING ... / OF NOTHING" (TLN 2657–59)

Hamlet's mocking suggestion to Rosencrantz and Guildenstern may echo Psalm 144:4: "Man is like to vanity: his days are as a shadow that passeth away."

4.3.52–53: "FATHER AND MOTHER IS MAN AND WIFE, MAN AND WIFE IS ONE FLESH" (TLN 2715–16)

Hamlet mordantly rephrases Genesis 2:24: "Therefore shall a man leave his father and mother, and shall cleave unto his wife; and they shall be one flesh." See also Matthew 19:5–6: "For this cause shall a man leave father and mother, and shall cleave to his wife," and Mark 10:8: "And they twain shall be one flesh."

5.1.31: "THE SCRIPTURE SAYS ADAM DIGGED" (TLN 3225)

The First Gravedigger seems to have in mind Genesis 2:15: "And the Lord God took the man, and put him into the garden of Eden to dress it and to keep it." Genesis 3:23 reports further that "the Lord God sent him forth from the garden of Eden, to till the ground from whence he was taken." Medieval interpretation saw in these verses a justification for the idea that Adam was a digger; compare "When Adam delved and Eve span, / Who was then the gentleman?" as preached by the radical priest John Ball in an open-air sermon at Blackheath shortly after the Peasants' Revolt of 1381.

5.1.68: "CAIN'S JAWBONE" (TLN 3269)

Hamlet's comparing a skull at Ophelia's gravesite to "Cain's jawbone" recalls Cain's slaying of his brother Abel in Genesis 4:8. The account there does not actually mention a jawbone, but the association was traditional. Compare above, 3.3.37–38, p. 271, where Claudius speaks of his murder of his brother as having "the primal eldest curse upon't."

5.1.185–86: "ALEXANDER RETURNETH INTO DUST, THE DUST IS EARTH, OF EARTH WE MAKE LOAM" (TLN 3396–98)

See above, 1.2.70–71, and pp. 269–70.

5.1.226: "NOW PILE YOUR DUST UPON THE QUICK AND DEAD" (TLN 3445)

Laertes, jumping into Ophelia's grave, echoes the Acts of the Apostles 10:42: "And he commanded us to preach unto the people, and to testify that it is he which was ordained of God to be the Judge of quick and dead." See also 2 Timothy 4:1: "the Lord Jesus Christ, who shall judge the quick and the dead," and 1 Peter 4:5: "Who shall give account to him that is ready to judge the quick and the dead." This biblical language is incorporated in the Nicene and Apostles' Creeds, and in the Church of England's Book of Common Prayer.

5.2.40: "AS LOVE BETWEEN THEM LIKE THE PALM SHOULD FLOURISH" (TLN 3542)

Hamlet's mocking quotation from Claudius's commission to the King of England recalls Psalm 92:12: "The righteous shall flourish like the palm tree."

5.2.200–01: "THERE'S A SPECIAL PROVIDENCE IN THE FALL OF A SPARROW" (TLN 3668–69)

Hamlet's reflection brings to mind Matthew 10:29: "Are not two sparrows sold for a farthing? and one of them shall not fall on the ground without your Father." See also Christ's Sermon on the Mount as reported in Matthew 6:28–30: "Consider the lilies of the field, how they grow; they toil not, neither do they spin / ... Wherefore, if God so clothe the grass of the field, which today is, and tomorrow is cast into the oven, shall he not much more clothe you, O ye of little faith?" The account in Luke 12:27–28 is closely similar.

APPENDIX C: SOURCES AND ANALOGS

1. FROM SAXO GRAMMATICUS, *HISTORIA DANICA* (1180–1204)

[The ultimate source for Shakespeare's *Hamlet* is Saxo Grammaticus's *Historia Danica*, also known as *Gesta Danorum* (late twelfth century). The portion of Saxo that is most relevant to Shakespeare's play is included here. A modern spelling of all nine extant books of Saxo's *Historia*, translated in 1894 by Oliver Elton, is available online at Project Gutenberg, with an extensive discussion by Douglas B. Killings and David Widger of Danish political institutions, customary and statute law, methods of war, social life and manners, funeral customs, magic, folk tales, and mythology.

Saxo's account embodies many features retained in Shakespeare's *Hamlet*: the bravery of the hero's father while he was alive, the murder of that chivalric ruler by his own brother, the incestuous marriage of the villainous brother to his own sister-in-law, the hero's use of feigned madness as a device to confuse his enemy, the use of a woman as a decoy, the eavesdropping by a counselor who is thereupon slain by the hero, the hero's confronting of his mother with the sinfulness of her marriage, the trip to England with the substitution in the letter of a commission ordering the execution of the escorts instead of the hero, the hero's return to Denmark, his reconciliation with his mother, and his avenging the murder of his father in the play's final scene.

Much too is changed, most notably the hero's relationship to the ethic of revenge. Saxo's story of Amleth is unapologetically a tale of revenge, derived from ancient Norse legends. Amleth must bide his time and feign madness because he is coping with a canny enemy, but the young man has no scruples about killing his uncle in cold blood. He plots his course of vengeance and then, assisted by his mother, carries it out with sudden violence. Saxo as narrator applauds the intrepidity of a hero who "not only saved his own life but also managed to avenge his father. Because of his skillful defense of himself and his vigorous vengeance of his father, it is hard to say which was the greater, his courage or his cleverness." Throughout, Amleth is seen as admirably cunning. Saxo's account savors the wit of Amleth's deceptions and half-truths; we take ironic pleasure in knowing the full purport of what the hero is misleadingly saying to his enemies. We are invited to nod approvingly as he takes his sexual pleasure with a young woman employed as a decoy against him. We hear no authorial disapproval of his deliberately stabbing to death the nosey counselor he finds in his mother's chambers; Saxo offers no counterpart to Hamlet's quick regret at his having mistakenly killed the unseen man whom Hamlet plausibly assumed to be his uncle. No pity or revulsion accompanies Amleth's disposing of the counselor's dismembered body in a privy frequented by swine.

Amleth never encounters his father's ghost and has no need to ascertain whether Feng is guilty of murdering his brother; indeed, Feng makes no secret of what he has done. The young woman in Saxo's story is not the old counselor's daughter. She does not go mad and then drown herself, as does Ophelia, nor does she have a brother. Amleth has no dear friend like Horatio in whom he can confide. The counterparts to Rosencrantz and Guildenstern are only unnamed escorts who convey Amleth to England and are killed in his stead, not his boyhood friends. The whole story of Fortinbras has only a distant connection to the saga as told by Saxo.

Shakespeare did not go directly to Saxo or to other Scandinavian legends. He knew François de Belleforest's free French translation of Saxo in his *Histoires Tragiques* (1576); see Appendix C2. He probably also knew a lost play of *Hamlet* acted in London in the late 1580s and early 1590s. Saxo is the ultimate source in the important sense that he first told the story.

The following selection from Saxo's account begins with the birth of Amleth (Hamlet) to his father Horwendil and mother Gurutha. Feng, younger brother of Horwendil and uncle of Amleth, is the equivalent of Claudius in Shakespeare's play. The "good fortune" referred to in the first sentence of this extract is Horwendil's having succeeded to the throne and Gurutha's having given birth to a son and heir.]

Such great good fortune stung Feng with jealousy, so that he resolved treacherously to waylay his brother, thus showing that goodness is not safe even from those of a man's own house. And behold, when a chance came to murder him, his bloody hand sated the deadly passion of his soul. Then he took the wife of the brother he had butchered, capping unnatural murder with incest. For whoso yields to one iniquity, speedily falls an easier victim to the next, the first being an incentive to the second. Also, the man veiled the monstrosity of his deed with such hardihood of cunning, that he made up a mock pretence of goodwill to excuse his crime, and glossed over fratricide with a show of righteousness. Gurutha, said he, though so gentle that she would do no man the slightest hurt, had been visited with her husband's extremest hate; and it was all to save her that he had slain his brother; for he thought it shameful that a lady so meek and unrancorous should suffer the heavy disdain of her husband. Nor did his smooth words fail in their intent; for at courts, where fools are sometimes favoured and backbiters preferred, a lie lacks not credit. Nor did Feng keep from shameful embraces the hands that had slain a brother; pursuing with equal guilt both of his wicked and impious deeds.

Amleth beheld all this, but feared lest too shrewd a behaviour might make his uncle suspect him. So he chose to feign dulness, and pretend an utter lack of wits. This cunning course not only concealed his intelligence but ensured his safety. Every day he remained in his mother's house utterly listless and unclean, flinging himself on the ground and bespattering his person with foul and filthy dirt. His discoloured face and visage smutched with slime denoted foolish and grotesque madness. All he said was of a piece with these follies; all he did savoured of utter lethargy. In a word, you would not have thought him a man at all, but some absurd abortion due to a mad fit of destiny. He used at times to sit over the fire, and, raking up the embers with his hands, to fashion wooden crooks, and harden them in the fire, shaping at their lips certain barbs, to make them hold more tightly to their fastenings. When asked what he was about, he said that he was preparing sharp javelins to avenge his father. This answer was not a little scoffed at, all men deriding his idle and ridiculous pursuit; but the thing helped his purpose afterwards. Now it was his craft in this matter that first awakened in the deeper observers a suspicion of his cunning. For his skill in a trifling art betokened the hidden talent of the craftsman; nor could they believe the spirit dull where the hand had acquired so cunning a workmanship. Lastly, he always watched with the most punctual care over his pile of stakes that he had pointed in the fire. Some people, therefore, declared that his mind was quick enough, and fancied that he only played the simpleton in order to hide his understanding, and veiled some deep purpose under a cunning feint. His wiliness (said these) would be most readily detected, if a fair woman were put in his

way in some secluded place, who should provoke his mind to the temptations of love; all men's natural temper being too blindly amorous
to be artfully dissembled, and this passion being also too impetuous
to be checked by cunning. Therefore, if his lethargy were feigned, he
would seize the opportunity, and yield straightway to violent delights.
So men were commissioned to draw the young man in his rides into
a remote part of the forest, and there assail him with a temptation of
this nature. Among these chanced to be a foster-brother of Amleth,
who had not ceased to have regard to their common nurture; and who
esteemed his present orders less than the memory of their past fellowship. He attended Amleth among his appointed train, being anxious
not to entrap, but to warn him; and was persuaded that he would suffer
the worst if he showed the slightest glimpse of sound reason, and above
all if he did the act of love openly. This was also plain enough to Amleth
himself. For when he was bidden mount his horse, he deliberately set
himself in such a fashion that he turned his back to the neck and faced
about, fronting the tail; which he proceeded to encompass with the
reins, just as if on that side he would check the horse in its furious pace.
By this cunning thought he eluded the trick, and overcame the treachery
of his uncle. The reinless steed galloping on, with rider directing its tail,
was ludicrous enough to behold.

Amleth went on, and a wolf crossed his path amid the thicket. When
his companions told him that a young colt had met him, he retorted,
that in Feng's stud there were too few of that kind fighting. This was
a gentle but witty fashion of invoking a curse upon his uncle's riches.
When they averred that he had given a cunning answer, he answered
that he had spoken deliberately; for he was loth, to be thought prone
to lying about any matter, and wished to be held a stranger to falsehood; and accordingly he mingled craft and candour in such wise that,
though his words did lack truth, yet there was nothing to betoken the
truth and betray how far his keenness went.

Again, as he passed along the beach, his companions found the
rudder of a ship, which had been wrecked, and said they had discov-
ered a huge knife. "This," said he, "was the right thing to carve such
a huge ham"; by which he really meant the sea, to whose infinitude,
he thought, this enormous rudder matched. Also, as they passed
the sandhills, and bade him look at the meal, meaning the sand, he
replied that it had been ground small by the hoary tempests of the

ocean. His companions praising his answer, he said that he had spoken it wittingly. Then they purposely left him, that he might pluck up more courage to practise wantonness. The woman whom his uncle had dispatched met him in a dark spot, as though she had crossed him by chance; and he took her and would have ravished her, had not his foster-brother, by a secret device, given him an inkling of the trap. For this man, while pondering the fittest way to play privily the prompter's part, and forestall the young man's hazardous lewdness, found a straw on the ground and fastened it underneath the tail of a gadfly that was flying past; which he then drove towards the particular quarter where he knew Amleth to be: an act which served the unwary prince exceedingly well. The token was interpreted as shrewdly as it had been sent. For Amleth saw the gadfly, espied with curiosity the straw which it wore embedded in its tail, and perceived that it was a secret warning to beware of treachery. Alarmed, scenting a trap, and fain to possess his desire in greater safety, he caught up the woman in his arms and dragged her off to a distant and impenetrable fen. Moreover, when they had lain together, he conjured her earnestly to disclose the matter to none, and the promise of silence was accorded as heartily as it was asked. For both of them had been under the same fostering in their childhood; and this early rearing in common had brought Amleth and the girl into great intimacy.

So, when he had returned home, they all jeeringly asked him whether he had given way to love, and he avowed that he had ravished the maid. When he was next asked where he did it, and what had been his pillow, he said that he had rested upon the hoof of a beast of burden, upon a cockscomb, and also upon a ceiling. For, when he was starting into temptation, he had gathered fragments of all these things, in order to avoid lying. And though his jest did not take aught of the truth out of the story, the answer was greeted with shouts of merriment from the bystanders. The maiden, too, when questioned on the matter, declared that he had done no such thing; and her denial was the more readily credited when it was found that the escort had not witnessed the deed. Then he who had marked the gadfly in order to give a hint, wishing to show Amleth that to his trick he owed his salvation, observed that latterly he had been singly devoted to Amleth. The young man's reply was apt. Not to seem forgetful of his informant's service, he said that he had seen a certain thing bearing a straw flit by suddenly, wearing a stalk of chaff fixed in its hinder parts. The cleverness of this speech, which made the rest split with laughter, rejoiced the heart of Amleth's friend.

Thus all were worsted, and none could open the secret lock of the young man's wisdom. But a friend of Feng, gifted more with assurance than judgment, declared that the unfathomable cunning of such a mind could not be detected by any vulgar plot, for the man's obstinacy was so great that it ought not to be assailed with any mild measures; there were many sides to his wiliness, and it ought not to be entrapped by any one method. Accordingly, said he, his own profounder acuteness had hit on a more delicate way, which was well fitted to be put in practice, and would effectually discover what they desired to know. Feng was purposely to absent himself, pretending affairs of great import. Amleth should be closeted alone with his mother in her chamber; but a man should first be commissioned to place himself in a concealed part of the room and listen heedfully to what they talked about. For if the son had any wits at all he would not hesitate to speak out in the hearing of his mother, or fear to trust himself to the fidelity of her who bore him. The speaker, loth to seem readier to devise than to carry out the plot, zealously proffered himself as the agent of the eavesdropping. Feng rejoiced at the scheme, and departed on pretence of a long journey. Now he who had given this counsel repaired privily to the room where Amleth was shut up with his mother, and lay down skulking in the straw. But Amleth had his antidote for the treachery. Afraid of being overheard by some eavesdropper, he at first resorted to his usual imbecile ways, and crowed like a noisy cock, beating his arms together to mimic the flapping of wings. Then he mounted the straw and began to swing his body and jump again and again, wishing to try if aught lurked there in hiding. Feeling a lump beneath his feet, he drove his sword into the spot, and impaled him who lay hid. Then he dragged him from his concealment and slew him. Then, cutting his body into morsels, he seethed it in boiling water, and flung it through the mouth of an open sewer for the swine to eat, bestrewing the stinking mire with his hapless limbs. Having in this wise eluded the snare, he went back to the room. Then his mother set up a great wailing, and began to lament her son's folly to his face; but he said: "Most infamous of women; dost thou seek with such lying lamentations to hide thy most heavy guilt? Wantoning like a harlot, thou hast entered a wicked and abominable state of wedlock, embracing with incestuous bosom thy husband's slayer, and wheedling with filthy lures of blandishment him who had slain the father of thy son. This, forsooth, is the way that the mares couple with the vanquishers of their mates; for brute beasts are naturally incited to pair indiscriminately; and it would seem that thou, like them, hast clean forgot thy first husband. As for me, not idly do I wear the mask of folly; for I doubt not that he who destroyed his brother will riot as ruthlessly in the blood of his kindred. Therefore it is better to choose the garb of dulness than that of sense, and to borrow some protection from a show of utter frenzy. Yet the passion to avenge my father still burns in my heart; but I am watching the chances, I await the fitting hour. There is a place for all things; against so merciless and dark spirit must be used the deeper devices of the mind. And thou, who hadst been better employed in lamenting thine own disgrace, know it is superfluity to bewail my witlessness; thou shouldst weep for the blemish in thine own mind, not for that in another's. On the rest see thou keep silence." With such reproaches he rent the heart of his mother and redeemed her to walk in the ways of virtue; teaching her to set the fires of the past above the seductions of the present.

When Feng returned, nowhere could he find the man who had suggested the treacherous espial; he searched for him long and carefully, but none said they had seen him anywhere. Amleth, among others, was asked in jest if he had come on any trace of him, and replied that the man had gone to the sewer, but had fallen through its bottom and been stifled by the floods of filth, and that he had then been devoured by the swine that came up all about that place. This speech was flouted by those who heard; for it seemed senseless, though really it expressly avowed the truth.

Feng now suspected that his stepson was certainly full of guile, and desired to make away with him, but durst not do the deed for fear of the displeasure, not only of Amleth's grandsire Rorik, but also of his own wife. So he thought that the King of Britain should be employed to slay him, so that another could do the deed, and he be able to feign innocence. Thus, desirous to hide his cruelty, he chose rather to besmirch his friend than to bring disgrace on his own head. Amleth, on departing, gave secret orders to his mother to hang the hall with woven knots, and to perform pretended obsequies for him a year thence; promising that he would then return. Two retainers of Feng then accompanied him, bearing a letter graven on wood—a kind of writing material frequent in old times; this letter enjoined the King of the Britons to put to death the youth who was sent over to him. While they were reposing, Amleth searched their coffers, found the letter, and read the instructions therein. Whereupon he erased all the writing on the surface, substituted fresh characters, and so, changing the purport of the instructions, shifted his own doom upon his companions. Nor was he satisfied with removing from himself the sentence of death and passing the peril on to others, but added an entreaty that the King of Britain would grant his daughter in marriage to a youth of great judgment whom he was sending to him. Under this was falsely marked the signature of Feng.

Now when they had reached Britain, the envoys went to the King, and proffered him the letter which they supposed was an implement of destruction to another, but which really betokened death to themselves. The King dissembled the truth, and entreated them hospitably and kindly. Then Amleth scouted all the splendour of the royal banquet like vulgar viands, and abstaining very strangely, rejected that plenteous feast, refraining from the drink even as from the banquet. All marvelled that a youth and a foreigner should disdain the carefully cooked dainties of the royal board and the luxurious banquet provided, as if it were some peasant's relish. So, when the revel broke up, and the King was dismissing his friends to rest, he had a man sent into the sleeping-room to listen secretly, in order that he might hear the midnight conversation of his guests. Now, when Amleth's companions asked him why he had refrained from the feast of yestereve, as if it were poison, he answered that the bread was flecked with blood and tainted; that there was a tang of iron in the liquor; while the meats of the feast reeked of the stench of a human carcase, and were infected by a kind of smack of the odour of the charnel. He further said that the King had the eyes of a slave, and that the queen had in three ways shown the behaviour of a bondmaid. Thus he reviled with insulting invective not so much the feast as its givers. And presently his companions, taunting him with his old defect of wits, began to flout him with many saucy jeers, because he blamed and cavilled at seemly and worthy things, and because he attacked thus ignobly an illustrious King and a lady of so refined a behaviour, bespattering with the shamefullest abuse those who merited all praise.

All this the King heard from his retainer; and declared that he who could say such things had either more than mortal wisdom or more than mortal folly; in these few words fathoming the full depth of Amleth's penetration. Then he summoned his steward and asked him whence he had procured the bread. The steward declared that it had been made by the King's own baker. The King asked where the corn had grown of which it was made, and whether any sign was to be found there of human carnage? The other answered, that not far off was a field, covered with the ancient bones of slaughtered men, and still bearing plainly all the signs of ancient carnage; and that he had himself planted this field with grain in springtide, thinking it more fruitful than the rest, and hoping for plenteous abundance; and so, for aught he knew, the bread had caught some evil savour from this bloodshed. The King, on hearing this, surmised that Amleth had spoken truly, and took the pains to learn also what had been the source of the lard. The other declared that his hogs had, through negligence, strayed from keeping, and battened on the rotten carcase of a robber, and that perchance their pork had thus come to have something of a corrupt smack. The King, finding that Amleth's judgment was right in this thing also, asked of what liquor the steward had mixed the drink? Hearing that it had been brewed of water and meal, he had the spot of the spring pointed out to him, and set to digging deep down; and there he found, rusted away, several swords, the tang whereof it was thought had tainted the waters. Others relate that Amleth blamed the drink because, while quaffing it, he had detected some bees that had fed in the paunch of a dead man; and that the taint, which had formerly been imparted to the combs, had reappeared in the taste. The King, seeing that Amleth had rightly given the causes of the taste he had found so faulty, and learning that the ignoble eyes wherewith Amleth had reproached him concerned some stain upon his birth, had a secret interview with his mother, and asked her who his father had really been. She said she had submitted to no man but the King. But when he threatened that he would have the truth out of her by a trial, he was told that he was the offspring of a slave. By the evidence of the avowal thus extorted he understood the whole mystery of the reproach upon his origin. Abashed as he was with shame for his low estate, he was so ravished with the young man's cleverness, that he asked him why he had aspersed the queen with the reproach that she had demeaned herself like a slave? But while resenting that the courtliness of his wife had been accused in the midnight gossip of a guest, he found that her mother had been a bondmaid. For Amleth said he had noted in her three blemishes showing the demeanor of a slave; first, she had muffled her head in her mantle as handmaids do; next, that she had gathered up her gown for walking; and thirdly, that she had first picked out with a splinter, and then chewed up, the remnant of food that stuck in the crevices between her teeth. Further, he mentioned that the King's mother had been brought into slavery from captivity, lest she should seem servile only in her habits, yet not in her birth.

Then the King adored the wisdom of Amleth as though it were inspired, and gave him his daughter to wife; accepting his bare word as though it were a witness from the skies. Moreover, in order to fulfil the bidding of his friend, he hanged Amleth's companions on the morrow. Amleth, feigning offence, treated this piece of kindness as a grievance, and received from the King, as compensation, some gold, which he afterwards melted in the fire, and secretly caused to be poured into some hollowed sticks.

When he had passed a whole year with the King he obtained leave to make a journey, and returned to his own land, carrying away of all his princely wealth and state only the sticks which held the gold. On reaching Jutland, he exchanged his present attire for his ancient demeanour, which he had adopted for righteous ends, purposely assuming an aspect of absurdity. Covered with filth, he entered the banquet-room where his own obsequies were being held, and struck all men utterly aghast, rumour having falsely noised abroad his death. At last terror melted into mirth, and the guests jeered and taunted one another, that he whose last rites they were celebrating as though he were dead, should appear in the flesh. When he was asked concerning his comrades, he pointed to the sticks he was carrying, and said, "Here is both the one and the other." This he observed with equal truth and pleasantry; for his speech, though most thought it idle, yet departed not from the truth; for it pointed at the weregild[1] of the slain as though it were themselves. Thereon, wishing to bring the company into a gayer mood, he jollied the cupbearers, and diligently did the office of plying the drink. Then, to prevent his loose dress hampering his walk, he girdled his sword upon his side, and purposely drawing it several times, pricked his fingers with its point. The bystanders accordingly had both sword and scabbard riveted across with an iron nail.

---

1 Compensation paid to an injured party's family by the person who committed the offense.

Then, to smooth the way more safely to his plot, he went to the lords and plied them heavily with draught upon draught, and drenched them all so deep in wine, that their feet were made feeble with drunkenness, and they turned to rest within the palace, making their bed where they had revelled. Then he saw they were in a fit state for his plots, and thought that here was a chance offered to do his purpose. So he took out of his bosom the stakes he had long ago prepared, and went into the building, where the ground lay covered with the bodies of the nobles wheezing off their sleep and their debauch. Then, cutting away its support, he brought down the hanging his mother had knitted, which covered the inner as well as the outer walls of the hall. This he flung upon the snorers, and then applying the crooked stakes, he knotted and bound them up in such insoluble intricacy, that not one of the men beneath, however hard he might struggle, could contrive to rise. After this he set fire to the palace. The flames spread, scattering the conflagration far and wide. It enveloped the whole dwelling, destroyed the palace, and burnt them all while they were either buried in deep sleep or vainly striving to arise. Then he went to the chamber of Feng, who had before this been conducted by his train into his pavilion; plucked up a sword that chanced to be hanging to the bed, and planted his own in its place. Then, awakening his uncle, he told him that his nobles were perishing in the flames, and that Amleth was here, armed with his crooks to help him, and thirsting to exact the vengeance, now long overdue, for his father's murder. Feng, on hearing this, leapt from his couch, but was cut down while deprived of his own sword, and as he strove in vain to draw the strange one. O valiant Amleth, and worthy of immortal fame, who being shrewdly armed with a feint of folly, covered a wisdom too high for human wit under a marvellous disguise of silliness! And not only found in his subtlety means to protect his own safety, but also by its guidance found opportunity to avenge his father. By this skilful defence of himself, and strenuous revenge for his parent, he has left it doubtful whether we are to think more of his wit or his bravery.

2. FROM FRANÇOIS DE BELLEFOREST, *HISTOIRES TRAGIQUES* (1576)

[François de Belleforest's free French translation of the Hamlet saga in 1576 provides many new details. Shakespeare may well have read it in French, as an English translation was not available at the time he wrote *Hamlet*. Belleforest's Hamlet suffers from an intense melancholy that is revealed through psychological descriptions. The imagined setting is more that of a Renaissance prince than a pagan Scandinavian warlord. Belleforest sees a Christian vindication in Hamlet's slaying of his adulterous and murderous uncle. The following selection, in a modernized text from an early-seventeenth-century English translation, shows Belleforest's florid characterization of Hamlet's uncle, Fengon, and Hamlet's mother, Geruth. The heavily moralized depiction of adultery and fratricide is Belleforest's way of making an ancient and pagan saga palatable to sixteenth-century Christian readers. Here, Fengon makes no attempt to conceal the fact that he killed his brother, choosing instead to argue that he has done so to rescue Geruth from being abused and threatened with death by her husband Horvendile. The portrait of Geruth is far more denunciatory and misogynistic than in Shakespeare's play. The condemnation of Fengon's flattering courtiers is no less morally severe.]

Fengon, brother to this prince Horvendile, who [not] only fretting and despiting[1] in his heart at the great honor and reputation won by his brother in warlike affairs but solicited and provoked by a foolish jealousy to see him honored with royal alliance, and fearing thereby to be deposed from his part of the government, or rather desiring to be only governor,[2] thereby to obscure the memory of the victories and conquests of his brother Horvendile, determined, whatsoever happened, to kill him; which he effected in such sort that no man once so much as suspected him [of killing his brother out of envy and lust], every man esteeming that from such and so firm a knot of alliance and consanguinity there could proceed no other issue than the full effects of virtue and courtesy. But, as I said before, the desire of bearing sovereign rule and authority respecteth neither blood nor amity, nor caring for virtue, as being wholly without respect of laws, or majesty divine; for it is not possible that he which invadeth the country and taketh away the riches of another man without cause or reason should know or fear God. Was not this a crafty and subtle counselor? But he might have thought that the mother,[3] knowing her

---

1 Being angered.
2 The sole ruler.
3 I.e., Geruth.

husband's case, would not cast her son into the danger of death. But Fengon, having secretly assembled certain men, and perceiving himself strong enough to execute his enterprise, Horvendile his brother being at a banquet with his friends, suddenly set upon him, where he slew him as traitorously, as cunningly he purged himself of so detestable a murder to his subjects; for that before he had any violent or bloody hands, or once committed parricide upon his brother, he had incestuously abused his wife, whose honor he ought as well to have sought and procured as traitorously he pursued and effected his destruction.

And it is most certain that the man that abandoneth himself to any notorious and wicked action, whereby he becometh a great sinner, he careth not to commit much more heinous and abominable offenses, and covered his boldness and wicked practice with so great subtlety and policy,[1] and under a veil of mere simplicity, that, being favored for the honest love that he bare to his sister-in-law, for whose sake, he affirmed, he had in that sort murdered his brother, that his sin found excuse among the common people, and of the nobility was esteemed for justice; for that Geruth, being as courteous a princess as any then living in the north parts, and one that had never once so much as offended any of her subjects, either commons or courtiers, this adulter[er] and infamous murderer slandered his dead brother that he [Horvendile] would have slain his [own] wife, and that he [Fengon], by chance finding him upon the point ready to do it, in defense of the lady, had slain him, bearing off[2] the blows which as then he [Horvendile] struck at the innocent princess without any other cause of malice whatsoever. Wherein he wanted[3] no false witnesses to approve his act, which deposed in like sort as the wicked calumniator himself protested,[4] being the same persons that had borne him company and were participants of his treason; so that instead of pursuing him as a parricide[5] and an incestuous person, all the courtiers admired and flattered him in his good fortune, making more account of false witnesses and detestable wicked reporters,

---

1 Craftiness.
2 Deflecting.
3 Lacked.
4 All of whom testified in the same false terms that the wicked slanderer Fengon had sworn.
5 One who kills his own father (though in this case, he killed his own brother).

and more honoring the calumniators than they esteemed of those that, seeking to call the matter in question and admiring the virtues of the murdered prince, would have punished the massacrers and bereavers of his life. Which was the cause that Fengon, boldened and encouraged by such impunity, durst venture to couple himself in marriage with her whom he used as his concubine during good Horvendile's life, in that sort spotting his name with a double vice, and charging his conscience with abominable guilt and twofold impiety, [such] as incestuous adultery and parricide murder; and that the unfortunate and wicked woman, that had received the honor to be the wife of one of the valiantest and wisest princes in the north, embased[1] herself in such vile sort as to falsify her faith unto him[2] and, which is worse, to marry him that had been the tyrannous murderer of her lawful husband; which made divers men think that she had been the causer of the murder, thereby to live in her adultery without control.

But where shall a man find a more wicked and bold woman than a great personage once having loosed the bands[3] of honor and honesty? This princess, who at the first, for her rare virtues and courtesies, was honored of all men and beloved of her husband, as soon as she once gave ear to the tyrant Fengon, forgot both the rank she held among the greatest names and the duty of an honest wife on her behalf. But I will not stand to gaze and marvel at women, for that there are many which seek to blaze[4] and set them forth, in which their writings they spare not[5] to blame them all for the faults of some one or few women. But I say that either nature ought to have bereaved man of that opinion to accompany[6] with women, or else to endow them with such spirits as that they may easily support the crosses they endure, without complaining so often and so strangely, seeing it is their own beastliness that overthrows them.[7] For if it be so that a woman is so imperfect a creature as they make her to be, and that they know this beast to be so hard to be tamed as they affirm, why then are they so foolish to preserve

---

1 Debased, degraded.
2 I.e., to her dead husband.
3 Bonds.
4 Proclaim.
5 Do not hesitate.
6 Form relationships.
7 Seeing that men are undone by their own carnality.

them, and so dull and brutish as to trust their deceitful and wanton embracings? But let us leave her in this extremity of lasciviousness, and proceed to show you in what sort the young prince Hamlet behaved himself to escape the tyranny of his uncle.

3. FROM *DER BESTRAFTE BRUDERMORD* (1710)

[A lost anonymous *Hamlet*, alluded to by Thomas Nashe in 1589 (see Chronology, p. 54), appears to have been popular enough in its day that it may have been acted by English actors traveling in Germany in 1586. (A later touring production of the play in Germany, in 1626, could obviously have been influenced by Shakespeare's version.) The only surviving evidence of such a touring version is *Der bestrafte Brudermord* (*Fratricide Punished*), derived from a now-lost manuscript dated 1710. Even though the text of *Der bestrafte Brudermord* could well have been altered in the years between 1586 and 1710, the play we have could still reflect features of the play as acted in Germany in the 1580s.

In any event, if the German text we have is anything like the lost *Hamlet* (and we should allow for the possibility that it reflects some details of Shakespeare's own play, since the 1710 date comes later), the resemblances point to materials that Shakespeare might well have used. In *Der bestrafte Brudermord*, as in Shakespeare's play, the ghost of Hamlet's father first appears to Francisco, Horatio, and others as they stand watch at night. When Hamlet joins them, the Ghost returns, laments to Hamlet the Queen's hasty remarriage, describes his own murder by means of hebona poured in his ear, and urges revenge. When players arrive from Germany, in *Der bestrafte Brudermord* as in Shakespeare's play, Hamlet instructs them in the natural style of acting and commissions them to perform a play before the King about the murder of a ruler by his brother, again by means of poison poured in the ear. The King's guilty response to this performance convinces Hamlet that the King is indeed the murderer of his brother, Hamlet's father. When Hamlet then finds the King alone at prayer, he postpones killing the King lest the man's soul be sent to heaven. Making his way to his mother's chambers, Hamlet stabs Corambus through a tapestry. Hamlet is sent to England with two unnamed courtiers. On his return from England, he engages in a duel with Leonhardus, who has conspired with the King to employ a poisoned dagger in the duel; a cup of poisoned wine is to be at hand if the poisoned dagger should fail of its purpose. The deaths occur much as in Shakespeare's play. The dying Hamlet urges that the crown of Denmark be bestowed on his cousin, Duke Fortempras of Norway, whose name has not been mentioned earlier in this play.

These extensive correspondences include many circumstances not in Saxo or Belleforest. At the same time the differences, some of them amusing, are also numerous. The deranged Ophelia in *Der bestrafte Brudermord* imagines herself to be in love with the foppish Phantasmo, a sycophantic figure who bears a slight resemblance to *Hamlet*'s Osric. This court creature, identified in the list of persons represented as the play's "clown," is tauntingly addressed by Hamlet as "Signora Phantasmo." Later, this court butterfly helps the clownish peasant Jens with a tax problem. Hamlet foils the unnamed persons who are escorting him to England and who are under orders to kill him. The deadly wine cup intended for Hamlet in the play's final scene contains as its fatal ingredient a finely ground oriental diamond dust. Ophelia is reported to have committed suicide by throwing herself off a hill.

In the modernized excerpt given below, Hamlet has been escorted by two unnamed Ruffians to an island where they are under orders from the King to kill him. When they inform him of their intent, he begs them to spare him and acts as if he is about to take a sword from one of them, but he is so clearly outgunned by their pistols that he appears to submit to grim destiny. Hamlet's only last request is that he be allowed to say a final prayer; when he raises his hands to heaven, they are to fire their pistols, one from each side. He falls forward at the critical moment in such a way that they shoot each other. Hamlet thanks heaven for having inspired him with this stratagem. He finds a letter on the body of one of them, clearly implicating the Danish King of a villainous attempt at murder which Hamlet will now avenge on his return to Denmark.

What is especially noteworthy about this selection is its use of slapstick comedy. Perhaps in this sense it functions as a lightening before death in much the way that Shakespeare's text suggests in the comic dialogue of the gravediggers (5.1.1–48) and also the absurd posturing of Osric (5.2.81–169).]

Hamlet, Two Ruffians.

HAMLET. It is a pleasant place here on this island! Let us stay here for a while and dine. There is a delightful wood, and here a cool spring of water. So fetch the best from our ship, and we'll make right merry here.

RUFFIAN 1. There's no dinner time here for you, my lord, since you will never leave this island, for here's the place destined for your grave.

HAMLET. What sayst thou, scoundrel, slave? Dost thou know who I am? Wouldst thou jest thus with a royal prince? However, on this occasion I pardon thee.

RUFFIAN 2. No, it is no jest, but grim earnest. Prepare yourself for death.

HAMLET. Wherefore this? What harm have I ever done you? I cannot recollect any; therefore speak out, why do ye have such wicked thoughts?

RUFFIAN 1. We have been ordered to do it by the King: as soon as we have brought Your Highness to this island, we are to take your life.

HAMLET. Dear friends, spare my life! Say that you have done it properly, and I will never return to the King as long as I live. Consider well, what do you gain by covering your hand with the innocent blood of a prince? Will you stain your consciences with my sins? What bad luck that I came here unarmed! If only I had something in my hand!

RUFFIAN 2. Take care of thy weapon, comrade!

RUFFIAN 1. I'll take good care. Now Prince, prepare yourself; haven't much time.

HAMLET. Since it cannot be otherwise, and I must die at your hands, by the orders of the tyrannical King, I must submit, although I am innocent. And since you have been bribed through poverty, I freely pardon you. Yet this murderer of his brother and my father must answer for my blood at the Last Great Day.

RUFFIAN 1. Eh! What is that great day to us? We must carry out our orders for today.

RUFFIAN 2. That's true, brother! Quickly to work; it must be so! You fire from this side, I from the other.

HAMLET. Listen to one word more from me. Since even the wickedest evildoer is not executed without being given time to repent, I, an innocent prince, beg you to let me first address a fervent prayer to my Creator; after which I shall willingly die. But I shall give you a sign: I shall raise my hands to heaven, and as soon as I spread out my arms, fire! Level both pistols at my sides, and when I say shoot, give me as much as I need, and be sure and hit me, that I may not suffer long.

RUFFIAN 2. Well, we may do that much to please him; so go right ahead.

HAMLET. [*He spreads out his hands.*] Shoot! [*He falls down forward between the two Ruffians, who shoot each other.*] Just Heaven! Thanks be to thee for thy angelic inspiration; henceforth I will ever worship the guardian angel who working through my thoughts has saved my life. But these scoundrels, as they worked, so were they paid out. The dogs move still; they have shot each other, but for revenge I'll give them the coup de grâce; otherwise one of the rogues might escape. [*He stabs them with their own swords.*] Now I'll search them, to see whether they have some warrant on them. This one has nothing. But here I find a letter on this murderer. I'll read it. This letter is written to an arch-murderer in England, so that should this attempt miscarry, they would hand me over to him and he would soon blow out the light of my life! But the gods ever stand by the just. Now I will go back again to my "father," to terrify him; but I will not trust to water again, for who knows whether the captain may not likewise prove a rogue. I shall go to the first town and take the post. The sailors I shall order back to Denmark, but these scoundrels I'll throw into the water.

APPENDIX D: DOMESTIC ISSUES IN *HAMLET*

1. MARRIAGE AND INCEST

[As Claude Lévi-Strauss has argued in his *The Elementary Structures of Kinship* (1969; *Structures élémentaires de la parenté* [1949]), incest is not an invariable taboo but one that takes various forms in different cultures. In Egypt in Cleopatra's time, for example, brothers and sisters of the royal family not infrequently married. Judeo-Christian tradition, on the other hand, forbade a man to marry his brother's wife, as proscribed by Leviticus 18:16: "Thou shalt not uncover the nakedness of thy brother's wife" (along with the same forbidding of sexual contact with father, mother, father's wife, sister, daughter-in-law, aunt, uncle, sister-in-law, and so on); and Leviticus 20:21: "And if a man take his brother's wife, it is an unclean thing." The Anglican *Book of Common Prayer* in sixteenth-century England adopted this rule for the English church; in "A Table of Kindred and Affinity, wherein whosoever are related are forbidden in Scripture and our laws to marry together," Item 18 specifies that a man may not marry his brother's wife (see list on p. 294). Henry VIII's marriage with Katharine of Aragon, the widow of Henry's older brother Arthur, was hotly contested: Rome's refusal to accept the marriage as legitimate led eventually to England's Reformation break with Rome. The marriage of Claudius and Gertrude in *Hamlet* violates the rule in Leviticus. Though this action is imagined to have taken place in Denmark in former times, the negative attitude of the Protestant English church toward marriage with a deceased brother's wife seems to have been carried over into Shakespeare's play, at least in the view of Hamlet and of his father's ghost, both of whom repeatedly condemn the marriage as incestuous; see 1.2.157 (TLN 341), 1.5.43 (TLN 729), 1.5.83 (TLN 768), 3.3.9.90 (TLN 2365), and 5.2.310 (TLN 3807–08).]

Wherein whosoever are related are forbidden in Scripture and our laws
to marry together

A man may not marry his

1. Grandmother
2. Grandfather's wife
3. Wife's grandmother
4. Father's sister
5. Mother's sister
6. Father's brother's wife
7. Mother's brother's wife
8. Wife's father's sister
9. Wife's mother's sister
10. Mother
11. Step-mother
12. Wife's mother
13. Daughter
14. Wife's daughter
15. Son's wife
16. Sister
17. Wife's sister
18. Brother's wife
19. Son's daughter
20. Daughter's daughter
21. Son's son's wife
22. Daughter's son's wife
23. Wife's son's daughter
24. Wife's daughter's daughter
25. Brother's daughter
26. Sister's daughter
27. Brother's son's wife
28. Sister's son's wife
29. Wife's brother's daughter
30. Wife's sister's daughter

A woman may not marry her

1. Grandfather
2. Grandmother's husband
3. Husband's grandfather
4. Father's brother
5. Mother's brother
6. Father's sister's brother
7. Mother's sister's husband
8. Husband's father's brother
9. Husband's mother's brother
10. Father
11. Step-father
12. Husband's father
13. Son
14. Husband's son
15. Daughter's husband
16. Brother
17. Husband's brother
18. Sister's husband
19. Son's son
20. Daughter's son
21. Son's daughter's husband
22. Daughter's daughter's husband
23. Husband's son's son
24. Husband's daughter's son
25. Brother's son
26. Sister's son
27. Brother's daughter's husband
28. Sister's daughter's husband
29. Husband's brother's son
30. Husband's sister's son

2. WOMEN AND OBEDIENCE

Wives in the early modern period (as in previous ages) were required to be obedient to their husbands, and children to their fathers, just as subjects owed obedience to kings, and as persons of all ranks owed obedience to the aristocrats above them in the social structure. In the same way, all humans owed obedience to God and to the church that embodied their religious faith. *Hamlet* associates the term "obedience" particularly with Ophelia as the daughter of Polonius, who informs the King that his daughter, "in her duty and obedience" (2.2.107, TLN 1134), has returned Hamlet's letters to him. Polonius reads aloud Hamlet's letter to Ophelia, emphasizing again, "This in obedience hath my daughter shown me" (2.2.124, TLN 1153). Ophelia's never-wavering obedience to her father leads to her tragic madness and death.

Gertrude's story takes a different turn. Her failure to remember her dead husband and her shifting of allegiance to Claudius so distress Hamlet that he sharply bids her to do two things by way of returning to a better sense of duty. "[G]o not to my uncle's bed," he instructs her (3.4.166, TLN 2543). Do not "Let the bloat King tempt you again to bed," and "for a pair of reechy kisses, / Or paddling in your neck with his damned fingers," "ravel all this matter out / That I essentially am not in madness, / But mad in craft" (3.4.189–95, TLN 2558–64). Gertrude is thus told that she must distance herself from her new husband to the extent of withholding the husband's right to carnal companionship and then in effect lying to him by not telling the truth about Hamlet's seeming affliction. And she may indeed prevaricate to Claudius a few moments later, when Hamlet has dragged off the corpse of Polonius and Claudius has found her profoundly sighing. "Where is your son?" he asks her. "How does Hamlet?" Her answer is perhaps something she knows to be untrue: "Mad as the sea and wind when both contend / Which is the mightier" (4.1.4–8, TLN 2590–94). In this interpretation, she is covering for Hamlet as he has asked, not giving away his important secret.[1] Similarly, in the play's final scene, she disobeys her new husband. She drinks a cup of wine to announce publicly her

---

1 An alternative interpretation is that the Queen thinks Hamlet is indeed mad and that she prevaricates to him, not to Claudius. Both interpretations appear viable according to the text, though the former seems to be supported by some lines that appear only in the unauthorized Q1: see Appendix E3, p. 299.

support for her son. "The Queen carouses to thy fortune, Hamlet." When Claudius orders her to desist—"Gertrude, do not drink"—she deliberately refuses to obey. "I will, my lord, I pray you pardon me" (5.2.274–77, TLN 3758–62). She thus goes to her death, whether having guessed that the wine is poisoned, or, perhaps more likely, not knowing it to be poisoned. In either case, she joins herself and her fortunes with those of her son in an act of disobedience to her husband.

The obedience of wives to husbands was a central requirement of marriage under the Church of England in the sixteenth century. For example, in "The Form of Solemnization of Matrimony" in the 1559 version of *The Book of Common Prayer*, the priest asks the man, "Wilt thou love her, comfort her, honor, and keep her, in sickness and in health?" The corresponding question to the woman adds servitude and obedience: "Wilt thou obey him and serve him, love, honor, and keep him, in sickness and in health?" Similarly, the man's vow "to love and to cherish" his bride is followed by the woman's "to love, cherish, and to obey" in return. The requirement of obedience for the woman has been dropped from this ceremony in more modern times, so that the oaths of husband and wife are more evenly balanced. The Renaissance version was based in part on Genesis, where God chastises Eve for eating of the forbidden fruit by telling her that she is now to bear children "in sorrow," and that "thy desire shall be to thy husband, and he shall rule over thee" (Genesis 3:16). The Anglican Church in the late sixteenth century (especially its Puritan-leaning component) was moving toward a companionate view of marriage, one in which a husband should treat his wife with generous forbearance rather than tyranny, but the husband's superior authority was not to be questioned in all this.

APPENDIX E: SOME TEXTUAL VARIATIONS IN QUARTO 1

1. ANOTHER "TO BE OR NOT TO BE," 3.1.57 FF. (TLN 1710 FF.)

[This famous soliloquy varies in many details from its Q2/F1 counterpart, with the order of the lines considerably rearranged; it is also placed considerably earlier in the action, at sig. D4v–E1 in Q1.]

HAMLET. To be, or not to be, ay, there's the point,
To die, to sleep, is that all? Ay, all.
No, to sleep, to dream, ay, marry, there it goes,
For in that dream of death, when we awake,
And borne before an everlasting judge,
From whence no passenger ever returned,
The undiscovered country, at whose sight
The happy smile, and the accursèd damned.
But for this, the joyful hope of this,
Who'd bear the scorns and flattery of the world,
Scorned by the right[1] rich, the rich cursed of the poor,
The widow being oppressed, the orphan wronged,
The taste of hunger, or a tyrant's reign,
And thousand more calamities besides,
To grunt and sweat under this weary life,
When that he may his full quietus make
With a bare bodkin? Who would this endure,
But for a hope of something after death?
Which puzzles the brain, and doth confound the sense,
Which makes us rather bear those evils we have
Than fly to others that we know not of.
Ay, that. Oh, this conscience makes cowards of us all.

---

1   Very.

2. DIFFERENT ADVICE TO THE PLAYERS,
3.2.14 FF. (TLN 1865 FF.)

[As in the later texts, Hamlet here enunciates his insistence that a good actor knows how to avoid the exaggerated gestures and stale jesting that is too common on the contemporary stage. In this version, however, at Q1, sig. F2–F2v, Hamlet provides some specific, rather homely, examples of the abuses of the Clown.]

HAMLET. And do you hear? Let not your Clown speak
　　More than is set down. There be of them, I can tell you,
　　That will laugh themselves, to set on some
　　Quantity of barren[1] spectators to laugh with them,
　　Albeit there is some necessary point in the play
　　Then to be observed. Oh, 'tis vile, and shows
　　A pitiful ambition in the fool that useth it.
　　And then you have some again that keeps one suit
　　Of jests, as a man is known by one suit of
　　Apparel, and gentlemen quotes his jests down
　　In their tables[2] before they come to the play, as thus:
　　"Cannot you stay till I eat my porridge?" and "You owe me
　　A quarter's wages," and "My coat wants a cullison,"[3]
　　And "Your beer is sour," and blabbering with his lips
　　And thus keeping in his cinquepace[4] of jests
　　When, God knows, the warm Clown cannot make a jest
　　Unless by chance, as the blind man catcheth a hare.
　　Masters, tell him of it.
PLAYERS. We will, my lord.
HAMLET. Well, go make you ready.

1　Ignorant.
2　Playgoers record the jokes in their notebooks.
3　My coat lacks a badge.
4　A dance.

[No other text provides what Q1 here offers at sig. G3–G3v: Hamlet explicitly urging his mother to aid him in his revenge as a way of purging her own guilt, and her vow of acquiescence. Whether Q1 can be taken as confirming Shakespeare's view of the Queen's final disposition—that her son is sane and her husband a villain—is uncertain. Like many vital questions of interpretation in this fascinating play, we are left once more with an authorial intention that may be deliberately ambiguous.]

QUEEN. Alas, it is the weakness of thy brain,
   Which makes thy tongue to blazon[1] thy heart's grief.
   But, as I have a soul, I swear by heaven
   I never knew of this most horrid murder.
   But Hamlet, this[2] is only fantasy,
   And, for my love forget these idle fits.
HAMLET. Idle? No, mother, my pulse doth beat like yours.
   It is not madness that possesseth Hamlet.
   O mother, if ever you did my dear father love,
   Forbear the adulterous bed tonight,
   And win yourself by little as you may.[3]
   In time it may be you will loathe him quite.
   And, mother, but assist me in revenge,
   And in his death your infamy shall die.
QUEEN. Hamlet, I vow, by that Majesty[4]
   That knows our thoughts and looks into our hearts,
   I will conceal, consent, and do my best,
   What stratagem soe'er thou shalt devise.
HAMLET. It is enough. Mother, good night.—
   Come, sir,[5] I'll provide for you a grave,
   Who was in life a foolish, prating knave.

---

1   Publicize.
2   I.e., Hamlet's insistence that he sees the Ghost.
3   I.e., win yourself, little by little, as much as you can, away from sleeping with Claudius.
4   I.e., God.
5   Hamlet speaks to the body of Corambis (Polonius).

4. THE QUEEN LAMENTS OFELIA'S DEATH, 4.5.76 FF. (TLN 2814 FF.)

[In Q1, sig. G4v, Gertrude interrupts Claudius's lines about Polonius's death making Ofelia mad. Her comment is understanding and empathetic; in Q2/F1 she has no voice at this moment, and Claudius is more interested in summarizing their political situation among accumulating woes.]

KING

Hamlet is shipped for England. Fare him well.
I hope to hear good news from thence ere long,
If everything fall out to our content,
As I do make no doubt but so it shall.

QUEEN

God grant it may. Heav'ns keep my Hamlet safe!
But this mischance of old Corambis' death
Hath piercèd so the young Ofelia's heart
That she, poor maid, is quite bereft her wits.

KING

Alas, dear heart! And on the other side
We understand her brother's come from France,
And he hath half the heart of all our land;[1]
And hardly he'll forget his father's death
Unless by some means he be pacified.

5. A SHORTER SCENE BEFORE THE DUEL

[This scene appears after the one numbered 4.5 in the later texts. It presents a conversation between Horatio and the Queen that, as Thompson and Taylor note, "is unique to Q1 and parallels the conspiracy between the King and Laertes in Scene 15 (4.7 in Q2)." It manages to dramatize in abridged form the Q2/F1 scenes in which Horatio and Claudius separately receive letters from Hamlet, and Hamlet relates to Horatio the adventures of his sea voyage. In Q2/F1 much of the material in this scene follows the graveyard conversation of Horatio

---

1   Support from half the population.

and Hamlet at Yorick's grave and Hamlet's struggle with Laertes at Ophelia's grave (5.1). The Queen's willingness to deceive her husband is more explicit here than anywhere in Q2/F1.]

[SCENE 14, SIG. H2V–H3]

Enter Horatio [with a letter] and the Queen.

HORATIO. Madam, your son is safe arrived in Denmark.
   This letter I even now received of him,
   Whereas he writes how he escaped the danger
   And subtle treason that the King had plotted.
   Being crossed[1] by the contention of the winds,
   He found the packet[2] sent to the King of England,
   Wherein he saw himself betrayed to death,
   As, at his next convers'ion[3] with your grace,
   He will relate the circumstance at full.
QUEEN. Then I perceive there's treason in his[4] looks
   That seemed to sugar o'er[5] his villainy.
   But I will soothe and please him for a time,
   For murderous minds are always jealous.[6]
   But know not you, Horatio, where he[7] is?
HORATIO. Yes, madam, and he hath appointed me
   To meet him on the east side of the city[8]
   Tomorrow morning.
QUEEN. Oh, fail not, good Horatio, and withal commend me
   A mother's care to him.[9] Bid him awhile
   Be wary of his presence,[10] lest that he
   Fail in that[11] he goes about.

---

1 Frustrated, opposed.
2 The packet containing the letters written by the King to the King of England.
3 Conversation.
4 The King's.
5 Give a deceptive appearance of sweet temper to.
6 Suspicious.
7 Hamlet.
8 The harbor, with its docks, where Hamlet may have landed.
9 Convey to him my motherly love and concern.
10 Bid him to proceed with caution at all times.
11 That which.

HORATIO. Madam, never make doubt of that.
  I think by this the news be come to court:
  He is arrived. Observe the King, and you shall
  Quickly find, Hamlet being here,
  Things fell not to his mind.[1]
QUEEN. But what become of Gilderstone and Rossencraft?
HORATIO. He being set ashore, they went for England,[2]
  And in the packet there writ down that doom
  To be performed on them 'pointed for him.[3]
  And by great chance he had his father's seal,[4]
  So all was done without discovery.
QUEEN. Thanks be to heaven for blessing of the Prince![5]
  Horatio, once again I take my leave,
  With thousand mother's blessings to my son.
HORATIO. Madam, adieu.

[*Exeunt.*]

---

1 Things have not worked out as he (the King) intended.
2 Once Hamlet had been set ashore, Gilderstone and Rossencraft proceeded on to the English court.
3 And in the packet of letters by Claudius intended for the King of England, Hamlet changed the sentence of death to contain the names of Rossencraft and Gilderstone instead of his own.
4 The royal seal used to authenticate documents.
5 Bestowing its blessing upon Prince Hamlet.

WORKS CITED AND SELECT BIBLIOGRAPHY

Adelman, Janet. *Suffocating Mothers: Fantasies of Maternal Origin in Shakespeare's Plays, Hamlet to The Tempest.* New York: Routledge, 1992.

Aristotle. *Poetics.* Ed. M. Heath. London: Penguin, 1996.

Artaud, Antonin. *The Theatre and Its Double.* Trans. Mary Caroline Richards. New York: Grove P, 1958.

Bate, Jonathan. *The Genius of Shakespeare.* Oxford: Oxford UP, 1997.

Bednarz, James P. *Shakespeare and the Poets' War.* New York: Columbia UP, 2001.

Bevington, David. *Murder Most Foul: Hamlet through the Ages.* Oxford: Oxford UP, 2011.

Boose, Lynda. "The Father and the Bride in Shakespeare." *PMLA* 97 (1982): 325–47.

Bowers, Fredson T. "Hamlet as Minister and Scourge." *PMLA* 70 (1955): 740–49.

Bradley, A.C. *Shakespearean Tragedy.* London: Macmillan, 1904.

Brown, Arthur. "The Play within a Play: An Elizabethan Dramatic Device." *Essays and Studies* 13 (1960): 36–48.

Bullough, Geoffrey, ed. *Narrative and Dramatic Sources of Shakespeare.* 8 vols. London: Routledge and Kegan Paul; New York: Columbia UP, 1957–75.

Callaghan, Dympna. *Shakespeare without Women: Representing Gender and Race on the Renaissance Stage.* London: Routledge, 2000.

———, Lorraine Helms, and Jyotsna G. Singh. *The Weyward Sisters: Shakespeare and Feminist Politics.* Oxford: Blackwell, 1994.

Campbell, Lily Bess. *Shakespeare's Tragic Heroes: Slaves of Passion.* Cambridge: Cambridge UP, 1952.

Campbell, Thomas. *An Essay on English Poetry.* Boston: Wells and Lilly, 1819.

Camus, Albert. *The Myth of Sisyphus and Other Essays.* New York: Knopf, 1967.

Charnes, Linda. *Hamlet's Heirs: Shakespeare and the Politics of a New Millennium.* New York: Routledge, 2006.

Charney, Maurice. *Style in "Hamlet."* Princeton, NJ: Princeton UP, 1969.

Clarke, Mary Cowden. *The Girlhood of Shakespeare's Heroines.* New York: G. Putnam, 1850–52.

Coleridge, Samuel Taylor. *Coleridge on Shakespeare: The Text of the Lectures of 1811–12*. Ed. R.A. Foakes. Charlottesville: UP of Virginia, 1971.

Cook, Ann Jennalie. *The Privileged Playgoers of Shakespeare's London, 1576–1642*. Princeton, NJ: Princeton UP, 1981.

Cutrofello, Andrew. *All for Nothing: Hamlet's Negativity*. Cambridge, MA: MIT P, 2014.

Dawson, Anthony B. *Hamlet: Shakespeare in Performance*. Manchester: Manchester UP, 1995.

de Grazia, Margreta. *"Hamlet" without Hamlet*. Cambridge: Cambridge UP, 2007.

Dent, R.W. *Shakespeare's Proverbial Language*. Berkeley: U of California P, 1981.

Derrida, Jacques. *Writing and Difference*. Chicago: U of Chicago P, 1978.

DiGangi, Mario. *The Homoerotics of Early Modern Drama*. Cambridge: Cambridge UP, 1997.

Dollimore, Jonathan. *Radical Tragedy: Religion, Ideology, and Power in the Drama of Shakespeare and His Contemporaries*. Chicago: U of Chicago P, 1984.

Dusinberre, Juliet. *Shakespeare and the Nature of Women*. New York: St. Martin's, 1975.

Eagleton, Terry. *Shakespeare and Society*. New York: Schocken Books, 1967.

Eliot, George. *Mill on the Floss*. London, 1860.

Engle, Lars. "Moral Agency in *Hamlet*." *Shakespeare Studies* 40 (2012): 87–97.

Faucit, Helena. *On Some of Shakespeare's Female Characters*. London, 1885.

Foucault, Michel. *Discipline and Punish*. New York: Vintage, 1977.

Freud, Sigmund. *The Interpretation of Dreams (Die Traumdeutung)*. 1899. New York: Macmillan, 1913.

Frye, Northrop. *Anatomy of Criticism*. Princeton, NJ: Princeton UP, 1957.

Garber, Marjorie. *Coming of Age in Shakespeare*. London: Methuen, 1981.

———. *Dream in Shakespeare: From Metaphor to Metamorphosis*. New Haven, CT: Yale UP, 1974.

Geertz, Clifford. *Negara: The Theatre State in Nineteenth-Century Bali.* Princeton, NJ: Princeton UP, 1980.

Gennep, Arnold van. *The Rites of Passage.* Chicago: U of Chicago P, 1960.

Goethe, Johann Wolfgang von. *Wilhelm Meister's Apprenticeship.* Trans. Thomas Carlyle. New York: Suhrkamp Publishers, 1962.

Goldberg, Jonathan. *James I and the Politics of Literature: Jonson, Shakespeare, Donne, and Their Contemporaries.* Baltimore: Johns Hopkins UP, 1983.

Greenblatt, Stephen. *Hamlet in Purgatory.* Princeton, NJ: Princeton UP, 2001.

Grotowski, Jerzy. *Towards a Poor Theatre.* New York: Simon and Schuster, 1968.

Gurr, Andrew. *Playgoing in Shakespeare's London.* Cambridge: Cambridge UP, 1987.

Hall, Kim. *Things of Darkness: Economies of Race and Gender in Early Modern England.* Ithaca, NY: Cornell UP, 1994.

Hamlin, William M. *Tragedy and Scepticism in Shakespeare's England.* New York: Palgrave Macmillan, 2005.

Hanmer, Thomas. *Some Remarks on the Tragedy of Hamlet, Prince of Denmark.* London, 1736.

Harsnett, Samuel. *A Declaration of Egregious Popish Impostures.* London, 1603.

Harvey, Gabriel. Manuscript marginalia by Harvey some time between 1598 and 1601 in Thomas Speght's edition of *The Works of ... Chaucer,* London, 1598, folio 422b.

Hazlitt, William. *Characters of Shakespeare's Plays.* Boston: Wells and Lilly, 1817.

Helgerson, Richard. *Forms of Nationhood: The Elizabethan Writing of England.* Chicago: U of Chicago P, 1994.

Hinman, Charlton, compiler. *The First Folio of Shakespeare.* New York: W.W. Norton, 1968.

Howard, Jean. *The Stage and Social Struggle in Early Modern England.* London and New York: Routledge, 1994.

Jameson, Anna. *Characteristics of Women.* London: Saunders and Otley, 1832.

James VI of Scotland. *Daemonologie.* 1597.

Jardine, Lisa. *Still Harping on Daughters: Women and Drama in the Age of Shakespeare*. Totowa, NJ: Barnes & Noble, 1983.

Jenkins, Harold, ed. *Hamlet*. The Arden Shakespeare, 2nd series. London: Methuen, 1982.

Johnson, Samuel, ed. "The Preface to Shakespeare," in his edition of the *Works*, 1765.

Jones, Ernest. *Hamlet and Oedipus*. 1910. Rev. ed. New York: W.W. Norton, 1949.

Jonson, Ben. "To the Memory of My Beloved, the Author, Mr. William Shakespeare," in *William Shakespeare's Comedies, Histories, and Tragedies*, 1623, the First Folio edition.

Jung, Carl. *The Psychology of the Unconscious*. Princeton, NJ: Princeton UP, 1991.

Kahn, Coppélia. *Man's Estate: Masculine Identity in Shakespeare*. Berkeley: U of California P, 1981.

Knight, G. Wilson. *The Shakespearean Tempest*. London: Oxford UP, 1953.

———. *The Wheel of Fire*. London: Oxford UP, 1930.

Knights, L.C. *An Approach to Hamlet*. London: Chatto & Windus, 1960.

———. *Explorations*. London: Chatto & Windus, 1946.

Kott, Jan. *Shakespeare Our Contemporary*. New York: Norton, 1964.

Kyd, Thomas. *The Spanish Tragedy*. London, 1592.

Lamb, Charles, *On the Tragedies of Shakespeare*. London, 1811.

Lesser, Zachary. *Hamlet after Q1: An Uncanny History of the Shakespearean Text*. Philadelphia: U of Pennsylvania P, 2015.

Lévi-Strauss, Claude. *The Elementary Structures of Kinship*. Boston: Beacon, 1969.

Lewis, Rhodi. *Hamlet and the Vision of Darkness*. Princeton: Princeton UP, 2017.

Mack, Maynard. "The World of *Hamlet*." *Yale Review* 41 (1952): 502–23.

Marcus, Leah. *Puzzling Shakespeare: Local Reading and Its Discontents*. Berkeley: U of California P, 1988.

McCoy, Richard. *Faith in Shakespeare*. Oxford: Oxford UP, 2013.

Montrose, Louis. *The Purpose of Playing: Shakespeare and the Cultural Politics of the Elizabethan Theatre*. Chicago: U of Chicago P, 1996.

Murray, Gilbert. *Hamlet and Orestes*. New York: Oxford UP, 1914.

Neely, Carol. *Broken Nuptials in Shakespeare's Plays*. New Haven, CT: Yale UP, 1985

Novy, Marianne. *Love's Argument: Gender Relations in Shakespeare*. Chapel Hill: U of North Carolina P, 1984.

Orgel, Stephen. *The Authentic Shakespeare and Other Problems of the Early Modern Stage*. New York: Routledge, 2002.

———. *The Illusion of Power: Political Theater in the English Renaissance*. Berkeley: U of California P, 1975.

Parker, Patricia, and Geoffrey Hartman. *Shakespeare and the Question of Theory*. New York: Methuen, 1985.

Paster, Gail. *The Body Embarrassed: Drama and the Disciplines of Shame in Early Modern England*. Ithaca, NY: Cornell UP, 1993.

Patterson, Annabel. *Shakespeare and the Popular Voice*. Oxford: Blackwell, 1989.

Pepys, Samuel. *The Diary of Samuel Pepys*, 1668 ff., any edition.

Rackin, Phyllis. *Shakespeare and Women*. Oxford: Oxford UP, 2005.

Raleigh, Sir Walter Alexander. *Shakespeare*. London: Macmillan, 1907.

Rose, Mark. "*Hamlet* and the Shape of Revenge." *English Literary Renaissance* 1 (1971): 132–43.

Schlegel, August Wilhelm von. *Lectures on Dramatic Art and Literature*. First published 1809. Trans. John Black. London: G. Bell, 1846.

Scoloker, Anthony. *Epistle to Diaphantus, or the Passions of Love*, London, 1604, "Epistle."

Shaftesbury, Antony Ashley Cooper, Earl of. *Characteristics of Men, Manners, Opinions, Times*. London, 1790; Cambridge: Cambridge UP, 1999.

Shannon, Laurie. *Sovereign Amity: Figures of Friendship in Shakespeare's Contexts*. Chicago: U of Chicago P, 2002.

Shapiro, James. *A Year in the Life of William Shakespeare*. New York: HarperCollins, 2005.

Sinfield, Alan. *Faultlines: Cultural Materialism and the Politics of Dissident Reading*. Berkeley: U of California P, 1992.

Smith, Bruce. *Homosexual Desire in Shakespeare's England*. Chicago: U of Chicago P, 1991.

Spencer, Theodore. *Shakespeare and the Nature of Man*. New York: Macmillan, 1942.

Sprengnether, Madelon. *Shakespearean Tragedy and Gender*.
Bloomington: Indiana UP, 1996.

Spurgeon, Caroline. *Shakespeare's Imagery and What It Tells Us*.
Cambridge: Cambridge UP, 1935.

Stoll, E.E. *Art and Artifice in Shakespeare*. Oxford: Oxford UP, 1933.

Stone, Lawrence. *The Crisis of the Aristocracy, 1558–1641*. Oxford:
Oxford UP, 1965.

Thompson, Ann, and Neil Taylor, eds. *Hamlet*. The Arden
Shakespeare, 3rd series. 2 vols. London: Thomson Learning,
2006, rev. 2016.

Traub, Valerie. *Desire and Anxiety: Circulations of Sexuality in
Shakespearean Drama*. London: Routledge, 1992.

Traversi, Derek. *An Approach to Shakespeare*. 2 vols. 3rd. ed. London:
Hollis & Carter, 1938, rev. 1968–69.

Turner, Victor. *The Ritual Process: Structure and Anti-Structure*. Ithaca,
NY: Cornell UP, 1969.

Weitz, Morris. *Hamlet and the Philosophy of Literary Criticism*.
Chicago: U of Chicago P, 1964.

Williamson, C.C.H., ed. *Readings on the Character of Hamlet, 1661–
1947*. London: George Allen and Unwin, 1950.

Wilson, John Dover. *What Happens in "Hamlet."* Cambridge:
Cambridge UP, 1935.

FROM THE PUBLISHER

A name never says it all, but the word "Broadview" expresses a good deal of the philosophy behind our company. We are open to a broad range of academic approaches and political viewpoints. We pay attention to the broad impact book publishing and book printing has in the wider world; for some years now we have used 100% recycled paper for most titles. Our publishing program is internationally oriented and broad-ranging. Our individual titles often appeal to a broad readership too; many are of interest as much to general readers as to academics and students.

Founded in 1985, Broadview remains a fully independent company owned by its shareholders—not an imprint or subsidiary of a larger multinational.

For the most accurate information on our books (including information on pricing, editions, and formats) please visit our website at www.broadviewpress.com. Our print books and ebooks are also available for sale on our site.

BROADVIEW PRESS
WWW.BROADVIEWPRESS.COM

The interior of this book is printed on 100% recycled paper.